MW01008328

Tokens

Tokens

The Future of Money in the Age of the Platform

Rachel O'Dwyer

VERSO

London • New York

First published by Verso 2023
© Rachel O'Dwyer 2023

1 3 5 7 9 10 8 6 4 2

Verso
UK: 6 Meard Street, London W1F 0EG
US: 388 Atlantic Avenue, Brooklyn, NY 11217
versobooks.com

Verso is the imprint of New Left Books

ISBN-13: 978-1-83976-834-7
ISBN-13: 978-1-83976-835-4 (UK EBK)
ISBN-13: 978-1-83976-836-1 (US EBK)

British Library Cataloguing in Publication Data
A catalogue record for this book is available from the British Library

Library of Congress Cataloging-in-Publication Data

Names: O'Dwyer, Rachel (Lecturer), author.
Title: Tokens : the future of money in the age of the platform / Rachel
O'Dwyer.
Description: Brooklyn : Verso, 2023. | Includes bibliographical references
and index.
Identifiers: LCCN 2023021466 (print) | LCCN 2023021467 (ebook) | ISBN
9781839768347 (hardback) | ISBN 9781839768361 (US EBK) | ISBN
9781839768361 (UK EBK)
Subjects: LCSH: Cryptocurrencies. | Digital currency. | Blockchains
(Databases)
Classification: LCC HG1710.3 .O38 2023 (print) | LCC HG1710.3 (ebook) |
DDC 332.4—dc23/eng/20230602
LC record available at https://lccn.loc.gov/2023021466
LC ebook record available at https://lccn.loc.gov/2023021467

Typeset in Sabon by MJ & N Gavan, Truro, Cornwall
Printed and bound by CPI Group (UK) Ltd,
Croydon CR0 4YY

For Ted

Contents

Introduction

It's a thing in a tiny circle shape ... and it's like gold ... and you pay for it ... and ... pfff!! C'mon! you know what money is, don't you?

Ted, aged four

The hotel off the Vegas strip is called the Tropicana. The carpets are the undefined brown of melted Neapolitan ice cream. When it gets warm they send up the smell of decades of stale cigarettes. I'm here for the Money20/20 Conference. In 1995 the Cypherpunks, the group that all but invented Bitcoin, stayed here for Defcon. They planned a meet-up in the lobby before something called 'Hacker Jeopardy'. I wonder if the Tropicana used to be great. Or was it always a dive? Can history happen in a place like this?

In the evenings I hang out in another hotel, the Venetian, with anthropologists whose universities are paying their way. We drink a famous cocktail with a desert flower in it. We wander the streets of Little Venice, with its indoor canal and its artificial sky and its real goldfish. We sit at a pool terrace and argue about crypto while a giant singing frog serenades us from the water. In the morning I get up early and walk the strip to the conference venue. At 8 a.m. it's already sweltering, a dry, candyfloss heat at the back of my throat. The only other people awake are cleaning the footpaths or on their way to a service shift. There are escalators and moving walkways on the street. There's piped Muzak from everywhere and nowhere. It feels like a giant outdoor mall.

It's 2015. The hallways at Money20/20, the world's largest fintech expo, are full of middle-aged men dressed like Bill Gates circa 1995 and a younger cohort dressed like Mark Zuckerberg, a collision of old-school finance and Bitcoin evangelism. These delegates are exhaustively male, and at every bathroom break I share a conspiratorial smirk in the mirror with whatever woman is at the sink beside me, breezing in and out while, outside, men squirm in line and miss the free cookies in the breakout zone. There are stages everywhere where CTOs pace, shilling 'cookies for the real world', or the 'robots in the sky' that will make credit decisions in the near future. An Israeli child prodigy who needs a stool to see over the podium showcases his smart contract locks for Airbnb. Below us is an exhibition centre the size of a football pitch. The sounds of 8-bit slot machines drift up from the casino on the ground floor.

At the far end of the expo, I stop at a small booth manned by an Irish man in late middle age. He has a soft, avuncular presence that's out of step with the swagger all around us. I suddenly feel a bit homesick. His company sells phone credit, or 'airtime', he tells me. A buyer can log on to their website, buy airtime for a mobile operator in another country, and choose the phone number they want to send it to. 'People can use our website to top up somebody else. Abroad, or ...' So what's a phone credit company doing in a fintech expo? What does buying airtime have to do with the future of money?

In inflation-ravaged Zimbabwe, airtime had begun to act as a de facto currency. Instead of taking a top-up code and using it to add credit to their phone, users started to text these codes to others as an informal means of payment. Sometimes they were cash – shops that had once given small change in sweets and condoms began, instead, to give out phone credit slips. Sometimes they were a token of affection – boyfriends sending minutes to their girlfriends. Sometimes they were remittances, a safe way to send wages home. Gradually, vendors emerged as cash-in and cash-out points, selling the phone credit and buying it back for a small fee. Some of these suppliers acquired loans on the back of the credit they accumulated. Airtime became ... money. Well, money*ish*.

Knowing this, I ask the man if his company is for international remittances. They are using phone credit as a way to send money back home without actually sending money – right? Phone credit is cheaper and faster to send than money via Western Union. And you don't even need a bank account, just a phone number. 'Is this money?', I ask. I feel rude posing such a direct question. 'Ah ... hmm, well ...', he says. He's apologetic, like he, too, feels it's rude that he can't just level with me. 'I mean, not exactly, but ...' – and he winks.

I tell the anthropologists about the wink over lunch. Anthropologists are big on winks, it turns out. There are different meanings wrapped in a wink, I'm told by Taylor Nelms, who is studying alternative currencies in Ecuador. The wink *says* something. A wink is deliberate, directed at a particular person, and used to get a message across that won't formally register with others.[1] Winks are part of an established code. Winks are layered with social meaning. The anthropologist's job, Taylor says, while the others around the table nod knowingly, is to catch these 'winks' and uncover their meanings. In the context of a fintech expo like Money20/20, when so much of the talk is hot air, I can see the point of a wink. This wink said something like: 'I can't say this out loud or readily admit to it because to do so would be to totally overhaul my business model and grapple with fund-transfer regulations; but yes, between you and me, we both know that this is to all intents and purposes a new kind of money, one that is issued and underwritten by a phone company.'

This book is about things that are almost but not quite money. Things that are money-*ish* – money with a wink and a nudge.

At various points in history, tokens circulated alongside 'real' money: as a way to shore up grey markets; to trade against stored assets; to pay wages for everything from jury duty to sex work; to grant the bearer access to secret societies; to pay for wars and infrastructure; to remember; to credit; to keep account. Under industrial capitalism, money – the state-backed money that we use to pay our taxes – largely took over. Tokens didn't disappear entirely, but they were driven underground, into games, gambling, gifts, charity, student union bars, and onto the Silk Road. Now tokens are returning and multiplying. Maybe money as we know it was only ever a blip?

Money is being replaced by online tokens. By tokens I don't just mean the NFTs that drove headlines in 2021, but all the ways in which digital platforms are issuing new kinds of money-like things, from airtime to loyalty, gift vouchers, game tokens, and customer data. Tokens are now used to turn invisible stuff into assets, to pay wages, to track purchases, and to programme and specify the terms of financial access and inclusion. To offer a few examples, Amazon, a retail conglomerate, pays some Mechanical Turk workers in Amazon Gift Cards. Meanwhile, its streaming site, Twitch, is denominated in 'Bits', an in-channel token that acts as payment for streamers on the site. Online games, from *EverQuest* to *Eve Online*, trade in multiple virtual currencies that have real-world value. Coined tweets and digital memes are sold for thousands. The Chinese super-apps WeChat and Alibaba, with legacies in gaming and online retail, operate the payments systems that are used by virtually all Chinese citizens. The apps support online and in-store purchases, gameplay and virtual gifting. In turn, the data produced by these activities is used to underwrite credit. M-Pesa, the largest banking and mobile payments system in the Global South, is a formal version of 'airtime trading', in which mobile phone credit acts as informal currency. It is also predominantly owned by Vodafone – a mobile network operator.

Many of the companies issuing these tokens have a legacy in social media, gaming, and communications – not money. Most don't even have a financial licence.

4

But tokens are also lively and subversive. Users online and on the ground remake them to be paid in informal economies, to communicate, to protest, and to reimagine money. Since the 2008 financial crash, there has been an upsurge in experiments with tokens, from local exchange trading systems (LETS) to time banks. In 2021, meme economies on Reddit drove an attack on Wall Street. Gig workers, streamers, gamers, and sex workers still find ways of transforming online gift cards, wish lists, skins, and gaming tokens into liquid cash. Tokens are coloured by dark subreddit humour, gamified like e-sports, memed like a viral TikTok.

Some of the questions this book will explore are: If money is shifting to online tokens, who controls the shape these will take? What does it mean when online platforms become de facto banks? What new types of control and discrimination emerge when money is tied to specific apps, or actions, or online identities? How are tokens creating new value streams for virtual and physical assets, from tokenised bullion to consumer data, GIFs, and land in the metaverse? How are tokens a regulatory sleight of hand, driving exploitation in the gig economy and the fintech space? What is the balance of power between the state and the platform when these tokens are issued and redeemed, and how does this play out in different contexts? And how might online subcultures, activism, and internet art be spaces for reimagining what money could be, now and in the future?

What Is a Token?

There is a widespread sense that tokens are an internet-native phenomenon, something that surfaced along with the Bitcoin whitepaper and surged with the Covid-19 pandemic. It would be more accurate to say that new tokens rework a range of practices that have always ghosted the 'real' economy. In 7500

BC, Neolithic tokens emerged alongside the development of agriculture. The first tokens responded to a need to store and trade goods collectively. Clay was fixed into simple shapes representing commodities – quantities of grain, oil, livestock, and human labour.[2] These tokens were not only the first example of accounting; they were also the first example of written record-keeping. They were made to keep track of things. Later, the clay tokens became exchange media in their own right. They conjured the ownership of real things in the real world.

Tokens *are a value-transfer layer*. They can capture the value in things that are intangible, like digital memes, moments in time, and famous people's farts. But just as often, tokens are a way of allowing solid things that are unwieldy and generally 'illiquid' to enter the market. This is true of tokenised soy listed on the blockchain in 2023, just as it was true of Mesopotamian grain tokens nearly 10,000 years ago.

Archaeologists uncovered more tokens from 5000 BC Athens. Surviving accounts suggest they *were used in democratic processes* – for allocating seats, for voting and paying jury duties, and for making sure these processes were fair and transparent.[3] But in 2009 the Bitcoin whitepaper outlined a new kind of token, where users did not need to trust in one another, or the state, or a bank. Instead, they would 'trust in the code'.[4] State-backed money might be replaced altogether by so-called 'trustless' tokens, the whitepaper suggested – and so might government, with cryptographic tokens used to vote and pay for services.

This idea was popular with the Cypherpunks, an anarchist list on the early internet that believed in 'a technological solution to the problem of too much government'.[5] They developed many of the technologies that eventually became Bitcoin. 'Trust in the code' appealed to libertarian capitalists who wanted to switch out the state for smart cities in the Nevada desert; but it was also attractive to anarchist socialists, some of whom wanted to use crypto to build a better society. (These two groups and their preoccupations often bleed together.) As Athenian tokens demonstrated, tokens have always played a role in politics. But whereas these ancient tokens were designed to complement the democratic process, today there is a sense that smart tokens and smart contracts might *replace* politics altogether – that the right token might stand in for the messy business of human cooperation.

Throughout history, tokens have littered the edges of the economy, where markets fade to grey and then to black. For the most part they *were privately issued – an extra-legal sleight of hand*. Spintriae tokens found in ancient Rome may have been used in brothels or for gambling, where official coinage was forbidden.[6] In other moments, tokens circulated alongside official money – as a way to meet a shortfall in official coinage, to boost local economies, or as a means to pay wages or finance wars when there wasn't enough real money available.

While tokens do most of the things that proper money does – store value, buy things, and pay wages – the agents issuing them may claim, like my fellow countryman at Money20/20, that they are *not really* money at all. As something that is 'not quite money', tokens blur the hard edges between legitimate and illegitimate work and legitimate and illegitimate transactions. With tokens, someone is 'not really' a vendor or an employer, just as someone else is 'not really' working. Unlike the sex worker or the babysitter or the cleaner, who do parts of the same job for money, a housewife's work is 'not really' work at all. It is just what good wives and mothers do; the lack of a wage proves it. Players mining axolotls and gathering herbs in online worlds are not working to feed their families; they are just playing a game. A streamer in a hot tub on Twitch is 'just chatting', and if other users choose to send her a token, then it's all good. But it isn't money.

This plausible deniability benefits the big players. It allows companies like Amazon to employ people without formally being an employer and to process payments without being a bank. It allows a start-up to issue tokens that are securities or Electronic Trade Transfers in all but name, but sidestep regulation. For a moment in 2019, it even looked as though this grey area might allow Facebook to issue a private token with more clout than the US dollar. Tokens benefit platforms, then, but they also play a role for precarious workers eking out a living on and off the internet. Streamers and camgirls turn online 'gifts' from patrons into money. Gamers use skins as collateral for online gambling. Students bet on an NFT of a pair of virtual Nikes in the hope of turning one month's rent into three. Extremists are paid in subscriber tokens to share their conspiracy theories when many traditional processors have frozen them out.

Tokens are not just value; they *communicate more than the terms of an exchange*. They also joke and bond and troll. In a twist that evokes the strange 'bragging rights' of NFTs, royal tokens called *jetons royaux* in medieval France had a value that was tied to their iconography more than to their named exchange value or weight in gold. They carried an insider language – different layers of meaning wrapped in symbols – that most people who encountered them couldn't decipher.[7] If you could, it meant you were somehow in on the joke.

In the 1990s, anthropologist Viviana Zelizer explored how general-purpose money was 'earmarked' and transformed into special-purpose tokens throughout the nineteenth and twentieth centuries.[8] Before then, much of the sociology of money, from Marx to Simmel, took the view that money reduced every exchange to a transaction and every 'thing' to its price. Zelizer showed that while money calculates, it is nonetheless a deeply social technology. By changing the function or the appearance of general-purpose money, a simple payment could be changed into a lover's keepsake, a treat, a gift, or a bribe.

As an image search of 'Bitcoin' proves, tokens are clearly coded to say 'money': 'a little gold thing in a circle shape', as my four-year-old, Ted, put it. But they were also capable of communicating more than their exchange value. This is particularly true when these tokens circulate via group chat and social media. People use payments apps like Venmo and WeChat Pay not only to send money, but to joke with their friends, troll celebrities, and even harass ex-partners who have blocked them.[9] In online games, tokens like skins and emotes (a kind of animated reaction) are de facto currency, but they can also be used to flex, insult, or celebrate. Bored Ape and Friends With Benefits NFTs are investment tokens, but they also codify membership to an elite group.

Unlike 'commodity money', which is worth its weight in gold or silver, one definition of tokens is that they *are a medium of exchange that is worth more than whatever they're made of*. The token is not supposed to be valuable for what it is *in itself*, in other words, but because of what it represents. This link between representation and so-called 'real value' is not only the biggest question surrounding the nature of money; arguably, it's the biggest question surrounding meaning since the early twentieth century. The link between representations and things is what key questions of language, art, and value boil down to. This question reared its head when Western countries abandoned the gold standard, and when artists decided to designate mass-produced objects as 'art', and when poststructuralist philosophers challenged the relationship between words and things. But it is clearly also in play when we try to understand today what makes a token of an Elon Musk tweet 'valuable', or a token of a Shiba Inu internet meme popular.

Users are social with tokens – and platforms are in the business of monetising social interactions. As cash goes digital and social media platforms begin to process payments, the 'real money' is often in the *data* on how digital tokens are circulated, transferred, and spent. Increasingly, this data is used to profile consumers, fine-tune logistics, or underwrite credit and risk. Platforms also repackage this transactional data for the state, which uses it to profile and survey citizens. What

9

strategies – from reclaiming cash, to money-burning, to Bitcoin laundering – have users evolved to keep their tokens a secret?

Tokens confer *identity and access*. In fourth-century BC Athens, tokens stamped with inscriptions functioned as passports, guaranteeing safe passage or favoured treatment. They were credentials. Tokens found in the Roman city of Palmyra, meanwhile, seem to have been used to grant access to exclusive feasts and gatherings.[10] In Ancient Rome, tokens issued privately by patrons bestowed free swag – meals, gifts, alms, wine, hospitality, admissions to games and public spectacles. Medieval alms tokens singled out the 'deserving' poor, giving them access to items of basic sustenance like bread, wine, and charcoal. Such tokens provided credentials ('you, the bearer, are worthy') and access ('this is what you get').[11] Today, platforms are competing to issue the token that will act as a digital passport for users, rolling together payments, permissions, and credentials.

Tokens also constitute *contracts*, capturing an agreement between a host and guest, a creditor and debtor, a suitor and their intended, or a bank and a depositor. By transforming or limiting the liquidity of everyday money, tokens could be programmed to curb the economic freedoms of particular social groups: scrip tokens for workers that could only be spent in the employer's own store; store credit for a wife; vouchers and food stamps for the poor. Tokens can thus also be a way of attaching special conditions to payments. They can bring spending, eating, parenting, and, well, *living* in line with the issuer's objectives. Not just value, then, but *values*. In the United States, for example, food stamps cannot be used to purchase alcohol or cigarettes or pre-cooked meals for your family. In the past, users found creative ways around these terms and conditions. But this is no longer always possible. Tokens are now *programmable*: rules are 'hard-coded' into exchange by way of smart contracts or software. Tokens are habitually tied to identity, to loyalty, to citizenship and refugee status, to employment, to life choices and social standing. This kind of tokenised authority affects some more than others. What values are written into tokens? And who writes this script – the state or the platform?

Technology is never neutral. Who shapes it and what it does have political consequences. As Langdon Winner noted, our 'artefacts have politics'.[12] Over time, as a technology moves from the shiny foreground into the background, these effects are fixed, even forgotten. Sometimes – particularly in moments of breakdown or unrest – these politics come back into view. Arguably, the financial crash of 2008 was one of these moments. People began to ask how money was made and might be made differently. Money was broken. How to fix it? A hum of experiments with alternative currencies, from basic income to babysitting circles, grew into a din: tokens with no leader; tokens that support local communities; decolonial tokens to repay centuries of inequality; tokens coined to account for things that are commonly external to the real economy, like care for others, or care for the environment; central-bank digital currencies managed by the state.

More or Less

As Clare Rowan and her co-editors point out, application of the word 'token' to this range of practices is so broad it's not always useful.[13] Tokens – from ether to Bits to NFTs – are for paying, but they also capture assets, access, bonds, identity, contracts, surveillance, control, prestige, and power.

Tokens, then, *are both more and less than money*. They are less because they are not legal tender. They usually have a limited functionality, making them less liquid than general-purpose money. They can be redeemed only for certain things or only by certain people, in certain places, or at certain times. But tokens are also more than money. A token can be a game, a passcode, a ticket, a social tie, a keepsake, a bribe, a secret message, a gift, a promise, a vote, an ownership stake, a joke, a meme, an art, a flex, a bet, a law, another token. Tokens deal in more than money. Tokens blur the lines between the market and the social, but they also show us where the lines are drawn in a society – between money and intimacy, work and play, artifice and authenticity, legitimate and illegitimate financial activity, and representation and value.

Tokens are not money. But by exploring their past and present we might begin to glean what money is, and what it might be in the near future.

The chapters that follow probe this 'more and less'. When I finished writing them, I had a better knowledge of the history of tokens and a speculative take on the future of Web3 – but I'm not sure if I was any closer to saying what tokens or money *were* exactly, or even how they were distinct. These stories follow the winks and the blurred edges, not to draw hard lines once and for all – because we can't. Values cannot be squared away, put to a vote, or written into a smart contract. This is what keeps them interesting.

1

A Bit of Cheer

In 2012 I was involved in a campaign against zero-hours contracts in the university where I worked. In the aftermath of the financial crash, my employer was careful to keep wages low for adjuncts and avoid anything that might later be used to claim employment rights. I carried a similar teaching load to a tenured academic, but for that I was paid in a semester what my permanent colleagues took home each month after tax. And I felt lucky. In some other universities, or so the whispers went, temporary staff were now being paid in multi-store gift cards, book tokens, and Amazon vouchers.

By such a token, money can be ritualised as a gift and distinguished from other payments, wages, or remittances. Transformed in this way, money is no longer payment due, but becomes, as sociologist Viviana Zelizer described it, a 'bit of cheer' or some 'little thing'.[1]

The gift card is also a way of paying without appearing to pay, from a legal perspective. As something other than a wage that registers on the books, the work it compensates can fade from view.

Amazon Gift Cards are not only a common form of payment for adjunct lecturers, foreign remittances, and Christmas bonuses, but also for informal online work, topping the wish lists of influencers, streamers, and cam models on sites like Chaturbate, Twitch, and OnlyFans. Amazon Gift Cards are tax-free and highly liquid and can be redeemed for anything in the Amazon store – which is to say, for just about anything. Gift card exchanges and resale forums appear online for trading and/or cashing a gift balance out. In some instances, Amazon Gift Cards denominated in dollars even trade above par on eBay and the dedicated Reddit forums. In countries where the local currency is unstable, being paid in Amazon dollars is a coup – an arbitrage that benefits both parties.

Amazon even pays its non-US and non-Indian Mechanical Turk workers exclusively in Amazon Gift Cards. These workers receive not a physical card that can be transferred, but a redeemable code that can only be spent on the site and only by the named party. Many of these workers live in areas that Amazon delivery does not reliably serve. Allegedly, some workers find ways around this problem by buying things for others at a discount and getting paid in bitcoins.

Here the gift card is 'scrip' – a wage paid in a token that is issued by and can only be redeemed through the employer. It was once common enough to pay workers in food, coupons, tokens, or trade checks. These tokens could usually be exchanged only for goods held by the company, in a special worker's store for example, including those goods the worker had toiled to produce – the coal you had mined, say, or the fruit you had picked. The token kept the flow of wages and profits in a closed loop. It made sure no value escaped the system.

In the 1800s and 1900s, laws known as 'Truck Acts' and 'Store Orders' forbade the payment of workers in anything but legal tender, with no 'scrip, coupons, punchouts, tokens or trade checks'.[2] These acts were repealed in the UK in 1986, ostensibly to pave the way for electronic transfers. Today, scrip wages are once more a common feature of the gig economy, where gift and store cards act as piece wages for hidden work.

The problem is, if you are paid in the boss's own token, they alone get to decide how it's used and how much it's worth. The worker is accountable to the employee's valuation process and subject to their terms of redemption. Universities paying workers in gift cards is 'precarious', in that it offers no contract; but scrip is precarious in another sense, as in 'at the pleasure or discretion of another'. These tokens let platforms do as they please.

Another example of this scrip is the issuance of Bits by Twitch, the Amazon-owned streaming platform. Viewers can purchase Bits with dollars and donate them (or 'cheer' them, in the vernacular of the platform) to streamers on the site. A hundred Bits can be purchased for roughly $1.40. Streamers can redeem these Bits for 70 per cent of their purchase price, while Amazon takes a 30 per cent cut.

For Twitch, Bits are a way of capturing value from content on the platform, but they are also a regulatory sleight of hand, a way of employing workers without a contract and processing payments without a financial licence. For streamers and users on the platform, though, these tokens can also be a way to express themselves and bond with others. Even more importantly, they are a loophole into the grey market, a way for workers to get paid for marginal and/or extra-legal work.

A popular ASMR streamer called Foxenkin is wearing animal ears and whispering seductively into a microphone. Her room is low-lit, like the seedy glow of a monitor in the dead of night. There's the obligatory convention of teddy bears lined up on a bed in the background, including a near human-sized specimen with an ESC key on its stomach, mansprawling across the frilly duvet. The technical setup includes two Neumann condenser microphones positioned shoulder-width apart and a binaural microphone with two silicone ears, engineered to give the auditory impression that the streamer is speaking from inside the viewer's head.

ASMR (autonomous sensory meridian response) consists of psychoacoustic effects designed to produce a tingling sensation in the listener, that 'shivers down the spine' feeling when something looks or sounds particularly beautiful. It's popular on YouTube, and so popular on Twitch that it has its own dedicated channel. Many enthusiasts fight to distinguish the tingles produced by ASMR from goal-orientated sexual arousal or orgasm – but, like a lot of things on Twitch, the lines are blurred.

Foxenkin's goal is clearly stated: for 5,000 Bits (roughly $50 after Amazon has taken its cut), she will lick the binaural ear for ten minutes. Alongside subscribing to her channel and gifting subscriptions to other viewers, Twitch viewers can donate Bits by typing a message into the chat box. They can also scroll down and click a link that takes them to her curated Amazon wish list and choose from her selection of gift cards, World of Warcraft figurines, and yoga mats, or to her pet's Amazon wish list (mostly collars and cat baskets).

Foxenkin taps her long acrylic nails along the shaft of a heavy-duty condenser mic, and runs them through her long black hair, making a tugging sound like a rope unfurling in my earbuds. Sometimes she pulls in other props – a jar of water, a pipe made of delicate blue glass, which she draws on, blowing a wisp of smoke across the microphone – whispering, gasping, purring like a big cat, responding, gently, to her viewers' in-channel descriptions of their crippling insomnia.

Twitch is the latest in a line of life-logging websites, the first of which was the Jennicam, a live-cam feed in the late nineties that logged both the mundane and sexual activities of camgirl Jennifer Kaye Ringley. Twitch emerged in 2011 from a streaming website called Justin.tv, a feed that saw the founder Justin Kan fix a webcam to his baseball cap, don a backpack full of hardware, and set about 'lifecasting' his every move. Users were given accounts called 'channels', and encouraged to broadcast their own live video content under headings like 'people and lifecasting', 'gaming', 'entertainment', 'music and radio', 'animals', and 'divas and dudes'. In 2011 the company created a new site geared to streaming gaming content – Twitch.

It goes without saying that gaming as a social or networked phenomenon – meeting co-workers in *Animal Crossing* during the pandemic, playing *Fortnite* with friends online – has grown in popularity in the past decade. So have platforms dedicated to watching other people play video games (growing up with five brothers, this was basically my childhood). Partly due to a boost during lockdown, when many live sports were cancelled, e-sports, as they are called, now boast revenue greater than many of their IRL counterparts. There are numerous websites dedicated entirely to e-sports: Facebook Gaming; YouTube Gaming; Nitro; Caffeine. Twitch is the most popular.

Twitch was acquired in August 2014 by Amazon in an all-cash deal for $970 million, after anti-trust regulation caused a similar deal with Google to fall through. But to say that Twitch is a game-streaming platform is to reduce the variety of live streams on offer, from crafting and drawing, music broadcasts and dancing, public eating, and political commentary, to vlogs, hot-tub streams, and ASMR performances like Foxenkin's.

Among the usual long tail of amateur streamers sharing niche content with only a few followers, there are also streamers who have shot to fame on the platform. xQc, aka Félix Lengyel, is a Canadian streamer with over 78,000 subscribers at the time of writing. He is famous for playing the multiplayer game *Overwatch*. Tarik, a first-semester college dropout, now makes a living playing *Valorant* on the platform, a first-person shooter game released during the pandemic. His streams average around 40,660 viewers at any one time.

Pokimane is a 'just chatting' streamer based in Canada, whose content bounces between cutesy talk about her cat and hairstyle of the day, sharing her opinions on big tech, and playing *League of Legends*. In contrast, Amouranth, a.k.a. Kaitlyn Michelle Siragusa, is the site's most popular 'hot-tub streamer', a glamour model who flirts with the boundaries of Twitch's acceptable nudity policies.

A streamer goes live. Viewers have the option of watching and/or actively engaging through games and a live-chat function. The feeling is one of messing around online, but streamers can monetise their content – whether playing video games, painting with their feet, or purring like a cat – in a number of ways, depending on whether they are partnered or affiliated with Twitch. Like YouTube, one source of revenue resides in in-channel advertisements and sales through affiliated links. In China, streaming sites have come full circle to resemble the live shopping channels of the 1990s. Streamers like xQc usually recommend equipment to their fans, and include links to the gaming equipment they use.

Another revenue source for affiliated streamers takes the form of paid subscriptions or 'subs', offering viewers the opportunity to support a streamer's feed on a monthly or annual basis, as a way to show support and access exclusive content. Pokimane, for example, earns $35,000 a month from her 9,500 subscribers. Subscriber perks include private chat rooms, where patrons can access exclusive content and exclusive 'emotes' (emojis) that can be used in the chat. Subscribers see themselves as fans or 'patrons', with the less specific financial support that term implies, rather than outright consumers demanding a specific return for their money.

Users can subscribe to a streamer, but they can also gift subscriptions to others in a channel. Subscription fees are normally split equally between the streamer and the platform, although a data leak in 2021 revealed that popular streamers may be able to demand more favourable terms. Many streamers will also have other interfaces for generating revenue: links to Amazon wish lists where viewers can buy personalised gifts, links to other platforms where exclusive content can be subscribed to such as OnlyFans or Patreon, or links to off-channel sites for donations.

Another source of income, particularly for streamers who are not affiliated with the platform, lies in in-channel donations through Twitch's token of choice, Bits. Previously, streamers would provide links to external PayPal accounts where users could send a donation if they felt like it. In 2016, Twitch introduced its own in-platform tipping system. Bits are a 'virtual good' that viewers can buy on the Twitch platform using PayPal or Amazon's preferred system of payment, Amazon

Pay. Revenue streams are split 70/30 between the streamer and the platform.

In the manner of in-game currencies, these tokens allow the viewer to interact in the channel using messages or animated 'emotes'; to show support for streamers; to send messages; to influence or shape content; to participate in live games; or to earn and unlock badges or virtual loot during special events. Twitch urges viewers to 'keep some on hand so you can join the conversation anytime you want'.

I sign up for an account on Twitch and use a credit card I share with my husband to purchase some Bits. I get a small discount as a first-time buyer. I choose my username almost at random, scanning the pile of books on the windowsill to my right and typing 'sick_of_nature', which seems to convey the unwholesome beta-male persona I somehow imagine lurks in Twitch's hot-tub streams.

Sick_of_nature enters a room where a woman, Katrina, who looks to be roughly my age, is blowing into a polka dot swimming ring. The performance hasn't officially started. This is the backstage – the business of getting ready to perform – but the camera and the streamer's body are carefully angled to give a view of jiggling flesh in hot pants as she wrestles with her giant pool toy. I choose a customised emote worth 100 Bits, a festive birthday streamer. Katrina pauses for a second, pulling her mouth from the valve. 'Thank you sick of nature', she whispers in a breathy voice (or maybe she is just out of breath). I feel a voyeuristic and slightly sick thrill of communion, hearing this name that I have just thought up whispered back to me on the channel. Hearing it back, I'm not sure I like it. I close my laptop down and go to get my child ready for swimming.

Sending a small number of Bits might result in a polite onscreen acknowledgement from the streamer. Sending a large number usually triggers more of a fanfare: animated *Ivan the Terrible*-style showers of coins raining down on the streamer, cutaways of the streamer celebrating, the sounds of crowds cheering, animated confetti streaming and money clinking into the chest, your name on the streamer's leader board, your name on the streamer's body, your name on the streamer's forehead. There are supercuts on YouTube dedicated to nothing but 'Bit Bombs' of 100,000 or more, with streamers mouthing in shock or breaking down and crying with gratitude and what looks like relief.

Through these reactions, the process of cheering and subscribing is turned into a game. A streamer will commonly specify targets that are denominated in Bits or subs: a spin-the-wheel game, a dance, a change of costume. For Amouranth, 2,000 Bits will see her don a horse's head mask and trot around the set, astride a sweeping brush. For CodeMiko, one of the site's most popular virtual streamers, the viewers' Bits can alter her appearance, adding or removing hair or altering breast size. The token is a logic gate; a set figure triggers a reaction on the screen or in the body of the performer.

If subscriptions are tied to a longer investment in a streamer, Bits are made to register instantly. The value of a stream is partly this sense of immediacy, that viewer and performer occupy the same moment in time. The cheer is not only about rewarding the streamer or a clever comment in the channel, then, it's also about ritualising this shared instant. Bits tokenise the now, designed to 'celebrate the moments you love with the community, all right in chat', according to Twitch's blog.

Researchers exploring streaming platforms in China have identified various motivations for sending gifts and virtual tokens to streamers. They indicate a desire to reward 'valuable content', or show support and appreciation for the streamer. But tokens are also a way to stand out from the crowd, to signal status or grab attention. Sometimes the token is a way to bridge and foster a lingering connection between the person cheering and the person on screen. More nefariously, tokens can also be used to communicate approval or disapproval, to say 'keep going' or 'stop'. In rare cases, they are also used to mark out territory, to assert domination over others in the channel or over the streamer themselves.[3]

Money Talks

'Money talks', Marshall McLuhan writes, because money is a metaphor, a transfer, and a bridge.[4] When theorists like McLuhan and Sybille Krämer argue that money is media, they are speaking about the ability of money to communicate price signals, or in some cases to signal something about the person wielding the bills.[5] Bits say more than the sum of their worth. They are put to work to 'cheer', but they are also used to roll your eyes, convey boredom, sarcasm, or surprise, and to nudge onscreen behaviour.

They are money-*ish*, but they are also a fast-paced language, full of jokes and burns and barbs. A cheer is not money or a transaction, Amazon is quick to confirm, but a particular kind of chat message, one with more clout, one with cooler emotes. Bits are 'communicated' rather than 'spent' or 'donated'.

I'm reminded of *The Hunger Games*, the book that single-handedly launched the young-adult dystopian (YAD) genre, in which twenty-four teenage 'tributes' fight to the death in a live-streamed competition. Survival depends not only on their ability to fight and think on their feet, but on gifts from wealthy viewers in the form of food, water, medicine, and weapons. Growing up, tribute Katniss Everdeen has had to resort to hunting in the forests around her district (and selling her kills on the grey market) to feed her family. In the arena, her survival hinges not only on things like shooting down other tributes with a bow and arrow, but producing and eventually manifesting real emotions for the audience watching at home. Like the authenticity work of streamers and influencers, the task involves more than surface acting, and Katniss ends up with something approaching real romantic feelings for another tribute. Meanwhile, Katniss's mentor Haymitch watches the stream from outside the arena. He uses the flow of gifts to send her messages from a distance, reinforcing certain behaviours and punishing others. Over time, she comes to understand the signals conveyed through the gift – that one staged kiss, for example, equals one vial of medicine, or one pot of broth.[6] This is a hunger game. But it's also a power game.

Amouranth's content spans hot-tub performances, ASMR, and a range of 'just chatting' streams. Some of this 'just chatting' takes place in front of her screen: Amouranth in a pink bra and fitted boy shorts, delicately tweezing edamame beans from a bento box with plastic chopsticks and complaining about the heat of a Texas summer. At other times it takes place outdoors at a local stables in Houston: Amouranth horse-riding with a go-pro attached to her helmet, gazing out between the horse's ears at the trail unfolding in front of her. The context – wedged between channels for *Outlaws* and *Red Dead Redemption 2* – lends these outdoorsy streams the feel of a Western game interface, where a first-person player rides through a virtual landscape on a CGI horse, fighting off wolves and hunting bounties.

When I log in today, she is doing squats in a hot tub. It's not an actual hot tub, but the kind of inflatable paddling pool you might blow up in the garden on a hot day. Amouranth has set hers up indoors, precariously close to her technical system. In line with Twitch guidelines, her underwear covers her nipples and vulva in non-transparent material. Her skin is branded with names, scrawled there with a black permanent marker. The interface on the screen suggests that these are the remnants of an interactive game. Five subs spins the wheel; ten gets your name on the streamer's body; twenty subs gets squats; two hundred gets your name on her forehead. Someone called Caedus has already made a donation worth $1,370, and their name is printed on her face in block capitals, and more legibly in neon font on the left side of the screen.

The spinning wheel is a homemade version of the classic gameshow kind, with segments of rainbow-coloured card labelled 'more squats', 'dare', and 'Q&A'. At the centre of the wheel is a giant cut-out of a surprised-looking Shiba Inu, the meme associated with Dogecoin. From ten lacklustre squats, Amouranth moves on to a quick Q&A session, climbing, dripping water, out of the paddling pool and leaning dangerously close to her monitor to read the messages in the chat: 'How – do – your – toes – not get – pruny – being – in – the water for so long? ... They do. They get *totally* pruny. I don't know why people think they wouldn't ...'

Amouranth has a real body that sweats in the Texas heat and prunes in soft water, that probably grows tired from excessive twerking. More recently, virtual streamers such as Projekt Melody and CodeMiko have entered the space. Virtual streamers take the form of 3D avatars, but they are animated by a real person wearing motion capture sensors fed to a 3D gaming engine. In the opening credits of her live stream, the avatar twerks robotically in front of a menu that lists various 'body morphs'. Changes to 'butt size' require from 60 to 600 Bits, depending on whether you want a subtle or more obvious modification, while various others control head size, neck length, musculature, weight, and breast size.

The token is a communication designed to express itself not only within the channel, but immediately and directly on the body of the performer. Nothing drives this home more than the work of tokens in the sex-camming platform, Chaturbate.[7] Like Twitch, Chaturbate enacts a tipping or donation system using in-platform tokens that are split between the platform and the cam model. Unlike Twitch, though, which flirts with the fuzzy boundaries of sexualised content, Chaturbate features full nudity and real sex acts. Tokens are solicited through interactive games, where donations are often tied to teledildonic vibrators that act directly on the cam model's body. For example, 15 to 99 tokens might equal ten seconds of vibration at a medium speed, while 100 to 499 might deliver fifteen seconds of high-speed vibration: 'Tease me with your tips,' a streamer's caption reads, 'make me cum with ur love'. Here, the token is a communication designed to register on the streamer's body, a voltage difference that makes a difference. It's money that can reach across space and literally touch the performer, stroke her, get inside her.

The virtual streamer Projekt Melody is currently the most famous cam model on Chaturbate. She also has a significant presence on Twitch, where she shares her semi-nude hentai artworks. Melody's backstory reveals she is an AI character, formerly designed to clean up email spam, before she was accidentally 'corrupted' by porn malware. Chaturbate now sees the avatar writhing in response to virtual tokens by way of a virtual Lovense, a popular teledildonic vibrator designed to translate tokens into, in this case, virtual sensations. (I keep using the word 'virtual' here, as though there's something novel about watching a fake orgasm on the internet. The joke of Melody is that of course there isn't, and it doesn't really matter.)

Like the names written across Amouranth's forehead, Bits register instantly on the channel. But as something more than a two-way market transaction (which is designed to settle instantly), they also forge a connection between the streamer and her public – they stick around, they linger. I picture Amouranth after the cameras have been turned off and the pool toys deflated, scrubbing patiently at the permanent marker on her cheek with a wet facecloth.

The next time I check in, Amouranth is dancing in the same bikini. She's a little awkward, approachable, more like a teenager at the Christmas disco than a glamour model doing seduction. The chat comes quick and fast, Kappa Demons and Miss Piggies cheering, and Kermit the Frogs staring agape, cmonBruhs, Gachigasms, streams of purple hearts, and other memes I don't really understand. Moderators – usually enthusiastic fans who have shown their loyalty to the streamer – are monitoring the chat feed, encouraging tips and deleting trolling or inappropriate comments before they have a chance to register. The atmosphere feels ... festive. One user redeems 1,000 Bits to make their chat message stand out in bright purple; another gifts five subscriptions to other members in the channel.

Different emotes carry different meanings, used to communicate sarcasm, celebrate, show gratitude, troll or call out trolling, be ironic – or, like the DoritosChip emoji, to celebrate or virtually share food. Much as in the world of online memes and emojis, Bit emotes have specific values, both on Twitch as a whole and within specific channels. The right token at the right time says you belong. It buys access in more ways than one.

Not only the variety of emotes but the ways they are used are sometimes difficult for me to follow. I can look up the meaning of common emotes like 'Kappa', a meme of the Twitch chat developer Josh DeSeno's face (used as a sarcastic eyeroll); Hahaa (cringing); the various Pepe memes (feelsgoodman/feelsbadman), for which it's debatable whether the alt-right symbology carries over to Twitch; or MrDestructoid, used for a glitch in communication, or to call out 'fake' or mercenary behaviour like view botting. I get to see this one in use when the sound and animation for Projekt Melody part company during a live feed, and again when CodeMiko's engineer appears to briefly lose control of her right breast. I can read about these symbols and even see them in operation, but, like a foreign language, I don't have the vernacular down. I'm an outsider searching through handfuls of change for the right token. *Was that a frog or was that money?* The meanings are hard to decipher, but that's the point. They're supposed to be.

In antiquity, possession of a token often regulated access to a privileged space, more key than currency. Coming to them centuries on, their meanings are locked up; they look like coined nonsense. Clearly, as professor Clare Rowan, a historian of token use in the Ancient Mediterranean, tells me, some tokens were 'designed *not* to facilitate wider communication'.[8] They traded on insider language. Your possession of the token and your grasp of its meaning marked you as an insider.

I cycle slowly through the list of Bits and emotes available to me. A stream of purple hearts is a safe enough bet, but a shamrock draws the channel's scorn. My choice of token says I don't belong.

Both memes and monetary transactions are what Sybille Krämer calls 'transmission events' – systems of exchange that include viruses, linguistic translation, and money.[9] As meme and money, the Bit contains competing messages that are at once symbolic, cultural, and economic. In other words, the Bit functions as a price and as a communication designed to signal to the streamer ('well done', 'keep going', or 'that was awkward'), but also as a broader cultural meme. A meme is a 'unit of culture' that moves from mind to mind.[10] Not unlike money, its survival depends on its being sticky enough to circulate, but rare enough to signal specialist knowledge. Just as money weighs supply and scarcity, memes flirt with the space between common and insider knowledge. As tokens, this is what Bits do so well, balancing inside jokes with a sense of belonging.

Twitch is not the only online token that blends memes and money. Emotes are also used in *Fortnite* to troll and celebrate. The payments app Venmo famously incorporates messages and emojis into its payments system – a playful account of everyday consumption. Different Unicode symbols become shorthand for different transactions: 'money with wings' for a remittance, or a plant emoji for weed. China's WeChat, a former social media and messaging platform, integrated payments into its messaging system. These are used not only to settle accounts, but also to reward other members – a boss might send hongbao ('red packet') envelopes for Friday drinks – or to tease other members of a group chat ('buy yourself an Alka Seltzer' the day after). Here, as on Twitch, the value is less in the monetary reward than the social meanings conveyed through the token. Users of the app are urged to 'let the red packet speak'.[11]

The most famous meme currency is Dogecoin, a fork of Bitcoin that built upon the popularity of the doge meme. The meme – we all know it – features an anxious Shiba Inu dog surrounded by fragmented thoughts that are, presumably, a Comic Sans manifestation of its own internal monologue. Much introspection. From its inception, Dogecoin blended internet money with internet memes. The jokey nature of the doge colours how it's used online – the right token for the right transaction. From its inception, Dogecoin was largely used to blend microtransactions into the broader fabric of online communications on sites like Twitter and Reddit, where users sent small amounts of the currency to 'tip' or 'thank' others for their contributions. As Sarah Jeong describes it, Doge is a token earmarked to reward 'socially valuable content' online. The transactions are usually small enough that their social and communicative function outweighs their role as money. As Jeong puts it, Doge transactions represent a payment in kind, a joke for another joke. Is this a lesson about the economy or is it, as Jeong suggests, a lesson about the internet?[12] When Elon Musk invested in Dogecoin on behalf of his progeny in 2021, and briefly flipped the Twitter bird logo to a Shiba Inu in 2023, it seemed like the joke was on us.

Like Doge, Bits are a currency whose primary use is to reward in-channel content, a monetary 'like' or 'follow' that sees social value outweigh exchange. But as memes themselves, with variable forms and expressions, they also *are* the cultural content.

Wishes

Bits drift between currency and communication, but this in-betweenness also makes them popular as an extra-regulatory payment. Performers can use their not-quite-money status to monetise the flows and quirks of typically non-market stuff like chatting, messing around, and forming relationships online.

Bits broker the in-between, flirting with very nuanced distinctions between money and 'some little thing', between work and non-work, message and price signal, authentic behaviour and performance:

- Hi everyone! Was wondering what you ladies put on you amazon Wishlists [*sic*] for only fans ☺ I want ideas ☺
- E gift cards, that's it. Don't have to worry about my address being potentially exposed and I can buy whatever. [*sic*] Want with the e-giftcards.
- Toys lingerie teddies video games household appliances. Add whatever you like!
- Ok! I put home stuff on there too just wasn't sure if that was appropriate haha. I also put some electronics ☺[13]

Unlike a lot of Chinese streaming platforms that fully embrace the idea of the virtual 'gift', Twitch relies on tokens that hover somewhere between donation, tip, gift, and payment, with all the uncertainty this implies. And yet, by Twitch's own terms of use, they are none of these things: the platform is quick to state in its guide to cheering that Bits 'have no monetary value' and that 'users cannot make a purchase, donate, or tip with Bits'.

Bits operate at the boundary between different kinds of transactions, then: not quite a payment, not quite charity, not quite a gift or a bribe. What's more, while Bits can be cheered and acknowledged and gambled and even tacitly encouraged, in accordance with Twitch's terms of service, they cannot be outright *requested*. Users cannot expect any quantifiable return from their Bits, and streamers cannot expect any specific return for their performance. They can link to wish lists and tip jars, but these are suggestions rather than price lists.

I spend a lot of time looking at these Amazon wish lists during work hours. I have to do this work on a separate computer, because my university's firewall won't allow me to visit streaming and adult websites – or, it turns out, even forums dedicated to the business of streaming and adult websites. I steal the old computer covered in dinosaur stickers my four-year-old uses to watch Netflix. Incidentally, his favourite show at the time is *Glitter Force* (*Smile Pretty Cure!* in Japanese), where magical teenagers collect tokens they use to battle evil. Or, as he describes it, 'you know ... the one where the pretty girls turn into love creatures and get money to fight'. I make a Post-it on the desktop. My husband reads from it incredulously one morning: 'black feather whip, animal ears, yoghurt, *How to Win Friends and Influence People*, Michael Kors clutch ...'

The gifts on the Amazon wish lists begin to soft-focus until they all look like the same woman. On OnlyFans and Chaturbate there is a lot of make-up, uncomfortable-looking shoes and underwear, headbands with animal ears. And interspersed with these obvious 'costumes', there are more pragmatic pieces of active wear, form-fitted leggings and sports bras (which feel like they might be worn in the streamer's downtime, but which may also be costumes). On Twitch, maybe in a nod to the geekier audience, the wished-for items veer towards quirky gaming and *World of Warcraft*.

There is quite a bit of home décor, presumably to furnish the streamer's set – things like throw pillows and strings of LED lights of the kind you might see strung up in a teenage girl's bedroom. They are domestic props that feel personal, hinting at, if not exactly a rich interior life, then at least the glimpse of something authentic. But they are also universal enough to have a broad appeal, to give the impression, like an IKEA showroom, that a basic set of protocols has been carefully skewed to produce the effect of a real domestic interior – of a *real interior life*. There's a dreamcatcher, a print that says 'coffee strong, lashes long, hustle on'. One item in particular catches my eye: an LED sign in a dusky pink that says: 'DO WHAT YOU LOVE' in sanserif font.

Some wish for the necessary technical equipment: ring lights, tripods, webcam stands. The list of wishes and wants is a mixture of what Erving Goffman called the front- and the backstage – although, as with the yoga pants, it's hard to say where the real stuff ends and the performance begins. Some of the gifts are here because patrons want to buy them, or at least imagine buying them, while others are part of the practical business of producing and editing an online stream.

There's the occasional book: one of my lists from a Chaturbate streamer calling herself Sweet_Ary includes *How to Win Friends and Influence People* directly underneath *The Automatic Millionaire* and an investor's guide to cryptoassets. Sweet_Ary has also earmarked a Dogecoin mousepad. There are lots of wants and wishes, but very few basic needs. There are lots of cat toys and treats, but only very occasionally children's clothes or toys.

In my experience, it's rare to find something that points outside, to the practical business of domestic care and maintenance. I see a cordless vacuum cleaner, but it's an aspirational Dyson. Once, a jumbo pack of paper towels. But mostly the items exist in a fantasy world. The business of turning flammable underwear into cash or groceries happens backstage. And then there are the gift cards for popular stores like Amazon, Sephora, and Starbucks, picked for their high liquidity.

On message boards, streamers talk the fine art of wish list curation: What is an acceptable gift to ask for? What is too practical? What is too much? What do patrons prefer to buy? What are some good ways of turning the gift into a payment without seeming too mercenary or calculating? What sites are best for selling gift cards at cost? What kinds of privacy issues or potential disclosures does the wish list involve – for example, will their name or home address be inadvertently revealed to the buyer in a receipt? What does it cost to rent a PO box, and is it worth it? 'It is *so* worth it.' There are frequent issues with cancellations and chargebacks that mean the gift balance should be spent as quickly as possible, or with patrons marking something as 'purchased' for a perk when it really isn't. There are companies like WishTender on here, advertising their

A BIT OF CHEER

wares as wish list go-betweens – for a fee, they allow patrons to experience the gift, but turn it into cash for the streamer at the other end.

Do What You Love

'Some of the earliest tokens were used for prostitution', people are fond of saying. Like the myth of barter: 'before money was invented, people traded goats for firewood ...', it's one of those potted economic histories that gets churned up when you stick your hand in. These 'Spintriae', as they were called, were made from base metals. The coin couples sex with numbers. Heads is a sex act, tails is a number.

On the surface, it seems simple, like the coin is naming its act and naming its price. And given that it was treason to pay for sex with a coin that bore the image of the emperor, and illegal for slaves to handle any kind of money at all, this theory makes sense. The token might have allowed the customer and the slave to transact without ever handling or exchanging 'real' money.

But there are problems with this theory, one being that there is no straightforward match between the sex act and the numeral; the same acts are shown alongside wildly different amounts on different tokens. Maybe this was because, like a lot of services, the cost was lower as you got further from the capital. Clare Rowan thinks it is more likely that the objects in question were game pieces or souvenirs – a token held in memory, like a cruder version of the lover's keepsake.[14]

Writing of the more recent history of brothel tokens in the United States, Carly Kocurek likewise argues that these tokens were advertisements and souvenirs more than they were ever utility tokens that changed hands for a hand job. The tokens' power is in fantasy, the 'fantasy of purchase' or acquisition of another.[15] They play at owning something that can't be bought, at least not for this price. On Twitch, the fantasy of the token is

31

not necessarily one of direct ownership, but of authenticity – of real connection.

Because tokens are not real money, they hide the transaction. They abstract the work away. They allow everyone to pretend that what is happening is 'just for fun', that it happens 'among friends'. In a May 2000 article on the rise of private currencies, journalist Diane Coyle writes that her babysitting circle used Monopoly money as a means of payment.[16] The toy token hid the act of payment between a group of affluent friends, but it still tallied who owed what.

Tokens negotiate the tender boundaries between markets and online authenticity. Tokens, as some 'thing' that is not quite money, can temporarily shrug off the transaction. But equally, they are part of the work of keeping these things – online work and online play, friendship and business – separate. The token draws a line between the business of getting paid and the business of 'doing what you love'.

When I talk about money or a living wage for their work, my art students are sometimes uncomfortable, or confused. They love what they do – most of them love it so much they would do it for free. And 'doing what you love' is supposed to be outside the world of payment. It's supposed to foreclose the possibility of exploitation.

In the 1970s, Silvia Federici penned a manifesto called *Wages against Housework*. I show these same students images of the campaign: women with centre partings and high-waisted jeans marching below a banner. For Federici, the fact that women's work in the home was so often framed as a 'labour of love' hid its significance to capitalism. Demanding a wage ripped the veil from the assumption that some forms of work – like childcare or homemaking – were natural to women; to demand payment is, in Federici's words, to 'refuse that work as the expression of our nature, and therefore to refuse precisely the female role that capital has invented for us'.[17] The banners say 'Wages for Housework', but Federici's essay replaces 'for' with 'against'.

The money itself is not really what's at stake, in other words; but demanding a wage brings this invisible labour into a market where it can be seen as work, and, more importantly, refused.

Writing of the earmarking of domestic money, Viviana Zelizer dealt with controversies surrounding married women's allowances in the twentieth century. Women's money often had a 'special vocabulary that set it apart from ordinary cash', known as 'pin money', 'egg money', 'pocket money', 'butter money', or 'dole'. There were also difficulties negotiating the transfer of domestic money from husband to wife. Should the money a husband gave to his wife be a payment, an entitlement, or a gift? The payment, Zelizer writes, implied something too close to a working transaction. In fact, 'paying' a wife was illegal, since it made her 'a menial and a servant in the home where she should discharge marital duties in devoted and loving ministrations'.[18] Framing it as an entitlement – something she was *due* – conferred a dangerous power. The gift, finally, implied subordination and precarity, being subject to someone else's whims and inclinations. In upper- and middle-class households, Zelizer writes, women rarely handled cash, but instead 'relied almost entirely on "invisible" dollars, crediting their expenses', and had to resort to 'asking and cajoling and begging' for additional cash. If this failed, there were always other 'underground' tactics, from 'home pocket-picking' to 'padding bills' – for example, getting a dressmaker to send a bill for an inflated sum and pocketing the excess.[19]

I have an awkward conversation with my mother, who was married in 1966, three weeks after her twentieth birthday: 'Your father decided that £5 a week would do it. That was to pay for my food Monday to Friday.' I check it later with an online inflation calculator. It amounts to just under €120. She lapses into calculations based on the pre-decimal system: 'The bus from Dublin cost nineteen and six ...'. And what about clothes and things like that?, I ask. 'Well, sometimes he was paid in postal orders and he would give them over to me to cash in. Those were for clothes and children's toys, days out, treats, that kind of thing.' The conversation hitches and stalls, as it often does with money and family. It feels intrusive. It feels too on-the-nose. By asking about money I'm asking her to sketch the power dynamics in her early marriage. But what if you needed something?, I hedge. What if you just *wanted* something? 'Your Dad was always very generous', she doesn't quite answer. 'He always bought me things to make life easier for me.' She recites the 1960s housewife's ultimate wish list: 'I had a dishwasher before any of my friends, hostess trolley, microwave, tumble dryer ... Wait! – I nearly forgot the fur coat.' Like our conversation, the token was indirect, a contract, wrapped up in a diamond. It skirted the issue.

Money threatened the performance. It showed the backstage. Without a wage, the fantasy of doing what you love can be maintained.

But what kind of a transaction is a Bit? Bits operate at the boundary between different kinds of transactions – not quite a payment, not quite charity, not quite a gift, and not quite a bribe. What's more, while Bits can be cheered and acknowledged and gambled, and even tacitly encouraged, in accordance with Twitch's terms of service, they can never be asked for. Users cannot expect any return from their Bits, and streamers cannot expect any Bits in return for their performance. Tokens, Bits and lists are for wishes and wants, but rarely for *needs*. They are for cheering and treating and spoiling, but never for outright *paying*. The necessary and costly work of cashing the token out happens somewhere else, offline – backstage.

Bounded Authenticity

While most streamers keep their real-world identities private, virtual streamer CodeMiko's stream includes a deliberate unmasking of her personality. When playing CodeMiko, 'the

34

Technician' – the female game developer responsible for voicing and animating the avatar – dons a motion-capture suit designed by MOCAP Design, and plays games, and interviews internet personalities. Viewers use their Bits to write on her body, animate her limbs, change her appearance, and shape her content. (A favourite choice is to use Bits to make animated corpses explode in the background.)

Alongside streams as CodeMiko in a rarefied virtual setting, the channel also features streams in downtime from the Technician, as she lies in bed or hangs out with her boyfriend in their apartment. In one, she has recently lost her voice from extensive streaming. She lies in bed joking about Amouranth's recent ban from ASMR streams, and pretends to lick and fart on her microphone. Her bedroom looks artlessly dishevelled and almost wilfully ugly; there's a folded drying rack in the corner; a nearby IKEA dresser is covered in Pepto-Bismol, kombucha, and hair scrunchies; the floor in the foreground is littered with discarded clothes.

If CodeMiko is the 'fake' version, the Technician seems to imply, this messy room, this girl stripped of a costume and make-up in a rumpled nighty, is without artifice. CodeMiko is a wink at the camera, but here is the real deal – the girl who hustles so hard in a motion-capture suit that she can hardly speak the next day. CodeMiko, the Technician suggests, is as fake and as real as any other streamer on the platform.

'As with other forms of service work,' writes Elizabeth Bernstein of sex work, 'successful commercial transactions are ones in which the market basis of the exchange serves a crucial delimiting function that can also be temporarily subordinated to the client's fantasy of authentic interpersonal connection'.[20] Money can distinguish romance from a sexual transaction, but also, if it is used right, mix up the two, so that a fantasy of real connection can be maintained.

The same argument can be made of the service of streaming online, where tokens like Bits draw a line between work and pleasure, between markets and the intimate self, between payment, tip, and gift. But the token also allows the line to be blurred. Bernstein calls this fine (im)balance 'bounded authenticity', describing the 'numerous ways that clients seek to signal authenticity in their commercial sexual transactions with strippers, including payments through gifts or cocktails (more personal than cash transactions) and their persistent interest in dancers' real lives and identities'.[21] So, too, sex workers, at one moment engaged in mere surface acting, also take on the work of producing real affect and attachment. Tokens allow these ties to be forged and cut with dizzying speed.

Bounded authenticity takes place on streaming sites and influencer platforms – any space where the content produced involves a genuine investment in what is framed as the authentic self. Every time we look at a streamer casually eating a bento box in her underwear or an influencer in a baggy grey hoody crying about her mental health, we are witnessing this work, not just as a superficial performance but as a real emotional good. This is real intimacy, but it is also real work – the work that produces the real.

Money is media because it is a bridge: it brings people and people, and people and things, closer together. But money also mediates 'immediate' contact. Where money and intimacy are involved, Zelizer argues, what matters is the ways the token is marked to manage the social relationship and distinguish it from other similar but distinct encounters: Coyle playfully swapping Monopoly notes with her affluent neighbours but paying the teenage babysitter in cash; my mother's food allowance, her postal orders, the occasional gift of an expensive fur coat.[22]

This is in stark contrast to classic economic philosophy, which maintains that markets and intimacy should never mix. By this token, markets corrupt intimate life because they put a price on what should not be for sale.[23] This is why the sociologist Georg Simmel objected to sex work, and why others reject the idea of money for surrogacy or paying for the right to pick

36

your children up a little late from crèche.[24] While 'market think' argues that goods are valued more highly when they are given a price, other entities, because they are not supposed to be for sale at all, are cheapened by the slightest hint of a transaction.

We might not know how to draw a firm line between what is inside and outside the market, but we usually know when that line has been crossed. In December 2000, the artist Santiago Sierra paid four sex workers the market rate for a hit of heroine to have a line tattooed across their backs. In classic thinking, the work is distressing because it mixes money with bodily intimacy – even slavery; Sierra made visible the kinds of 'desperate exchanges' often presumed in situations of addiction or extreme economic destitution. It reads as a general symptom of a world where intimacy is a token and everything has its price. But using Zelizer's lens, we might say that the work is distressing because the money and what it is exchanged for do not match. Or, rather, they match too well; they show up the exchanges that we would rather not see.

Zelizer calls this line of thinking 'hostile worlds', to frame the idea that markets and intimacy are separate spheres. But by focusing on money as purely a market phenomenon, Zelizer argues, we fail to grasp the complex range of characteristics of money as a social medium. Instead, when we look more closely, the quantitative is always qualitative, and all intimate connections contain within them a germ of calculation.[25]

Coyle's Monopoly money did not pay the bills, but it still kept track of who did what in the cosy babysitting circle. My mother was a cherished new wife, but an engagement ring was three and a half times a monthly salary, and a weekly allowance that was five times the bus fare from one side of the country to the other ought to do it. The ways in which transactions are marked and named play a crucial role in defining a social encounter, in saying by this token what it is, but also what it is not.

Tokens underscore power dynamics. Tokens bring people together – separate them out. A good deal of work goes into matching intimate relationships with the appropriate token, with distancing similar but morally different relationships from one another.[26]

In *The Purchase of Intimacy*, Zelizer writes of the use of tokens in taxi dancing in 1960s dancehalls, where a dance with a woman could not be bought outright but could be exchanged for tokens purchased on the way in. The tokens looked like the stubs you might buy in a church raffle. They were denominated in units of time; each time a buzzer sounded, the token had been spent. It hid the seedier aspects of paying a woman directly for her time and attention.

Alongside the denominated token, Zelizer writes, the dancer and her patron frequently evolved other forms of donating and gifting, including redeeming pawned items, down payments on goods, and ration coupons. The practices were framed as 'treating', though never as payment.[27] The token also made space for an invisible trade-off between the dancer and the venue, in which a token was cashed out in a 50/50 split with the dancehall owner once the lights were turned up and everyone had gone home.

At the Edge

- My fake job is making me more money than my non fake job
- If it's not a job, why tf am I paying taxes? Going to stop that immediately!
- If its [*sic*] so fake why am I working 10 hours d y [*sic*] 5 days a week!!!?? Correction, More like 7 days a week
- I hate it when I see comment [*sic*] about how all we do is click a button on our phones [*sic*] OnlyFans is harder than my day job and I'm a care worker with 14 hour shifts. 😩[28]

For many working-class and middle-class women, streaming, camming, and OnlyFans are ways of paying off student debt or battling with the uncertainty of the job market – first in the aftermath of a global depression, and later in the midst of a global pandemic. Streamers frequently battle a perception that the work they do on these websites is not real work at all. It's 'just chatting' or 'just clicking a button', despite the fact that most streams require vast amounts of scripting, set and stage design, lighting, make-up, interface and game design, post-production, and promotion. Most streamers describe the job as a seven-day endeavour with extremely long hours, many of which are spent backstage, preparing and editing live-streamed content.

Just as Bits are used to blur distinctions between real and transactional encounters, they are also used to blur the lines between legitimate and illegitimate work. Tokens litter the edges of the 'real' economy: for beer in a student union bar that does not have a beer licence to serve alcohol; for a meal at a Buddhist temple that does not meet the required health-and-safety regulations to operate as a restaurant; for a live sex show when it is illegal to pay for or solicit online sex – and so on. Tokens draw the edges between work and non-work, legitimate and illegitimate economic activity, payment and gift. They mark the point where markets blend from white to grey, and from grey to black.

There is a new emote on Twitch. It's called 'Illuminati', and is used to call out conspiracy theories. Financing the alt-right became much more difficult in 2021. Just as all culture became digital culture, the queer and politically transgressive edges of that culture were smoothed and rounded out. A series of regulations made platforms more liable for the content they hosted, at least if their servers and infrastructure were under US jurisdiction. In response to controversies surrounding fake news and algorithmic manipulation, large social media conglomerates committed themselves to maintaining the integrity of the news circulated and shared on their platforms.

Because groups had previously gamed the feed to circulate conspiracy articles, Facebook refined its Edge algorithm so that articles circulating from less reliable sources would be ranked accordingly. PayPal cut ties with far-right internet personalities whose primary revenue was drawn from online donations. Twitch quickly became not only a soapbox for extremists, but also their payments processor. Groups struggling to receive attention or payments elsewhere migrated to Twitch, making a living in Bits.

The problem is that, with extremism, the more extreme the communication, the more the Bits flow in. A streamer can dial the flow of money up or down simply by adjusting how they communicate or express themselves. Bits reward outlandish claims and conspiracies as opposed to even critique. Sensationalism and emotive content plays (and pays) well on the platform. In 2022 Twitch became a source of pro-Russian sentiments, with affiliated streamers earning millions in Bits and subs for propaganda and conspiracy theories. QAnon found a home on the platform when it was filtered from Twitter and Facebook.

Bits also play a role at the margins of online sex work. Twitch expressly forbids adult content such as sex acts or nudity (there's even some debate about sexy banana-eating). Nonetheless, many users make use of hot-tub and ASMR streams both to earn Bits on the platform and as gateways to advertise their content on other platforms, such as OnlyFans. As we have seen, Projekt Melody has an online presence on Twitch, where she streams game-playing and chatting, but also on Chaturbate, where she leverages her Twitch audience for adult performances. Hot-tub streams make use of contextual exceptions in Twitch's terms of use that allow for semi-nudity in appropriate settings, such as pools, hot tubs, and beaches. Twitch has commented in the past that, while it has guidelines in place for sexually suggestive content, 'being found to be sexy by others is not against our rules, and Twitch will not take enforcement action against women, or anyone on our service, for their perceived attractiveness'.[29]

Twitch Bits, like other tokens, have a strong extra-regulatory function: they are a means of being paid without seeming to be paid. This is why they are so popular for forms of work that hover on the threshold between what is legally and fiscally recognised as labour and what is *just* chatting or *just* dancing provocatively in a hot tub, *just* messing around, playing games, expressing political opinions or ideas.

Platform Capitalism

But, as on many other platforms, the issuance of a token also functions in an extra-regulatory sense for the issuer. It is the issuance of a token, these Bits that are 'cheers' – deniable as money – that allows the platform to be a bank without appearing to be a bank, to be an employer without appearing to employ, and to pay piece wages and process payments without having to meet the legal requirements associated with either. They are a regulatory sleight of hand, a way to extract value and offset risk.

Twitch's owner Amazon is, for all intents and purposes, a bank. Without yet applying for a financial licence, Amazon has its own payments processor, a line of credits and loans, credit cards, and store cards, in-store payments and merchant services, and experiments in special monies. In *Ghost Work*, Mary Gray and Siddharth Suri explore the human labour built into seemingly automated systems, as well as how this work is remunerated. Amazon, they observe, is 'like both an ATM and a company store' for Mechanical Turk workers.[30]

Twitch payments are not the first time that Amazon has experimented with the use of tipping. Like Amazon's experiment with an Allowance Token for children and teenagers, they are one of a number of payments features trialled by the company in the past. In 2001 the company introduced a service called the Honor System, in which users could use a one-click button to donate between $1 and $50 for online content they thought was worthwhile – jokes, essays, recipes.

In an article, 'Thanking Web Sites, with Cash', published in 2001, Michelle Slatalla interviewed Jeff Bezos. Why, she asked, would users feel compelled to pay for something they could get for free? 'If you get something you value,' Bezos explained, 'you should pay for it.' 'Like love?' Slatalla asks, a little slyly. 'Like pineapples', Bezos said, recounting a wonderful experience with an honour box on a recent holiday to Hawaii. Maybe, Bezos continued, it would help readers to think of the Honor System in the same way as they think of tips: a little something to say 'thank you'. Amazon would charge a fifteen-cent transaction fee to issue every honour payment and take a 15 per cent cut of the transaction when it was cashed out at the other end.[31]

So Amazon is a bank. But Amazon is also an employer. Despite the social contract that the exchange of Bits entails, with Amazon taking a cut of all subscriptions and Bits, the platform is careful not to frame itself as an employer, with the obligations and duties that title suggests. Instead, it is an intermediary, providing a platform and audiences for up-and-coming content creators without the risk or the responsibility of providing them with security or regular wages. Amazon is very careful to distinguish the Bit from a currency or a payment, stating in its terms of use that Bits have no monetary or exchange value. But Bits are a de facto currency, and streamers, just like Amazon's Mechanical Turk workers, are de facto employees, ghost workers, paid in scrip.

In some cases, tokens subsidise the gap between wages and the cost of living. Platform tokens pay for invisible work – streamers are paid in Bits and subs, Amazon workers in gift card balances. Informal exchanges in food and childcare keep the economy afloat, something we saw more clearly during the pandemic than at any other time. Food stamps shore up piece wages. In Pennsylvania and Ohio, one in ten Amazon workers rely on them to make ends meet. In Arizona, that figure is one in three.

Economic anthropologist Bill Maurer speaks about money as both a token and a rail, as information and infrastructure.[32] These rails are multiple. In the publicly mandated money system they include institutions such as the Federal Reserve or the Central Bank, which issue and guarantee currency. Increasingly, they also include platforms and internet service providers that issue new tokens, controlling their conditions and how they are cashed out. PayPal, for example, is a private rail that sits on top of the public clearing-house system, giving the experience of synchronous settlement by effectively fronting the recipient money while it clears through the banking system.

Tokens ride their own rails and function in separate eco-systems. Someone or something has to connect these rails to make the tokens flow into other payments systems. In the above example, PayPal is a rail between peer-to-peer payments and the sludgy clearing house. Amazon, meanwhile, provides a rail for the in-channel donations of Bits, but it also bridges this token and the publicly mandated system. Websites like Reddit's r/giftcardsx build a shaky sort of bridge between the value in token gift cards and fiat money.

In the Twitch ecosystem, Bits are the token and Amazon is the rail. In the early days of Twitch, streamers provided their own 'tip jars', with links to PayPal accounts for donations. These off-channel donations formed a vital sub-economy. Amazon's introduction of Bits in 2016 was a coordinated strategy to capture the informal value streams that were leaking from the platform.

The not-really work of influencing, streaming, and sex camming is being reorganised. As viewers, we are still inclined to think about this work as a side gig – something an enthusiastic amateur does in their spare hours to make some spare cash. But this work is now an institution. While one Reddit poster may describe the exhaustive list of tasks she coordinates personally, from writing her scripts to designing her sets, programming her interactive content, and editing her own cutaways and promotions, today many streamers are choosing to enter into partnerships. These partnerships might be informal and supportive arrangements with other workers, such as what Crystal Abidin describes as the 'influencer pod', or Angela Jones calls the 'camily', but frequently they are formal arrangements with production studios or 'streamer guilds' that coordinate their work like any other job.[33] The guild's role is to institutionalise and scale informal work. The advantages are a support team dedicated to pre- and post-production – and, if all goes well, greater income security.

The drawbacks include set targets for engagement and set hours of work. These contracts usually include exclusivity, minimum working hours, and targets in the form of minimum donations or gifts. The guilds also influence streamer content. Streamers may be obliged to repeat content or behaviour that is lucrative, with less freedom to choose their own modes of expression. More than ever, their job is now to follow the money.

For virtual streamers, there is a whole extra degree of complexity. Their work is often produced by an entire team. The grandmother of the space, Kizuna AI, a Japanese virtual streamer coined in 2016 by the start-up Activ8, is rumoured to be voiced by several actors. (While viewers like watching the Technician, they tend not to like these accidental backstage glimpses, maybe because they feel as if they aren't being let in on the joke – that they are being duped by something less than real intimacy. #MrDestructoid.)

In a streamed interview following criticisms from real-life cam models that the virtual streamer Projekt Melody bears none of the risks and stresses associated with exposing yourself on the internet, her creator Digitrevx replied: 'While they [human streamers] are risking their identities, we are risking piles of

44

cash. It takes a lot of money to make tech run.'[34] Digitrevx is closed-lipped about the specific technologies used to animate Projekt Melody, except to enumerate the 'space shuttle' level complexity involved. Projekt Melody is described by her creator less as an individual personality than in technical terms as 'software talking to other software' and 'multiple computers chained together' – not a friend online, but a sexy Bitcoin rig mining coin.[35]

Tokens are a way for the platform to capture value at the edges.[36] But unlike the industrial factory that Marx diagrammed (where a good capitalist invested in materials and wages to produce a good sold at a profit), platform capitalism relies on ownership rather than extensive organisation of, or investment in, labour. As a value stream, this is in many ways closer to a pre-capitalist 'rent' or a cottage industry.[37]

In the pre-capitalist system, a landlord extracted value by virtue of ownership rather than through any direct organisation of workers. Platforms are just the same: they are the slumlords and feudal kings of the internet. Amazon is not investing in paying its streamers wages, providing them with the technical equipment required to produce and edit their streams, or organising their content or working hours, but simply providing a stage for streaming live content and a rail for processing payments, and positioning itself at the centre of that process. By controlling the issuance and redemption of tokens – how they are cashed in and cashed out – Amazon extracts revenue.

The purchase and the sale price of a Bit are different. While 100 Bits cost approximately $1.40, depending on the currency they are purchased in, for a streamer receiving them, they are worth $1. In the cashing in and cashing out, forty cents goes to the platform. Similar arrangements are in place across platforms such as Chaturbate, which splits tokens 50/50 with models, and OnlyFans, which takes a 20 per cent cut but requires that streamers not only produce their own content, but recruit their own audiences or fans from work carried out off-site.

Here, platforms are not just holding stations or processors, because payments are articulated differently at either end of the process – a situation that Antonia Hernández, a researcher who has diagrammed the distribution of tokens on Chaturbate, describes as the 'digital gentrification' of the internet.[38]

There are similar issues with payments on the Mechanical Turk platform. Users wishing to crowdsource tasks (called HITs) can pay the platform for them in advance using any major credit or debit card. They also pay Amazon a fee for posting and processing the task. The payments process is frictionless if you're sourcing work from the platform. But on the other end of the transaction, Mechanical Turk workers who perform these tasks experience numerous issues with cashing their payment out. For a start, new workers must wait ten days to be paid for their work. After this initial waiting period, US workers have the choice of transferring their earnings onto an Amazon Gift Card balance or to an Amazon pay account, and from there to their bank account of choice. For the latter, they pay Amazon a cashing-out fee. International workers, on the other hand, can only be paid in Amazon Gift Card balances.

The exception to this rule is India – though the process is still far from straightforward. Indian workers first have to submit their personal account number (the equivalent of a social security number), and then wait a week for verification. They then need to wait again to have their bank account verified. After this process, Amazon will mail the worker cheques or deposit their earnings into a bank account – once again, for a fee.

Similarly, the rails in and out of the Twitch ecosystem are different depending on whether you are a viewer or a streamer. The former are given a smooth passage from one payments ecosystem to another; the latter endure a service that is rickety and full of holes. A viewer can buy Bits through any major payment processor, while a streamer often has difficulty cashing out, leaning on automated clearing house (ACH) transfers and wire transfers, depending on where they are based. While

46

tips, donations, and Amazon wish lists and Gift Cards provide space for informal remittances, Amazon has found a way to bring marginal tokens, tips, links, and wish lists back into the platform ecosystem, extracting a cut from a whole range of otherwise invisible work.

Tokens of Excess

And yet, Twitch is not all closed loops and private rails. The mutability of tokens means that value is recruited into but also constantly leaking out of the platform into other value streams across gaming sites, payments processors, online retailers, and spaces like OnlyFans. Projekt Melody has a presence on Twitch, OnlyFans, and Chaturbate. Twitch, in this instance, provides its own value stream, but also a store-front for the streamer to build an audience that follows them to other adults-only parts of the internet.

Amouranth, whose hot-tub streams have caused controversy on the platform, gives links to her Patreon and OnlyFans page, where viewers can subscribe for adult content. Other streamers make use of additional platforms and overlays on their About pages. StreamElements, for example, a streaming overlay used by CodeMiko, includes its own link to a separate donations system, allowing fans to bypass the Twitch interface if they choose. And yet these loopholes are harder to find. There are no escape routes when Amazon is synonymous with the internet, when it is your employer and your bank and your grocery store.

In a post to the Extropian mailing list in March of 2000, a forum for technological futurism, Eliezer Yudkowsky, now an AI scientist, gushed over the launch of PayPal: 'Inertialess cash at last!' The coming age of electronic cash, Yudkowsky argued, would

47

herald the dawn of micropayments, take a huge bite out of the dominance of cash, eventually kick over the credit-card system now used, and perhaps create a great Webbed structure of cash applause. For some years now, I've visualized a system where, each time one visits a sufficiently great Website, one clicks a button that sends a few cents to the owner. Websites, mailing posts, bon mots, good causes, great ideas – all upheld and rewarded by a system of cash applause that, with the rise of ultraproductivity, may become a dominant part of the social system.[39]

At the time, PayPal charged no fees for credit-card transactions between users with US email addresses. What Yudkowsky didn't foresee was that these new platforms would take a slice of the 'cash applause', a bit of the cheer. And nor did he see that friction – like the future – would not be evenly distributed.

2

Money Talks, Tokens Track

In September 2020 my family moved to a rural town on the west coast of Ireland. We stayed for nearly two years. We didn't think we would survive a winter lockdown in a flat in Dublin. While most of my teaching was online, I still had to make the occasional trip to the city, a three-hour train journey, followed by a taxi to our house. Most places in Ireland now accept card payments, but the rural taxi driver is a sticking point. Hailing a taxi from outside the train station means having cash in hand to pay at the end of the journey.

This particular car is retrofitted for Covid. A plexiglass screen separates the front and back seats, with a hatch for paying at the end of the journey. The driver and I both wear masks. Even the passenger door slides open and shut without either of us touching it. There's no contact at all until we pull into my driveway and I fumble in the dark to find a €20 note, which I slide through a hatch in the screen. The driver fishes out €5 in change. But before he slides it over he squirts a generous blob from a bottle of sanitiser and smooths it across the surface of the note. I thank him and tuck the soggy paper into my wallet.

While I know the alcohol has killed off any germs, this money *feels* dirty. It's oily and sticky. Every time I open my wallet for a card or receipt, my fingers glance off it – *that* particular note from *that* taxi journey – until I pass it off at a market a few weeks later. I'm reminded of Sartre's famous essay on stickiness, the disgust he feels at plunging his fingers into a pot of honey. Stickiness is a trap, he writes; like a parasite, it undoes the boundary between the self and the outside world:

'I want to let go of the sticky and it sticks to me, it drowns me, it sucks at me'; it 'haunts me as value haunts my being'. Stickiness, Sartre argues, reverses the natural order of things: 'when I believe that I possess it, behold by a curious reversal, it possesses me'.[1] The sticky note takes hold. A bearer instrument bears up its owner.

The Kula was an exchange system of shells made of necklaces and armbands in the Massim islands, Papua New Guinea. It is among the earliest documented gift economies. Kula was also sticky. The token picked up value as it moved from hand to hand. Alongside the token – Kula – the term 'Keda' (meaning road, or path) was also sometimes used to describe the journey the shells took and the people they encountered.[2] Kula were ranked according to the history of their movement through a network of exchange. Their value fluctuated with the reputations of those they encountered. Kula flipped money on its head – instead of users ascribing a value to the token, the token took the measure of the user.

An interest in how money moves has led to projects such as Where's George? – a website that tracks the circulation of US dollars. Similar projects exist around the world, such as Where's Willy? for Canada and EuroBillTracker for Europe. It works like this: bills are manually entered into the database by a user, who lists the unique serial number marked on the note and their zip code on the website, marks the note with the URL, and finally spends it back into circulation. The hope is that future users will see the tag, look up the registered note online, and add further information about its current location to the database.

In tracking the circulation of these bills, a new layer of data is brought to light. Scientists have used data from the currency-tracking site to visualise the movement of paper money, and to find out what these traces can tell us. Theoretical physicist Dirk Brockmann discovered that money in the US generally moves in relatively local arcs. Brockmann scraped data from

Where's George? using network theory to draw the geographic lines that notes were unlikely to cross. The result was a map that overwrites state lines. In some places the lines faithfully followed state borders, but not always; Missouri was divided into eastern and western territories, as was Pennsylvania. The 'Chicago catchment area', as Brockmann refers to it, also included a significant chunk of both Indiana and Wisconsin.[3] In taking money as a totem for human mobility, the map illustrates how real communities of exchange do not necessarily observe official borders. More recently, data from sites such as Where's George? and EuroBillTracker have also been used to model and understand the spread of disease.

Where's George? reveals the stories hidden in the movement of cash – unmined data about human mobility, epidemiology, community, or commerce. But it takes something more for these stories to surface – to become 'actionable' data. Even with Where's George? there is a limit to how much information can be drawn from a paper token. The project asks its users to tag their bill with their zip code, illustrating where the bill has travelled to since it was first registered on the website. From this data you can't tell what a note is being spent on, or who spent it – just where it has travelled to and when. A user has to make the decision to give data to the system; a marked bill might interest them enough to log on to the website and register a hit, but nobody forces them to. In a world where 'opting out' is off the table, it seems like a lot of hassle to purposely opt in – but more than 305 million unique notes have been registered on the site.

When we pay electronically, there is no physical exchange of a token – only an issued instruction to update an electronic record. Cryptocurrencies, for example, don't rely on physical or even virtual coinage, but instead produce a shared database of electronic transactions to keep track of the 'movement' of funds. The token and the ledger entry (or 'record', or 'data') are one and the same. Digital tokens surface the traces hidden in cash – or maybe it is more accurate to say that they are all trace, and no token.

Digital tokens flatten the difference between money as instrument and money as information, but these tokens also expand what kind of information is recorded in a transaction. The new channels for payment cache transactional data alongside a range of other demographic, psychographic, social, and biometric details about payers and payees. And digital payments have produced a new class of platforms that store, retrieve, and act on this data.

A Brief History of Tokens as Recording Devices

The earliest tokens are thought to date back to 7500 BC, when settled farming communities began to track stocks of grain and precious metals. Mesopotamian clay tokens in the shape of cones, spheres, ovoids, and cylinders stood in for a recorded quantity of barley or silver in storage.[4] These clay tokens were a 'stored memory' of stored assets.[5] Later, around 3200 BC, grain harvests were centralised in state warehouses in both Babylon and Egypt. Tokens represented an individual's share in the store. These tokens were first-order records – receipts and proto-money in one.

Tokens that represent a share in a physical asset are not exclusive to proto-money. In the seventeenth century the goldsmith's receipt tallied deposits of jewels and bullion. These receipts were a precursor to the bill of exchange and the banknote.[6] The gold standard, in place throughout the Bretton Woods agreement, recorded gold bullion held in reserve, which the authorities agreed to exchange for circulating currency. In the early 1990s, companies began to experiment with 'digital gold' – online tokens backed by reserve bullion. Today, assets including bullion, precious metals, fine art, and even grain and soy are stored in warehouses that act as de facto 'banks' for these assets, and are represented by a token. Even the speculative value of NFTs is a kind of first-order record, a token of the ownership of a digital image or file.

First-order records operate at the moment *before* the token enters into circulation or exchange, and by some accounts are not proper money at all. Stephanie Kelton argues that money is a record not just of an asset, but of an asset *and* a liability.[7] It doesn't fully exist until a contract has occurred. Not only is money just valuable stuff, then, but it also entails our relationship with other people with respect to that stuff; it embodies claims upon and debts onto others.

To highlight this distinction, it is worth returning to Mesopotamian tokens. When these clay tokens entered into an exchange, they were stored inside hollow clay balls, and the signatures of the transacting parties were printed on the outside. The resulting object was a token of an asset, wrapped in a contract. This contract was a second-order record.

Tokens set down obligations: bonds were rendered in things. Another example is the tally stick: two pieces of wood that represented a creditor–debtor relation. The wooden split tally was used in medieval England as a receipt of taxes paid and debts owed to the exchequer.[8] Grooves etched in the wood fixed the contract. The token was then split in half, with the creditor and debtor each taking a piece. The debt was etched into the tally, but the bearer's identity was not. The tokens were transferable, so that an initial lender could use his credits as a means of exchange.

This movable 'contract' is probably clearest in the case of paper money. At first, paper money took the form of non-transferable receipts or bills of exchange – legal debt instruments issued by a named person who promised to redeem a specific sum of money on or by a specific date to the payee, also named on the document. Gradually, these receipts became transferable bearer instruments that circulated as currency. Earlier bills name a specific person, but modern banknotes are promissory notes issued by a bank and payable to 'the bearer' on demand, making them fully transferable. The role of these bills gradually shifted from a contract between specific named individuals to a fungible token.

In the eighteenth century a strange literary genre emerged (Mary Poovey calls it the 'literature of social circulation').[9] Thomas Bridges's *Adventures of a Bank Note* (1759–75) and Charles Johnstone's *Chrysal; or, the Adventures of a Guinea* (1760–65) are both narrated by money. The coin or note tells the story of all the people it meets on its journey and the conversations it overhears as it passes from hand to hand. Chrysal the Guinea describes its journey through the networks of colonial trade, from North America to England, to Holland and Germany. There is a reason it's a talking banknote and not a talking umbrella. Money was represented as having, as Chrysal put it, 'a power of entering into the hearts of the immediate possessors and reading all the secrets of their lives'.[10] The token bears witness to everything surrounding it. Talking notes, like Sartre's honey pot, dissolved the boundaries 'between possessor and possessed'. They reversed the order of things. Instead of humans measuring the worth of the token, it was now the other way around. Money could spy on and weigh up its owner.

Third-order records give an 'account' of how tokens are moved and circulated. Accounting gave more details about transactions: records of what people spent their money on, or when and where a particular transaction took place.

A simple 'memorandum' book was used until the nineteenth century, but third-order records became more detailed as merchant operations grew, moving from small businesses to larger department stores. Detailed store receipts soon captured the transfer of funds, often including the name of the issuing party, the date of the transaction, the amount of money transferred, details of what was purchased, and the nature of the tender.[11] In the twentieth century, bookkeeping expanded alongside electronic cash registers, lasers, machine-readable barcodes, and data processing, and merchants were encouraged to record ever more detail about each transaction.

Benedetto Cotrugli argued in *Della mercatura e del mercante perfetto* that the merchant 'should not rely upon his memory in his business dealings'.[12] Similarly, Alexander Malcolm warned against 'giving our Memory too much Trust, and neglecting to write down every Transaction of our Affairs'.[13] Accounting was artificial memory, something to be brought to mind. Much better to task a machine. Justin Wickett, the CEO of Informed.IQ, a company that verifies customers for financial institutions, echoed this sentiment nearly 500 years later, when he observed that financial algorithms were necessary because 'folks' memory is just limited, whereas a computer can do so much processing'.[14]

Crucially, accounting allowed the merchant to draw on the past to account for the future – to make projections about upcoming profits, and to expand their operations and dealings with others. Stores began to use the data gleaned from their accounts to analyse customers' purchasing habits. In 1929, for example, the Chicago clothier Capper & Capper attached coded punch-cards to its customers' nameplates, using coloured tabs to indicate which department the customer had shopped in, sales totals, seasonal spending, and (if they were female) their marital status.[15]

In this way, third-order records could be used to calculate returns and expected income, or to make predictions about future consumer behaviour. Some stores also invested in colour-coded cards that allowed them to visually 'sort' their customers according to risk. In one store the scheme was 'red for no credit, black for $25, blue for $50, green for $100 and gold for $150 or more'.[16] In the 1920s, Rand Visible Filing Systems were marketed with their own transparent celluloid tabs in various colours for this specific purpose. In one system, all files started out white, but were permanently stained to blue or red in the case of delays or non-payment.[17]

Predictions based on these systems were fourth-order records, a kind of actionable knowledge that measured the past to account for the future.

Everybody Eats, Even Bonnie

In the United States, the most popular payments system is Venmo, an app, owned by PayPal, for sending money to family and friends. Users share details of their transactions on a social feed. You can see the same emojis and happy birthday messages you can find on a Facebook Wall, except that in this case the messages are all about money.

In Venmo you have to use the memo function every time you send or request money. Accounting is integral to the payment. While the specific amount can only be seen by the transacting parties, each message details the identities involved in the transaction, the date and time, and an answer to Venmo's 'What's it for?' question. And so Venmo has become a space for what Thorstein Veblen called 'conspicuous consumption' – for showing off, in other words – but also for stalking ex-boyfriends and trolling celebrities. A man sends a small sum and an abusive message to the ex-lover, who has blocked him elsewhere. A disgruntled fan invoices Ben Affleck on Venmo for a cinema ticket refund for his latest crap movie.[18]

Until June 2021, Venmo's global feed was a constantly changing menu of tantalising, if oblique, stories. It included mundane 'pizza' or 'knife and fork' and 'money with wings' emojis and celebrations like 'red envelope money' around Chinese New Year, but also cryptic messages: 'heat miser', 'ill think about the rest [sic]' or 'everyone eats, even Bonnie'; a miserable 'please leave me alone', or the romantic 'nice try – save it for when we move in together x'. I started to collect them in a Word file. I could get caught in an endless scroll-and-refresh more absorbing than my Instagram feed.

I learn this activity has a name: it's called 'Venmo stalking'. Along with the money zipping from one account to another, the messages carry the story of a social encounter. Who is this frenemy Bonnie, who is constantly on a diet and pissing everybody off with her thigh gap? Is the author of 'nice try' at the start of a new relationship where money sours the romance? I think 'heat miser' is probably a passive-aggressive micropayment to a housemate who guards the thermostat. But maybe I am using my own social histories to fill in the gaps.

In a design informatics project, artist Hang Do Thi Duc illustrated Venmo data in an artwork called *Public by Default*, revealing just how much could be gleaned from the company's public API.[19] The designer used Venmo's public transactional data to trace the lives of five users she had never met, including a romantic couple, a food cart owner and his most popular customers, and a weed dealer operating out of Santa Barbara, California.

Other researchers subsequently reverse-engineered the Venmo feed to pinpoint members of AA, drug deals, users with a chronic gambling problem, illicit romantic affairs, and sex work. Transactions could tell the story of an acrimonious breakup through a flurry of invoices for half a couch, or one of a set of matching candlesticks.[20] As on Twitch, money was once more an expressive token – but the expressions, and the desires they communicated, might be worth more than the transaction itself.

A controversial option in the app also allowed users to see each other's lists of contacts. When a *Washington Post* article revealed that President Biden had Venmoed money to his grandchildren, journalists were quick to trace the president's broader contacts on Venmo, including family members and the first lady. In the wake of scandalised Buzzfeed articles, Venmo removed its global public feed in 2021.

What does a simple Venmo message really tell us? Is 'heat miser' soon going to need a new roommate? Is marriage or a family on the cards for 'nice try'? Maybe Bonnie has an eating disorder that will require medical treatment, or even lengthy hospitalisation. All of these stories have financial implications. Many speculate that the money is in the data gathered through these transactions – data on who sent money to whom and for what, on what these surfaced stories can tell advertisers, retailers, and insurance companies about users.

With electronic payments, this involves a shift from a business model based on generating revenue through transaction fees alone (moving money from place to place) to one based on transactional data (what the movement of money can tell you about people or things), or a combination of the two. From a user's perspective, it is not that the toll or fee disappears from the transaction; instead, the cost of transacting is extracted through a rent on personal data. The token becomes a proxy for the 'intimate secrets and desires' of its users, as Chrysal the talking guinea once put it. Data is money.

Following Venmo's presidential privacy breach, the company appears to be focused on interchange and withdrawal fees. Venmo also introduced new charges for retailers, ostensibly in line with new protections for buyers using the app. The company developed a partnership with Amazon called 'Pay with Venmo', and launched a new 'Cash to Crypto' function to allow its users to convert money in their wallet from dollars to crypto and back again. But as things stand at the time of writing, PayPal does not make much revenue from the transaction fees it charges Venmo users.

There is a sense that the data from payments is a cash crop that will yield fruit soon – but it is often not clear exactly how this is going to happen. How might these traces and stories and potted histories, laid bare, transfer into real-world value? Or do they simply trade on the hope that someday they may be worth something, even if only as training data for the algorithms of the future?

The key business models for transactional data are advertising, inventory management, and risk analysis. At this stage, we are all familiar with the fact that our past purchases are used to profile us as consumers. Amazon has a record of every product I have ever bought on the platform since the beginning of internet time. My profile runs along a strict graduate-student path for some time, only to diverge quite suddenly in 2016. Suddenly my orders are an advertiser's wet dream: an inflatable gym ball; a book from La Leche League with the cloying title *The Womanly Art of Breastfeeding*; lanolin cream; essential oils; arnica tablets – the list so specific to a pregnant woman of a certain class that I could almost be trolling the platform. Almost. I wasn't writing my biography; I was just buying the things I thought I needed to have a baby.

Targeted advertising is about targeting not only the 'right' consumer, but also the 'right' location and the 'right' moment to push a coupon or promotional offer. Such specific information might not be gleaned directly from *your* transactional data, but is often inferred through comparison with a small subset of existing data. For example, a large retailer might use a small database of women known to be pregnant – who have registered a wish list for a baby shower or applied for a specific promotional offer – and index their purchases against the wider population to infer who else might be expecting, as in one well-known story of targeted advertising gone wrong.[21] As Venmo suggests, such advertising can even occur on a peer-to-peer basis: scrolling a friend's Venmo feed might suggest a new lunch spot or prenatal yoga class in a 'word-of-mouth' fashion.

A second business model makes use of transactional data for what's called 'inventory management': deciding what products to stock in stores or send to distribution centres. Here, transactional data allow companies to forecast what customers might buy in the future, and tweak supply chains accordingly. Amazon's 2014 patent for anticipatory shipping – a logistical model using transactional and browsing history to predict future purchases – is one well-hyped example. Instead of waiting to

59

process an order, the company can ship items it predicts a customer will buy later to a warehouse near them. The platform might well have predicted my 4 a.m. order of *The Baby Sleep Solution* in 2017.

In 2021, Shopify also acquired a deep learning system that includes 'predictive inventory placement', using purchasing habits to move goods nearer to customers for the moment when they eventually click 'Add to basket'. Meanwhile, Palantir Technologies, a company developed by PayPal founder Peter Thiel, is looking to integrate consumer transactional data with sensors in the user's environment – tags on clothing, beacons in stores, sensors in their home fridge – to fine-tune inventory-flow management.

A third and rising trend is the use of transactional data to underwrite credit and insurance – the 'fourth-order records' discussed earlier in this chapter. Companies now specialise in credit offerings based on mined transactional data. They target users who have limited access to financial services – the 'underserved' or 'unbanked' – but also users whose credit, in the aftermath of a crash and a global pandemic, might be deemed subpar, a vulnerable category Joe Deville and Lonneke van der Velden have dubbed the 'digital subprime' market.[22]

Social Credit

My mother grew up in Kilkenny, a town in south-east Ireland. The family lived over their shop on the High Street, in a building that is now the local Credit Union. As we wait to be called to the counter, she describes the old layout. 'Where we're standing now was the shop floor and over there would have been our kitchen and the dining room. My grandparents' bedroom was directly above us.' We visited the Credit Union often because my parents had a small business that supplied financial institutions with desktop calculators, filing systems, and basic office equipment. (One of my jobs as a teenager was to program these calculators to convert the Irish punt to the incoming euro).

I applied for a Credit Union loan the September I started college – just a small amount to bridge the gap until I could draw down my grant. The loan was granted largely on the basis that the manager, a middle-aged man with a friendly paunch pushing against his suit, 'knew my mammy'. He came out from my mother's kitchen, and they talked while I filled out the paperwork. In small communities, credit is always social credit, underwritten by local knowledge and community ties.

Credit is an exchange, but it is also a bet, wagered on a promise to pay at some point in the future. All credit comes down to a social calculation, then: a decision about whom we trust and invest in. It's a risky business. The formal practice of scoring and quantifying this risk first emerged in the 1840s in the United States. Merchants always had ways of making their ledgers talk, but by the 1830s these personal ways were less effective. The financial collapse known as the 'Panic of 1837' was a crisis of confidence, as inflated land values and wildcat banking eroded trust in the financial system. But it was also the panic of a dissolving social order. Migration and trade between cities had begun to chip away at the old confidences – the trust necessary to wait to be paid or repaid.

There was still room for local credit dealings, but for those trading regionally or nationally it was becoming hard to gauge the worth of trade partners. Merchants were left clutching at worthless paper promises from virtual strangers. One of these was Lewis Tappan, a silk merchant from New York State. Bankrupted, he established the Mercantile Agency in 1841, a bureau established to collect detailed credit information about merchants and quantify the risk they represented.

Thirty years later, Tappan's agency had expanded in two ways. First, credit surveillance had grown from merchants to accommodate the relatively new (and much larger) category of 'consumers'. Second, credit evaluation had advanced from straightforward 'blacklisting' (the 'little list of names' of poor prospects, kept in mind or tucked beneath the counter) to what was called the 'affirmative/negative' system. Beyond singling out the worst offenders, the system used intelligence (Tappan's agency now employed over 10,000 correspondents) to rank the nation according to a scale that ran from deadbeat to upstanding citizen. Tappan was quick to defend the integrity of the bureau, claiming in one advertisement that it was 'not a system of espionage, but the same as merchants usually apply – only on an extended plan – to ascertain whether persons applying for credit are worthy of the same and to what extent'.[23]

Whatever Tappan said, credit scoring was the dawn of surveillance capitalism: the gathering and monetisation of data at the behest of a private organisation. The bureau's data was also repackaged and sold to retailers, who used it to market consumer goods and services.

Handwritten reports, stored in giant reference books in the agency's New York offices, were gradually translated into code. The legend '1 6 8 11 14 17 21 25', for example, stood for 'making money', 'economical', 'business not too much extended', 'does not pay large interest', 'good moral character', 'credits prudently', and 'not sued'.[24]

From the 1950s onwards there were attempts to model the process mathematically. Underwriting credit was an industry where number crunching, so crucial in World War II, found a commercial application. A technique recently developed by the English statistician (and eugenicist) Ronald A. Fisher became popular. 'Discriminant Analysis' allowed researchers to distil the information from credit applications into a set of discrete variables, each with a value and weight reflecting its statistical association with payment or default. Income, it turned out, was not a good predictor of anything, and nor was marital status – but things like room-to-child ratio and having a telephone in the house were. While statistics told the credit analysts that certain variables were important for predicting risk, they were often unable to say why.

Hindsight presents these techniques as immediately persuasive – an 'avalanche of numbers' that swept away all trust in human judgement. But in the 1950s the credit space was still a balancing act between intuition and calculation. Like the Credit Union manager who knew my mother, credit men clung to the confidence that one should *just know*, to a 'feeling – perhaps rather vague and indefinable', that some person was, by the sum of a gut, a good or a bad bet.[25] Many agents were suspicious of techniques that strayed too far from the calculus of 'good sense'. And yet, finding ways to model and abstract that good sense was now a serious mathematical preoccupation. The practice of ranking and scoring consumers was never just about the 'economic facts'; but when gossip was dressed up in codes and figures, it began to look like objective data. And 'data' feels more persuasive somehow than 'I know your mammy', even if it is reduced to the same thing.

In the early noughties, the complex credit scoring, reporting, and sorting of borrowers made way for the securitisation of home mortgages into risk-structured financial instruments. The subprime lending boom distributed this risk across homeowners through the use of new, complex financial products such as collateralised debt obligations and credit default swaps. When a system that was too big to fail went into full crisis, financial institutions went through what anthropologist Bill Maurer calls a period of 'de-risking'.[26] In much the same way as the Panic of 1837 drove a revolution in underwriting, the credit crunch ushered in new financial technologies, all designed to produce, once and for all, an accurate measure of risk. Today there is more than the whiff of a hope that, with enough data and intelligence, financial institutions can capture and model the uncertain future.

Until 2021, access to financial credit in China was controlled by Alipay. On launching an app that allowed its customers to buy products and send money instantly, the multinational realised that all this data about who buys what and sends money to whom could also be used to underwrite credit. In a culture where grandmothers use their smartphones to pay for groceries and the homeless don QR codes to accept passing donations, there is plenty of data to choose from. Alibaba's three-digit 'Zhima Score' dictates the terms of a personal loan based on variables such as what degrees its customers hold, data from their social networks, and how many video games they have purchased in the past month – but it also affects visibility on Chinese dating sites, employability, and even access to a Schengen Visa.

In Europe, a lending service called Kreditech attempted to build the 'Amazon of consumer finance', by mining the clues hidden in the Facebook data its customers voluntarily shared. Meanwhile, in the United States, Zest AI (formerly ZestFinance), the brainchild of Google's former CTO Doug Merrill, uses transactional data to rank customers whose credit rating never recovered from the subprime mortgage crisis. From the perspective of Zest AI, when users buy most things online and post their relationship status on social media, 'all data is credit data'.[27]

In the 1950s, statistical modelling was limited to twenty or thirty variables, distilling the user down to the pithy legends housed in Tappan's reference library in New York. Moving beyond repayment histories and credit-utilisation ratios, Zest AI claims to have built a system that gathers up to 10,000 details about each customer from their online activity to make a split-second credit decision. But 'not creepy data or anything like that', CEO Mike de Vere hastens to clarify.[28]

Many AI systems now also use natural language processing to 'extract cash flow data from bank statements', including information from how consumers 'pay their bills to their various sources of income, their assets and even their employment status'. Such details include the content of SMS messages; online browsing behaviour and purchases; education history;

64

online money transfers; data use; phone type; and activity on Facebook, Twitter, and Pinterest – as well as similar information from a borrower's social network: the data shadows cast by friends and acquaintances. How precisely having wealthy Facebook friends, playing Pokémon Go, and using an Android phone reflects creditworthy behaviour is unclear; but more than a decade after the financial crash, we're urged to trust that the numbers don't lie.

The new credit scores use a dimension of artificial intelligence known as machine learning, often intended to replace human input. While Zest AI's Doug Merrill describes 'building a whole bunch of math' to capture data points, Matt Flannery, the CEO of Branch, a for-profit using smartphone adoption in Kenya to underwrite credit, speaks of a benevolent 'robot in the sky' crunching numbers in the cloud.[29] In a step beyond statistical scoring, machine learning doesn't predetermine the rules by which an algorithm acts upon datasets, a kind of 'charitable donations = good / video games = bad' equation of risk; it involves teaching the algorithm how to refine and re-refine the functions that make decisions on personal data autonomously – often in ways that are fairly inscrutable from the outside. For example, people who filled out early Zest AI loan applications in capital letters were deemed to be riskier borrowers than those who wrote in upper and lower case. Merrill didn't know why. With some tentative reverse engineering, others discovered that categories as nebulous as browser type and screen resolution played a role in the constitution of Zest's credit scores.[30]

Despite the fact that nobody fully understands how they come up with the figures that they produce, a core argument made by the likes of Branch, Alipay, and Zest AI is that these automated scores are not only more *accurate* than legacy systems when it comes to revealing the inner character of loan applicants, but also more *fair*. 'It's better at choosing people than any person could ever be', Flannery boasted at Money20/20.[31] Where credit decisions were previously made by humans whose deepest grudges found their way into even standardised tests, the scoring algorithm 'sees beyond' the trumped-up prejudices that skewed access to credit in the past.

But classification has always harmed some more than others. As recently as 1935, whole neighbourhoods in the United States were classified according to their credit characteristics. For example, a 1935 map of Greater Atlanta in the National Archives comes colour-coded in shades of blue, yellow, and red. An accompanying note reads: 'light blue – best, dark blue – still desirable, yellow – definitely declining, red – hazardous'. The handwritten legend recalls the period when perceived credit-worthiness was calculated according to location data, and an individual's chances of receiving credit for a mortgage were sharply determined by their current geographic status.

The neighbourhoods that received a 'hazardous' credit rating were frequently poor or populated by racial and ethnic minorities. The scoring practice, known today as 'redlining', acted as a device to reduce mobility and to keep African American families from moving into neighbourhoods dominated by whites. The 1970 Fair Credit Reporting Act and the 1974 Equal Credit Opportunity Act in the United States were attempts to rectify these discriminatory practices.

Today – or so the narrative goes – we have detailed and unbiased scoring algorithms that are perceptually blind to gender, class, and ethnicity in their search for a creditworthy individual. And yet, burgeoning studies of how machine-learning algorithms classify and make decisions show that they mirror historical forms of racial, economic, and gender discrimination, leading critics such as Cathy O'Neil and Frank Pasquale to point to emergent practices of 'weblining', in which algorithmic scores embody the same old credit castes and inequalities.[32]

Critics often point to the inherent bias of those who write the code, but also to the fact that the machine learns from a wealth of historical transaction data that is chock-full of old inferences and resentments. It has been shown, for example, that

66

having an African-American name negatively affects the new algorithmic credit scores. Meanwhile, Amazon Prime's same-day delivery areas follow the contours of these historical maps of credit exclusion. Redlining is still there in the background – a stain that won't shift. And when an algorithmic score stands in for the messiness of real-world decisions, those outcomes are harder to contest.

In 2019, Zest AI shifted its business model from that of credit provider to present itself as a company offering an automated machine-learning suite to other financial institutions such as banks and credit unions. In 2022, the company partnered with Equifax, one of the world's three largest credit-reporting firms. The company claims it has since introduced measures to 'de-bias' the decisions made by its software, using one machine-learning system to underwrite credit and another to test whether the decision made by the former is 'fair' or 'not fair': the system would make a judgement and also judge if that judgement had judged well. The Zest Race Predictor, for example, is an algorithm that aims to identify a user's race based on their name and location, and then use this data to add an additional layer of due diligence in underwriting decisions. It is unclear how this double-check might occur, or how exactly it escapes its own constraints to avoid the pitfalls that characterise any other training data suite.

The State of Transactional Data

I tend to think of data surveillance as an anxiety that grew in the wake of the Snowden and Cambridge Analytica revelations, but transactional surveillance was a popular topic on the Cypherpunk forum, a 1990s mailing list dedicated to digital cash and the use of cryptography. The Cypherpunks, however, were more concerned about what the government might do with their payment histories than corporations. 'Make no mistake', wrote founder Timothy May in 1992, 'a government-run cash-less society will be worse than Orwell's worst'.[33]

As governments explore the development of central bank digital currencies (CBDCs) – digital tokens tied to the central bank – the possibilities for direct government transactional surveillance loom large. Hyun Shin of the Bank for International Settlements spoke evocatively of the CBDC as money with memory, predicting that 'computing and technology can come to the rescue, and fulfil the vision of a shared ledger of all past transfers'.[34] This would produce a state-backed money where nothing is ever forgotten, 'the power of memory driving everything into the light by linking it all together and making escaping into the shadows an impossibility'.[35]

Even before the Covid pandemic, which saw many countries introduce new incentives to 'go cashless', governments were driving a push to move from cash to traceable electronic payments. India, for example, saw an overnight demonetisation of all ₹500 (US$7.70) and ₹1,000 banknotes in November 2016, allegedly to crack down on the use of cash in shadow economies.

The pursuit of a cashless society has been as much a project of the nation-state as it is of private platforms, then, but for different reasons. Platforms and commercial banks are motivated by interest fees and transactional data. The state's interest is usually centred on questions of national security (anti terrorism) and cracking down on the loopholes and blind spots that dumb cash can facilitate (tax evasion, money laundering). Secondary data gathered by platforms is often repackaged and sold to governments, where it is used for these purposes. Transactional data is increasingly marshalled in the service of security, governance, and law enforcement – for example, in the targeting of money laundering or tax evasion. An example is the Italian Redditometro, an algorithmic income meter designed to compare people's spending patterns with their income to detect possible tax fraud. Such data might also be used to profile citizens as a terrorist or security threat (helpful hint: don't purchase a pressure cooker and a backpack on the same weekend).

In the United States, Thiel's Palantir Technologies currently forms a link between US tech companies and the US state. Its main customers are federal agencies. Palantir Gotham provides these agencies with transactional data for counterterrorism and fraud investigation. The United Nations World Food Programme, Team Rubicon, the National Institutes of Health, and the Polaris Project (an organisation specialising in combatting sex trafficking) have all used Palantir's transactional datasets.

Platform-driven experiments with algorithmic credit scoring might also be pilot studies for future state surveillance. Alipay's Zhima Credit was a testbed for the launch of China's social credit system – a haphazard national policy that provides citizens with a unique social score based on their compliance with government directives. In November 2020, the Chinese government suspended the platform's $37 billion IPO (some believed as a backlash for public criticism by founder Jack Ma of the Chinese state's regulatory system). In 2021 China's regulators went further. After six years as a commercial company, Zhima Credit was coerced into sharing its consumer credit data with the Chinese central bank. The company and its operators were folded into a financial holding company that fell under the People's Bank of China. Platforms and their private R&D were stepping stones on the way to a state-backed system.

The acquisition of Alipay fell under what President Xi Jinping described as the Chinese state's vision of 'data-driven governance'. I remember hearing a talk in early 2020 in which a visiting researcher described arriving at a Chinese university only to be treated to images and data trails of his journey from the airport to the campus. It was a tone-deaf demonstration of the surveillance systems in place. How shocking. But as it stands, social credit is less a unified, totalitarian vision than a kludge of regional initiatives. It is fragmented, and surprisingly analogue. It seems, in 2022, as if social credit might act most forcefully as a Western imaginary of state surveillance happening 'elsewhere' – one so perfect in its dastardly awfulness that we are distracted from the realities playing out in our phones and wallets – ones that are a little less novelesque, less suited to the capitalist realism of a Netflix series. Social credit is the spectre by comparison with which a surveillance programme seems tame because 'at least we're not China'. But we don't need to look to China to see the machine at work.

Erasing Tokens

What kind of tactics, if any, exist for hiding from transactional surveillance?

One response is to reclaim cash. Along with the portraits and the serial numbers and the hidden visual codes designed to prevent counterfeit, other secret messages sometimes make their way onto paper money. Artist Cildo Meireles's *Insertion into Ideological Circuits 2: Banknote Project* (1970) probed the relationship between money and media. At the time Meireles made the intervention, Brazil was experiencing a particularly oppressive period in its military dictatorship. The artist printed anti-imperialist messages onto Brazilian banknotes ('Yankees Go Home') before spending them quietly back into circulation.

Once spent, cash enters another system of exchange. There is a tension here between the control and issuance of a token by the state and the ability of a person on the street to use this public medium for critique – to send a signal back to power, or out into the world. Because the messages are anonymous, they are safe to convey. Cash acts as an analogue point-to-point medium, something that everybody uses but nobody quite controls. Even with social media these practices continue, maybe because there is nothing quite so immediate as defacing a banknote. In Ireland, where a controversial system known as 'Direct Provision' detains asylum seekers for years as they await the outcome of their applications, my sister-in-law points me to euro notes bearing the slogan: 'No Borders: End Direct Provision'. Sometimes the messages are just for fun. In 2015, Canadians paid tribute to the late Leonard Nimoy by trans-forming the face of seventh prime minister Wilfrid Laurier on the $5 bill into Dr Spock. Cash is a meme, a proto-social media.

During the pandemic, I notice that using cash starts to feel in bad taste. A handwritten sign in my local shop thanks me for using contactless payment. Cash carries all kinds of stuff, from bacteria to illicit drugs. One polymer note can carry the live flu virus for up to five days; for paper money, it's closer to seventeen. Along with microbes and foreign contaminants, studies show that the vast majority of cash also carries trace amounts of illegal substances it has come into contact with; around 80 per cent of British banknotes contain traces of drugs, and this percentage rises significantly in urban areas. Notes carry 'molecular echoes' – bodily fluids and parasites and traces of what people in a particular neighbourhood like to eat for lunch.

At the start of Covid, governments around the world took measures against the cash-based transmission of the virus. In the United States, money was quarantined as a precaution-ary measure. China and South Korea used UV light to kill any lingering germs, or in some cases took the money out of circulation altogether and burned it. Governments around the world launched incentives to go cashless, reducing the fees and limits for cashless payments to encourage citizens to forgo paper money.

For journalist Brett Scott, the pandemic was a keystone in the ongoing 'cold war against cash' – a push to wean people from physical, public tender onto traceable tokens. The way Scott sees it, all digital money – whether issued by a crypto start-up, or PayPal, or a commercial bank – is nothing more than private scrip, drawn on the deferred promise of redemp-tion through state-backed money. It is only when we exchange these private tokens for cash – when we, literally, 'cash them out' – that we exit the private system.[36] Far from a frictionless dream, the cashless economy ties us in.

Cash may be the last blind spot in a world where all economic exchange is subject to surveillance: 'If everything is traceable you start thinking about your purchasing behaviour', the Piratebay's Peter Sunde argued, shortly after his release from prison in 2014 for copyright infringement. 'You need cash for anonymous behaviour.'[37] Cash does not record its own traces or the identities of its bearers, or what they put it towards.

An engineer who worked for the Scottish Electricity Board in the 1970s once told me that women sometimes used their home meters as a 'bank', stockpiling coins at the start of the month and, later, calling out one of the company's engineers to issue a refund. Cash is still central for rural, unemployed, unbanked, elderly, and vulnerable people. It is particularly important for low-income households, where welfare is sometimes paid out in cash, and where physical coins and notes are used in household budgeting.[38] Cash is still tucked under the mattress or secreted in jars or envelopes, a practice known colloquially in parts of Ireland as 'the manage'.[39] It seems there is something about physical money that makes it easier to keep and harder to spend.

In moments of financial uncertainty, people fall back on the money they can see and touch (Nigel Dodd's *The Social Life of Money* opens with the striking image of Greek citizens hoarding cash in their freezers).[40] Cash is also important for charity: 'it is certainly hard to imagine beggars trading in their cups for card-readers', James Gleick wrote in 1996, in an article on the death of cash, when QR-code donations were still in the future.[41] Edging out cash is the latest form of digital gentrification. What makes this stranger is that it is often endorsed in the name of financial inclusion – of bringing the poor and the unbanked, with their sprawling fistfuls of change, into the virtual fold.

Alongside Scott's creeping war, though, it seems like there is a growing recognition of what we have to lose when we surrender cash. In Sweden and Norway, two countries that enthusiastically embraced the call to go cashless, regulators are now working to ensure the availability of cash to underserved parts of the country. The Eurosystem 2030 Cash Strategy, for example, now includes a remit on the importance of physical tender for financial inclusion, and has committed to upholding the acceptance of cash in all retail spaces.[42] The strategy also acknowledges that cash is that rare space where a consumer's right to privacy is still protected.

'Cash is dying', James Gleick wrote in 1996, as he pointed to the private tokens that were squeezing out the dollar – the chipped phone cards, frequent-flyer miles, and electronic food stamps riding the newly minted web. But also, cash isn't going anywhere anytime soon.

Anonymous Payments

A recent Harris poll of the American public began by introducing respondents to all the consumer benefits of the information superhighway. Then respondents were told that in order to make such systems economically viable, payment transaction data would have to be gathered and used for purposes such as making special offers to them. But the majority of respondents still objected to any use, other than consummation of the payment, and they gave privacy as the primary reason.[43]

In July 1995, the US congress convened a series of hearings on the future of money, inviting experts to debate a payments solution for the internet. David Chaum, the inventor of an anonymous electronic payments system called DigiCash, was among the invited speakers, wedged between representatives from Visa and Mastercard. Privacy concerns, Chaum argued, would only grow with the internet. And there was no way consumers would trade privacy for convenience. The solution had to be a digital token with the same anonymity as cash.

Chaum is the grandfather of Bitcoin you have probably never heard of. His 'vault system', described in his 1982 doctoral dissertation at University of California, Berkeley, detailed many of the innovations that later appeared in Nakamoto's blockchain.[44] Chaum's 'Security without Identification: Transaction Systems to Make Big Brother Obsolete' was published in 1985.[45] In everyday transactions, Chaum writes, individuals now hold a variety of private 'tokens' issued by organisations, alongside public money. These tokens make way for new types of surveillance, where 'consumer data would be used to infer individuals' life-styles, habits, whereabouts, and associations'.

In Chaum's DigiCash, tokens were anonymous. The scheme used a system of public and private keys. It relied 'on individuals keeping secret keys from organizations and organizations devising other secret keys that are kept from individuals'.[46] Private keys were a bit like a password or a PIN, not to be disclosed to anyone, while public keys were like a bank account number, with the difference that they weren't directly associated with a real-world identity.

In the 1990s, the online Cypherpunk community also debated types of anonymous money. Alongside Tacky Tokens, DigiFrancs, and GhostMarks, there was Magic Money, an email-based currency designed by the pseudonymous Pr0duct Cypher. These tokens were sent via email and run through an anonymous remailer to remove identifying details. As the names suggest, they were playful tokens that didn't take themselves too seriously. (DigiFrancs were redeemable for sixteen-ounce cans of room-temperature Diet Coke, held in a reserve at the UniBank 'vault' in Washington, DC). But they were also attempts to remake the nameless and point-to-point medium of cash as a digital token.

Bitcoin emerged in 2008. It drew on many of the innovations Chaum had developed for DigiCash, including blind signatures and chains of authentication. The cryptocurrency offered early adopters *some* anonymity, because, as with Chaum's tokens, the transactions used public and private keys. An encrypted currency should be untraceable, Chaum argued; there should be no way to reconstruct the user's real identity from their digital pseudonym.

In many ways, though, the Bitcoin protocol was *more* revealing than other payments systems, because the entire history of all tokens was publicly available. Anonymous data on the blockchain and identifiable data on message boards, public forums, and social media networks could be pieced together to match real identities to Bitcoin addresses. This is now the aim of anti–money laundering units worldwide, which spend time connecting known identities to anonymised transactional data. As Bitcoin transactions have become more traceable, other coins have attempted to foil surveillance by scrambling these traces.

With Bitcoin 'laundering' or Bitcoin mixers, for example, it is possible to cover your tracks by mixing funds together into a shared wallet with other trusted individuals. Others make use of chain-hopping, strategically moving money from one digital token to another, hiding their pathways in a mesh of false traces. At the time of writing, the most popular token for anonymous transactions on the dark web is Monero. Alongside a public and private key, Monero uses an additional 'stealth' token, a one-off key for each transaction that cannot be linked back to a user's public identity.

Another long-standing approach to online anonymity involves switching out personal credit cards and accounts in favour of prepaid options. Prepaid gift cards, once the remit of those without access to credit, are now strategically used for their anonymity and privacy benefits. So are virtual credit cards. Privacy.com, for example, creates a new card number for every transaction, marketed as a solution to increased online fraud, but also to data mining.

Obfuscation

Electronic payments can be extremely hard to opt out of. Finn Brunton notes the strain of navigating everyday life in metropolitan China without using WeChat Pay: 'These are spaces where not using digital cash has already passed from the archaic to the eccentric and bizarre.'[47] For Brunton, a scholar of internet activism, such trends are a preview of what we might soon or already be experiencing – maybe that whisper of a feeling that I had yesterday in the doctor's office, when my hand glanced off a €50 note in my bag but I still decided to pay with my phone, because it seemed … more polite? Hygienic? I couldn't say for sure, but the receptionist held the card reader up to the Plexiglas screen between us, and I held up my iPhone to the other side, and … *bloop*. Maybe that subtle 'feeling' will slowly morph into an obligation, a norm, or a law.

This is why Brunton is such a big believer in obfuscation: a whole suite of techniques designed to hide meaningful data in noise. Obfuscation includes tactics that hide money's footprints in a mesh of false traces; that work to erase the traces left behind by digital money; or, by swapping accounts and tracking objects (SIM cards, loyalty cards) within a group, that produce false or confusing data. Imagine the little bit of uncertainty that is added to your consumer profile when you buy gardening gloves for your mother or books for a friend, but at a much larger scale.

In 2003, computer scientist Rob Carlson created an online card-swapping system for loyalty cards from the Giant supermarket in the Baltimore and Washington, DC areas. Participants could enter their card numbers into a form on his website, and then print out and paste someone else's bar-code onto their loyalty card. 'Rob's Giant BonusCard Swap Meet' was designed to jumble together a user's purchasing data with data on many other customers' shopping at the retail superstore, destroying its market value to the corporation. Carlson admits that while his project was an attempt to digitise something hacker groups were already doing face-to-face, it never really worked as an obfuscation tool. It was more like a proposition than a working prototype – an extra piece of administration any human circa 2020 would be unlikely to sit down and actually *do*.[48] And, already in 2003, Giant was making it harder for customers to share loyalty cards, linking gasoline discounts and promotions to individual card numbers. The extra noise has an expressive more than a disruptive function. It was a way of registering protest, but it isn't always a way of throwing off the platform.

In 2021, MIT Media Lab student Alex Berke developed an obfuscation tool combining Amazon's locker system and mutual-aid networks. Lockers are frequently used by customers who want their real identities to remain private – such as streamers or cam models whose wish list items are a vital source of income from fans. In Berke's system, users can anonymously 'ask' for items they need and specify a locker location. Others can buy and donate random items and deliver them to a locker, adding a bit of noise to their profile.[49] The obfuscation tool does not try to reimagine e-commerce. It just builds on top of the infrastructures – wish lists, lockers, Amazon Prime – that are already in place.

Obfuscation and anonymity come in for criticism because these hacks can be used for crime and tax evasion. Recently, a number of crypto mixers, designed to maintain privacy, have faced government sanctions over alleged money-laundering or been blacklisted by the US Treasury.

The Paris attacks of November 2015 were also partly funded through anonymous prepaid debit cards. 'So then, I guess you "like" terrorism, do you?', an irate man once shouted at me at a privacy conference. No, I don't like terrorism. But national security is often used as a blanket justification for the rollout of widespread surveillance.

Burning Money

We could just destroy the token and its record altogether.

My interactions with Bitcoin zealots have made me wary of men who want to single-handedly redesign the economy, but Jonathan Harris is surprisingly down to earth. He came to money burning in 2007 off the back of a personal financial crisis. 'There's nothing like bankruptcy to push you back into a cash economy', he observes.[50] But, like a lot of people, Harris's foray into crippling debt in 2007 broke something else: a taboo on money.

At a moment when everyone was coming to recognise that money was just an entry in a virtual ledger, Harris was asking what money was made of, and what kind of special power it had over him. 'I'd thought about burning money for about two years,' he tells me, 'to the point where my own resistance to actually doing it became the thing that interested and fascinated me – why was I so reluctant to destroy this object?' Eventually he earmarked a £10 note and set a date, 23 October 2007. He invited his son and his now ex-wife to witness the ritual. I asked what he felt. 'I felt like I wanted to incant something, to say some words. The words that came to me were "release all", and it did feel like a release. What really is this stuff? What is our relationship to it?'

After deferring philosophy at the University of Warwick, Harris undertook a degree in economic history from the London School of Economics (LSE) at the age of twenty-nine. He was interested in the philosophy of money, but didn't know such a thing existed until he spotted Simmel on a lone shelf in the library during his final year. Upon graduation, Harris didn't go into economics or banking, like many LSE alumni. In 2000 he founded a website with his now ex-wife Sally called 'Natural-Sex' – a domain name he had acquired some years before in the belief that it was 'marketable'. The website featured erotic stories, descriptions and photos of their sex life, cameos

78

from friends, and a weekly interactive live-cam show. Sally Harris gave up a career as an NHS nurse and carer to pursue NaturalSex full time. To watch the live broadcasts, you had to subscribe. The most popular option was a monthly subscription for £19.95.

Jon and Sally Harris were partners in the scripting of the content, but Jon's role was largely on the technical side of things – everything from website design to payments processing and digital photography. Payments were an ongoing issue. They used a processor in Florida. It was hard to find one willing to manage subscriptions. Major credit cards are famously averse to sex work – Harris calls them 'the moral arbiters of money' – not only because of the regulatory issues involved, but also because of frequent issues with chargebacks: 'I don't know how this charge for a porn website ended up on my credit card ... '. While processing the payments, Harris undertook some stealth consumer research of his own into the website's subscribers. The transactional data was revealing. From the information provided, he could 'practically tell the surfer's shoe size', where they worked, and their age band (from thirty to fifty).

In 2021, Harris retrospectively describes the website as an ethical OnlyFans with a proposal for an issued token called XXX currency. It was a 'joyful time', he says fondly. 'Maybe a little too joyful.' The internet was undergoing a shift from a subscription to a free-content model, and small adult enterprises like NaturalSex struggled to survive. By 2007, they were overcome with debt and declared bankruptcy. Today, Harris is a van driver and makes slightly more than the minimum wage. He has no assets, and rents his house.

With money burning, the initiative stems less from a desire to erase the promise inscribed on a banknote than from a desire to erase the contractual obligations of the money relation altogether, revealing what one burner describes as 'our blind fixation on money as an object through the act of destruction'. Choosing to burn a token, or otherwise permanently remove it from circulation, shrinks the overall supply of that currency. The act of destruction has a deflationary effect that increases the value of the cash still in circulation. And because what is destroyed is merely a document of the thing and not the thing itself, the act does not destroy anything beyond the record of the bearer's claim on society. As Noam Yuran puts it, 'burning money, of whatever amount, disrupts the cosmic double-entry bookkeeping system that dominates our relation to the economy'.[51]

Harris began burning money regularly, penned *The Money Burner's Manual*, and established festivals where money burners came together to destroy tokens. His latest website, burnyourmoney.org, features a record of the tokens that have been burned to date, including their serial numbers. So far, £70,000 has been destroyed – a debt that, at least theoretically, can be wiped from the Central Bank's ledger. *Burning Issue*, a magazine edited by Harris and directed at the 'money burning community', describes a number of tactics to destroy currency, including those for 'burning' digital money. I am reminded of a performance by Geraldine Juárez in Berlin in early 2014, where the artist transferred bitcoin onto an XD card and toasted it, marshmallow-style, over a campfire outside the Haus der Kulturen der Welt.

At the end of our conversation, instead of paying Jonathan Harris for his time, I burn some money. It was my first time and, like Harris, I'm not sure where my hesitancy had come from. Until shortly after my money-burning exercise, I believed that what I was doing was illegal. By burning money, I was not only defacing the economy but also somehow severing my relationship with the state. It turns out this was a misconception on my part: it's not illegal to deface or destroy small amounts of currency in the EU.

Before burning my note, I show Harris another artefact, a tight brick of shredded euros I had been given several years back by a member of the Central Bank of Ireland, Paul Molumby.

The brick contains somewhere between €10,000 and €15,000 in destroyed euros, all shredded and withdrawn from circulation. 'My daughter uses it as bedding for guinea pigs', Molumby told me at the time. 'It's soft, but absorbent.' The brick is surprisingly heavy and just fits in the flat of my palm. As objects go, it's quite beautiful – tiny strips of festive colour, the odd fragment of a serial number, a denomination.

I withdrew the €20 from an ATM in Sligo the day before. Ever fewer of them are operational. Throughout our conversation on burning, I play with the note, turning the watermark to the light, pondering the burn and all of the other things that I could do with my money besides taking it out of circulation. 'Ah, that's a nice paper note', says Harris appreciatively when I show him my crisp €20. 'Not like those new polymer ones. They require a different burn technique. They tend to curl up, and you have to keep the flame applied to them.' He tells me to write down the serial number – TC0998492834. This is an important part of the ritual. I light the far corner just right of the identifier. 'Hold the note down', says Harris as the flame sputters and threatens to go out 'and let the flame travel up … mind your hand!'

Burning money is a sacrifice, says Harris. At times it can feel like a hammy ritual, a suburban swingers' party with a touch of Bacchanalia to add to the spectacle. In making the burning of money a sacrament, I ask Harris, are you not just feeding into the fetish of money? Why give the token so much sway? 'I see it as a ritual of disenchantment', Harris explains, 'a *de*-fetishisation of money, a rite that paves the way for a new narrative.' Burning the token makes room for a new story, maybe even a new economy.

Alongside money burning, Harris's festivals feature music and chanting and even live sex acts – until Covid made certain aspects of the ceremony 'unviable'. But they also feature pragmatic discussions about what money could or might be. Something else happens when you burn a note. Every destroyed token reduces the overall monetary supply of tokens circulating in the economy, having a real, if small, deflationary effect. But, for Harris, the real material effect of money burning happens at the level of the individual, in the way that we feel. We can be told something and read the whole LSE library catalogue, and still we might not know what money *is*.

Burning the token puts us in touch with an affective space that is beyond exchange, beyond the economy. 'Every time we spend money, we invoke a future', writes Lana Swartz.[52] And, strangely, burning money does the same thing. Burning money invokes, for a moment, the possible unfolding and suppressed futures in your hand – the money that could have been donated to charity or spent in a local shop or saved or gifted to a friend or turned into food, but also the possibilities of a different economy, and another kind of future.

3

Programmable Butter

The tokens come in a booklet with the recipient's name on the front. This one belonged to Bridget Connell of Ballina, Co. Mayo. The booklet has a friendly crease down the middle, as though the vouchers have been folded into a pocket or a hall drawer. There's a drink ring in the top-left corner, like they sat out on the kitchen table beside the tea and the marmalade. Inside, two columns of text in the state's official languages detail their proper use: 'Butter vouchers are issued to social assistance recipients to enable them to purchase butter at a reduced price for consumption in their own households. The vouchers must be used only by the persons to whom they are issued or by other persons acting on their behalf and MUST NOT BE EXCHANGED FOR ITEMS OTHER THAN BUTTER.'

In the early 1980s the common EU agricultural policy led to the oversupply of dairy produce in Ireland. The state called it a 'butter mountain', as warehouses were piled with Kerrygold bullion, a mountain of grease you could slide down.[1] On the other side of this mountain was the struggling welfare system, padding out dole payments with food stamps. The tokens recall a period of mass unemployment and emigration ('it was a given that most of you would grow up and leave', my mother says, with a shrug, about the 1980s). But it seems now that they are also remembered as a token of a different Ireland, before every corner shop was switched out for a franchise.

What people remember most about the butter voucher is not the drudge of living on welfare stamps, but usually all the ways the butter vouchers *were not* used for butter: the creative accounting, how shopkeepers turned a blind eye to the small print. Local shops routinely ignored the terms and conditions attached to the token. 'Shops would take them for bread, sardines and eggs', my friend Clare says. She seems a little defensive. She wants to stress that she was very hard pressed, 'living in actual poverty … but most of my friends were too … unemployed, in bands or writers'. 'Anything else?' I ask. 'Beans … sometimes a decent shop owner would take them for cigarettes or rollies', she says. 'Ten smokes', says another friend's mother. 'We called them baccy vouchers.'

In fact, the vouchers were accepted as payment for tobacco, for Buckfast Tonic Wine, for groceries, for children's treats. They were passed around. People even put them to non-transactional uses – as a decoy for insurance discs displayed on a car's windshield – one official paper masquerading as another.[2]

There is a space between the bureaucratic token and the token on the street. This is the space between state policy and what James C. Scott called the 'weapons of the weak'.[3] Something less than outright resistance, it is the foot-dragging and muttering and feigned ignorance that wears away at the operation of power.

Maureen's in Stoneybatter, Co. Dublin, closed in 2021. She was a crabby institution of a woman who had no truck with the gentrifying crowds swarming Manor Street for Sunday pancakes. 'She wouldn't sell me a can of COKE!' My husband is apoplectic. It is 2019, and he has just returned from rushing our toddler to the GP with a fever. He was in such a rush that he forgot to bring coins for the parking meter and ran into Maureen's to buy anything to break a note. She refused to serve him on the grounds that he was 'only looking to make change for the parking'. Maureen's was cash only. 'I asked her what I could get for a tenner', one customer recalls, 'and she gave me two fives.'[4] Maureen stocked, but hated selling, phone credit. Maureen's accepted butter vouchers.

Money Flows, Tokens Filter

'It is the nature of money to flow freely, to be like water', writes Mary Douglas. Tokens, on the other hand, 'reduce liquidity by blocking, earmarking and funding it in various ways'.[5] Tokens are usually only accepted for a limited range of goods or services, and only transferable to specific people. They are 'special-purpose'. Unlike money, which Douglas calls 'an instrument of freedom', tokens can be instruments of control; issuing one can be a way of closing certain economic possibilities down, of channelling and prescribing the limits of an exchange.[6]

Tokens, Douglas writes, mean 'closed doors, restriction and control'.[7] If money flows, tokens filter. But equally, tokens find the cracks in the legitimate economy. Tokens, rather than legal tender, are the route exchange takes when the normal channels are closed. They are usually *just liquid enough* to find the other way through.

For economic anthropologist Karl Polanyi, the validity of some object as 'money' rested on five criteria: the temporal, the territorial, the economic, the social, and the local. Did the object expire over time, or did it hold its value? Did it have spatial limits? Did it account – and could it be redeemed – for a broad variety of things, or only for specific things? Could it be used by everyone, or only by a select group? Were there restrictions attached to its use?

Money was 'special-purpose' if it served less than all of these five functions. If modern Western money was 'all-purpose' and fungible, Polanyi observed that primitive money was usually of the special-purpose type. It belonged to a time when money-like things – Yap stones, wampum, totemistic feathers – were grounded in rituals and social hierarchies. It operated only in certain sections of the community, or for certain transactions. Special-purpose tokens were culturally richer than modern exchange media, but not as economically useful. On this basis,

Polanyi concluded that modern societies did not deal in special-purpose money.[8]

This strikes me as an odd conclusion to draw at any moment in modern history, but it is especially jarring now. By Polanyi's definition, butter vouchers are clearly special-purpose money. And, also by Polanyi's definition, all money is to some degree 'special-purpose'. There is no token that is universally accepted in any time and place for anything. It seems more accurate to say, as Friedrich Hayek does, that we are dealing with a spectrum of exchange media. Instead of a hard line between fungible and non-fungible tokens, we have 'a range of objects of varying degrees of acceptability which imperceptibly shade at the lower end into objects that are clearly not money'.[9]

Polanyi's conclusions are jarring because we are now surrounded by things that skew across the five functions, to the point where it feels like a whole range of bespoke tokens might crowd out the fungible: money that straddles the cracks in the economy, money that can only be redeemed through specific channels or for very specific things, money that is tied to our identity or that circulates in niche circles, money that comes with strings attached.

Viviana Zelizer also calls these 'special monies'. Unlike Polanyi, she sees them everywhere: media of exchange that are earmarked for a particular purpose. Earmarking happens *in everyday use* when we distinguish between payments, tips, and gifts, or between 'dirty', 'clean', and 'bitter' money, Zelizer writes. But money is also earmarked *at its source*, to restrict the freedom it represents – especially when it comes into contact with poor or marginalised communities.

Zelizer's focus was on the earmarking of money for the poor throughout the 1800s. Straightforward cash transfers to the poor were seen as a 'dangerous form of relief', open to abuse, and the charitable organisations distributing aid were determined to make money 'as safe as groceries' for those receiving it.[10] They did this by replacing cash with special tokens.

86

Sometimes money was even substituted for in-kind relief ('food, clothing, or fuel, but *not* money') or grocery orders ('provisions for necessary support only').[11]

Charity workers also felt entitled to channel relief funds, and even collect wages from the poor, in order to '"launder" them into legitimate monies'.[12] Zelizer describes how collecting agencies intervened to earmark poor people's wages into 'fuel funds' and 'shoe clubs' and other savings societies. Convinced that the poor were fiscally and morally incompetent, agencies turned their money into 'stamps of various colors and denominations that were then pasted on a card'.[13] These stamps were non-transferable, and shops were forbidden to sell detached stamps 'lest they should be used for barter'.[14]

'Earmarking sends a message', writes Bruce Carruthers.[15] These special tokens were 'instructional currencies', designed to drive home a lesson about frugality and proper spending as much as they were made to give material relief. There was a morality to the token. Not value, then, but 'values'.

These values go back even further. In the fourteenth and fifteenth centuries, charitable tokens were branded with the items they could be redeemed for (bread, meat, wine, charcoal). Others marked the right to be excused from a toll. A token specified the quantity and type of goods it could be redeemed for, but also, crucially, who was to be given access to charity.[16] The charitable tokens could distinguish between the 'deserving' and the 'undeserving' poor. If you did not hold a token it was because, by some moral calculation, you did not deserve one.

In the United States today, the Supplemental Nutrition Assistance Program (SNAP) is a special-purpose benefit for the purchase of food for low-income families. The benefit is still sometimes referred to as 'food stamps', remembering a time when relief took the form of a paper token that could be spent on groceries. These tokens had pictures of harvested grain, of two parents and a child holding hands and facing a sunrise beneath sky writing that spelled out 'healthier families'.

Unemployment cheques could be redeemed for orange food stamps at cost. These bought groceries in participating stores. In addition, the bearer received a book of blue stamps for free, which could be redeemed against surplus goods like butter, eggs, oranges, flour, cornmeal, and beans.

Like the butter vouchers, food stamps were a double-sided market – they fed starving families in the aftermath of the depression, and, by restricting the token, they also helped to support food prices. Today, SNAP benefits come pre-loaded onto an Electronic Benefits Transfer (EBT) card. SNAP earmarks the tokens at source. SNAP benefits are 'not the same as monetary assistance'. They are not 'for general spending' or 'to receive cash-back services'. They can be used for fresh food and produce. They cannot be used for hygiene products, vitamins or medicines, or alcohol or tobacco. They can be used for cold deli food, but not for hot meals.[17] (Why cold pre-cooked meat but not half a rotisserie chicken? It seems there is something too 'easy' – too idle, maybe – about buying a hot meal for your family using benefits.)

In 2018, the Trump administration tabled an overhaul of the existing SNAP programme, replacing a portion of monetary benefits that could be spent on food with in-kind 'harvest boxes' – a 'USDA Foods package, which would include items such as self-stable milk, ready-to-eat cereals, pasta, peanut butter, beans and canned fruit, vegetables, and meat, poultry or fish'.[18] The proposal was framed as improving nutrition and targeting benefit fraud. If earmarking sends a message, here it is that the poor are underhand and do not know how to feed themselves. A poisoned gift from a toxic state, by any definition.

In Australia's Northern Territory, the federal government's Department of Human Services issues the Basics Card, an electronic relief token that can only be used on pre-approved items and in pre-approved stores.[19] Like SNAP, the Basics Card frames those experiencing hardship as somehow to blame for their circumstances. Poverty, as in the days of Zelizer's relief tokens, is an outcome of poor moral judgement. This personal failing (being poor) is tackled through personal change. The card is designed to 'support or induce the adoption of more responsible behaviours in particular communities by, for example, placing conditions on eligibility for welfare payments or on how welfare payments may be spent'.[20] It works by siphoning a portion of a citizen's social welfare into a special fund. The fund is accessed through an electronic card that can only be used to purchase essentials such as food, fuel, and clothing. Much like the SNAP card, prohibited items include alcohol, tobacco, pornography, and gambling services and products – but not unhealthy food items.

As Zelizer delves further into the history of charitable tokens, it becomes clear that surveillance and distrust of the poor went hand-in-hand with relief efforts. Charities were closer to investigative than relief agencies, spying on the poor, cataloguing their spending, and developing technologies for their moral rehabilitation. Virginia Eubanks describes an incident in 2014 in which former Maine Republican governor Paul LePage lambasted families receiving a small relief cash benefit called Temporary Assistance for Needy Families (TANF). The governor accused these families of defrauding tax payers by misspending their benefits. The allegation drew on 36,000 recorded cash withdrawals from an EBT card to show 3,650 transactions in which recipients had made a withdrawal in off-licences or smoke shops. Despite the fact that the data did not show how or where the money was spent, it spurred a bill requiring TANF families to submit twelve months of receipts for auditing. The poor are the test subjects for future surveillance: 'You should pay attention to what happens to us', a mother on welfare payments warned Eubanks. 'You're next.'[21]

And yet, alongside this earmarking at the source, Zelizer also observes how users were able to re-channel their special-purpose money, making it flow in unintended directions. Some of these were tokenistic – such as a poor housewife's insistence that she carried the funds herself on an otherwise supervised shopping trip with a charitable organisation. Others involved tacit arrangements between merchants and customers, much like the butter vouchers circulating in Ireland. A little creative accounting let coupons for coal or food be channelled into debts or rent. Charitable grocery orders were sometimes turned into cash or used as extra-legal tender in poor communities.[22]

Zelizer describes how an Italian widow managed to persuade her participating grocer to let her buy bread at an Italian bakery instead. He would then pay her weekly bill and add the amount to her authorised grocery order in his store. The arrangement only broke down when she went too far and started to add cheese and macaroni to her weekly shop.[23]

My neighbour Fiona remembers that butter vouchers were basic tender. She grew up in the Irish midlands, in a house over a grocery-pub. There would have been Guinness on tap, but also boxes of cornflakes in the window. She worked behind the till at weekends and after school, and remembers taking butter vouchers into the register and deducting them against the customer's total. They were 'not necessarily for buying butter … just a voucher that you would subtract the cost of groceries from'. Older people still carry a mental map of the shops like Fiona's that overlooked the fine print on the butter vouchers. 'Noel's used to take them. What a man Noel was!'[24] Special-purpose tokens were contested waters. Users often found ways around token relief – ways to repurpose and otherwise appropriate it.

Programmable Tokens, Programmable Scripts

You had to take those pieces of paper with you when you went shopping … It seems so primitive, totemistic even, like cowrie shells. I must have used that kind of money myself, a little, before everything went on the Compubank – I guess that's how they were able to do it, in the way they did, all at once, without anyone knowing beforehand. If there had still been portable money, it would have been more difficult.[25]

This is an extract from *The Handmaid's Tale* by Margaret Atwood. As Gilead rises to power, Offred goes to the shop to buy a packet of cigarettes and pays with her Compucard. The woman who normally works behind the counter is not there. She has been replaced by a stranger, a man who studies the card and keys in the numbers one by one. He obviously hasn't done it before: 'Sorry, he said. This number's not valid … See that red light? Means it's not valid.'[26]

When the Gilead administration comes to power, it uses identifying data to freeze any Compucard accounts held by women overnight. In one of many echoes of real-world events (IBM's punch cards allowed the German government to rapidly identify Jewish citizens), data meets wholesale action. *The Handmaid's Tale* imagined a future where access to payments is severed from half the population by changing a few instructions in a digital ledger. The light is red. The number is no longer valid. The computer says no.

In Offred's present, the handmaids use paper tokens again – objects resembling the rationing coupons of Atwood's World War II childhood. They have pictures of the things they can buy on the front – oranges, chickens, eggs. It is unclear if the tokens are part of a rationing system. Offred mentions war-torn supply chains in the same breath as she bears up a token and dreams of fresh oranges from California, but this might also be because women and slaves (and, really, the handmaids are both) were not permitted to handle money directly.

I'm re-reading the story, and wondering why the handmaids' money is a dumb token, a simple ration booklet kept in the kitchen under the watchful eye of the Marthas, when Offred mentions that the token's identifying numbers are keyed into a system at the point of sale. Tracked after all.

If stories like Offred's were called upon to justify their existence, Atwood wrote in 2013, they might be seen as imaginary tools: '*This is where the road seems to be heading*, they might say. *This is its possible destination. Do you really want to go there? If not, change the road.*'[27]

I keep trawling through images of the old Irish butter vouchers online. Butter vouchers and food stamps were earmarked at their source, but there was flexibility in how they were exchanged on the ground. 'Everything was analogue so [it was] impossible to trace the goods exchanged, really', Fiona says. The token was renegotiated at the point of sale when somebody handed over a butter voucher and got a packet of Marlboros. Butter vouchers became 'baccy' vouchers, became car insurance. Who could say which was which? This was not the 'coined liberty' of proper money, but it was a little bit of freedom, anyway.

By the mid 1990s, however, they came with a bar-code for machine readability. Rules were hard-coded into the token. Unlike the food stamps they replaced, for example, the use of the SNAP card provides the US Department of Agriculture with tools to 'identify, track, and take action' against fraudulent activity such as exchanging a card for cash, or using it to purchase non-approved items.[28]

Earmarking sends a message. It writes a 'script', a story with an intended use and an intended user. Such technological scripts, Madeleine Akrich argues, pose two questions. The first is how a thing and its script conditions how users can relate to the object and to each other. What kinds of imagined users does a token call forth? The deserving poor feeding their children? The nuclear family rising from the ashes of the Great Depression? A mythical 'welfare queen' who needs moral instruction? What kinds of strings are attached to its use, from gender and identity to social norms about propriety or proper nutrition? What can't you buy with a Compucard or with SNAP benefits? The second is the extent to which users are able to throw off, refuse, or rewrite the scripts or roles offered to them.[29] Can users re-channel the token to their own ends and desires? Is this still even possible?

In the past there was still a degree of latitude. Users found the workarounds. Tokens could change hands, or a shopkeeper or almsgiver could look the other way. In the era of programmable tokens, this is harder to do. There is one way through – no other way to go or to look to. For the most part, paper money as an object does not restrict its own use. (An exception happens if you try to scan or photocopy a banknote. Then, a strange little constellation of stars printed on the surface is registered by the photocopier and prevents the note from being duplicated. Instead you'll get a pixelated image, or maybe a printed error message that copying money is an offence. Suddenly the 'dumb' token feels a little more knowing.)

Tokens are now smart or 'programmable', which is to say that the conditions governing their use, redemption, and transferability are hard-coded in an object. The 'script' is no longer a set of terms and conditions printed on the note that we can turn a blind eye to. Alongside software, many of these programmable tokens also involve the use of what are called 'smart contracts' to automate the terms and conditions of an exchange. If the conditions are right – the right amount, the right denomination, the right person, the right credentials – then a transaction is triggered.

Nick Szabo first described the smart contract in 1994 as 'a set of promises, specified in digital form, including protocols within which the parties perform on other promises'.[30] For Szabo, much of the work required to implement, verify, and enforce a transaction might be taken from merchants and lawyers and given, instead, to cryptography. Instead of contracts where notaries are responsible for drawing up the terms of an agreement, and where institutions work to enforce and react to breaches, conditions might instead be 'embedded in the world' with hardware and software. Szabo gave the example of a vending machine as an already-existing smart contract at work, where programmed switches stand in for humans in the sale of a can of Coke. Although Szabo did not offer a specific technical implementation for his smart contract in 1994, he speculated that many of the blockchain-adjacent innovations being explored at the time – such as public-key encryption and blind signatures – could be used to make them happen.

Today, smart contracts consist of code that is stored, verified, and executed on a blockchain. While the Bitcoin script supported the kinds of contractual arrangements necessary for transferring money to and from addresses, Ethereum developed a programming language that could express all kinds of contractual relationships. Applications include the transfer and resale of property, but also gig-work contracts, welfare payments, and voting. As well as facilitating contractual relationships between people and other people (or collections of people), the smart contract also allows for contractual arrangements between things and other connected things.

In his memorandum, Szabo suggests that the smart contract is a straightforward translation of the cultural and normative legacies inscribed in contract law into code. You take something that was previously realised through norms or laws or markets, and delegate it to software. But what exactly happens in this translation from social to judicial, to machine-readable code? Inferred agreements, accepted norms, legally binding clauses, and smart contracts are all very different. How are smart contracts linked to transactions as we know them?

First, with a smart contract, contractual clauses are expressed in *machine-readable* terms. While transacting is still by nature a social interaction, smart contracts give the process over to the kinds of if-then-else statements that govern code. Second, these contracts are designed to execute *automatically*. A traditional contract has no action built into it. The action happens somewhere else – off the paper. If these traditional contracts are implemented on a computer, they have no algorithmic relationship to the code that executes them. With a blockchain 'smart contract', though, execution and verification are in the weft of the contract.

This 'automatic' execution changes how a contract is arbitrated in the case of a dispute – or, more accurately, forecloses the possibility of dispute altogether. A traditional contract is a voluntary agreement. Its clauses are expressed in natural language. These clauses need humans to validate and execute them. Such contracts are, by their nature, not directly binding.[31] They contain possible recourse (because of conditions such as 'undue influence, incapacitation, unconscionability').[32] Contracts can be broken – some might say they are even *made* to be broken. But there is no space between clause and execution in a software-defined arrangement, no room for varied interpretation or uncertainty. This means that smart contracts by design do not allow for refusal (or even compliance, in the truest sense of the word).

As Vitalik Buterin, the now twenty-eight-year-old founder of Ethereum, admits, 'smart contracts' might not be the best phrase for the process. The term 'contract' assumes an external legal framework that may be brought to bear, as well as the possibility for non-compliance. A 'persistent script' might be a better word, Buterin muses – a set of automatic rules that work without the need for external enforcement, because they foreclose refusal altogether.[33]

The smart token seeks to do away with two things, then: the space for selective interpretation and refusal and the messy business of external oversight. The two go hand in hand because it is the possibility of the first that invokes the second – the care and maintenance when things don't go to plan. A welfare agency does not want to have to monitor welfare fraud. A bank would rather not have to pay for third-party validation for cross-border transfers or inter-bank settlement. Vendors would rather not have to rely on a third party to hold funds in escrow until a sale was completed.

A History of Programmable Tokens

An early script for programmed money was the IBM dollar, proposed by Edward de Bono (better known as the father of lateral thinking) and published by the Centre for the Study of Financial Innovation in 1994. The mission statement claimed that the centre had no ideological agenda beyond a belief in 'open and efficient markets' (as though markets were ideologically Switzerland). De Bono suggested that 'IBM would issue its own currency', one that took the form of what he called 'target currencies', backed by and redeemable for IBM products on some future date and which, for the time being, could be purchased at a discount – say 80 per cent of its cash value.[34]

Not only should IBM issue target currencies, de Bono argued; all kinds of large corporations 'should create their own special currencies which would be exchangeable for or "targeted" on their products'.[35] British Airways could issue a token based on airline seats. Sainsbury's supermarket could issue a token backed by the products in its UK stores. Both examples resemble the loyalty points and air-miles that now function as money-like things in the token economy.

Governments could also write currencies that might be 'targeted at particular areas of the economy, geographical or sectoral ... exchangeable for designated types of goods or in chosen parts of the country like development zones', de Bono argued.[36] Wages paid could be split between fungible and target currencies. While such tokens might have a bad reputation because of their resemblance to 'scrip', which companies once forced employees to accept and spend back into their own stores, De Bono argued that we should not let that put us off.

The IBM dollar was wedded to IBM's legacy in computation and data processing. IBM would use its expertise to manage supply and inflation, but also, crucially, to create money with a new programmability. This token was a 'smarter' kind of money, driven by the fact that computers 'now make it possible to run a system with multiple target currencies'.[37] De Bono's dream currency never graduated beyond the paper proposal. Instead, twenty-four years later, IBM filed a patent for a Bespoke Programmable Crypto Token. The patent describes a conscious money, in which a one-of-a-kind token is associated with particular requirements or 'the performance of an activity'.[38] When proof of that activity is tendered through a mechanism known as 'proof of performance' – when these requirements are satisfied – the token is shucked over to its new owner.[39] The process remains vague, yet all-encompassing. IBM's 2020 patent describes applications including the provision of social benefits and refugee credit, as well as the automatic enforcement of economic embargoes.

Fintech consultant David Birch believes that programmable money will emerge 'amid the fusion of reputation, authentication, identification, machine learning and AI. This is money that has a memory, but it's also money that has an API – that can make decisions about you. Different actors might produce it or coproduce it. Different transactional communities might form around the values hard-coded into different tokens. 'It might be', Birch suggests, 'a type of money that will prevent people from using it unless they have a track record of upholding its values.'[40]

In a step up from the 'vending machine sells cokes' or the 'fridge buys milk' scenario, programmable tokens could be tied to specific values – a car might be rented only when it is shown to be compliant with particular emissions tests; or, like conditional cash transfers today, a relief token might be deposited in a parent's bank account following a child's enrolment in school, or engagement with social or health services, or the uptake of a nutritional supplement. It might be geared towards particular environmental incentives, such as emissions testing or green energy transaction markets; tied to gender, as with the electronic money in Gilead; tied to your reputation, as with tokens explored on the Cypherpunk mailing list back in the

1990s; or tied to our digital identity, as in countless examples of non-transferable scrip now issued by employers, welfare departments, and relief agencies worldwide. Such currencies might be tied to specific locations or specific goods, like targeted relief aid, or maybe even to a specific timeframe, made to expire or lose value over time, like 'demurrage' tokens, which have surfaced throughout history in moments of financial instability.

Writing on a cashless society in 1992, Cypherpunk founder Timothy May reasoned that e-money might soon be 'non-fungible'. 'It is fairly easy', May observed, 'to attach various restrictions to the electronic databases which hold the money.' By updating a database, conditions can be attached to electronic tokens, rules about who could use it and what they could use it for. In a speculative post called 'Scenario for a Ban on Cash', May argued that these non-fungible tokens might play a role in the exercise of state power in the future – in particular through '"welfare reform" by restricting the allowable expenditures that can be made'.[41]

In the wake of the Covid pandemic, several proposals emerged for smart relief payments: to cover furlough, benefits, or loans in the form of what was called 'money with constraints'.[42] In a project that emerged from a German hackathon, developers devised a government-distributed and blockchain-based relief voucher that could only be redeemed in specific stores in economically struggling areas. Like the butter voucher or IBM's targeted currency, the token might prop up struggles on either side of the transaction, but without any of the old escape routes.

Following the Russian invasion of Ukraine, Binance, the company that runs the world's foremost crypto-exchange, issued a refugee crypto card for Ukrainians forced to seek asylum throughout Europe. The company is currently working with charitable organisations to funnel aid through its card scheme. The money was framed as targeted relief without the usual border wrangling or clearance issues. Instead, the card required the usual Know Your Customer (KYC) regulations (proof of a Ukrainian address, proof of identity), as well as an existing or new Binance account. The token would be a special kind of crypto, tied to the user's global identity and place of origin, but also to their refugee status.

Identity Tokens

Unlike cash, tokens are often linked with identity. Foundling Tokens, for example, were special keepsakes lodged with orphans in London institutions in the 1700s. The admissions process instructed parents to 'affix on each child some particular writing, or other distinguishing mark or token, so that the children may be known thereafter if necessary'.[43] The object was tucked into the admissions papers. Both were placed in a sealed envelope. If a mother reclaimed her child in the future, the unique token in the envelope acted as the means of identification. I scroll through a repository of these tokens until my chest hurts. Surely the fact of them, here, means that these promises were not redeemed? Sadly, the original curator didn't see the need to preserve the link between each named child and their unique identifier when they were first put on display. Now they are just free-floating tokens of affection: a little hazelnut on a string, a handmade paper heart, a thimble, a William III sixpence, a pendant with the words: 'You have my heart though we must part.' These tokens are deeply personal, as identity should be. Their singularity – their humanity – is at odds with the bureaucratic schemes that turn subjects to numbers in a database.

With a physical token, there is still room for creative interpretation. It is possible for the identity token and the bearer it identifies to be switched out or separated. With programmable tokens, that is not the case. In 2016, the World Food Programme trialled a system that issued payments through the use of iris-scanning technology. The token allowed refugees to purchase items from participating shops using their biometric data as a credential. The project was a collaboration between the World Food Programme, Jordan Ahli Bank, the Middle East Payment Services, and the UNHCR – UN Refugee Agency. When a user scans their iris to pay for an item, the system refers to a database held by the UNHCR to confirm their identity. From there, they are directed to the payer's Jordan Ahli account via Middle East Payment Services to confirm their account credits. The system connected two previously disparate systems – biometric registries and payments technology – so that a singular array of melanin under infrared light updates a ledger in another location.

Similarly, Sam Altman, best known as the CEO of ChatGPT parent OpenAI, is also the co-founder of Worldcoin, a project to combine a global identity system (based, again, on tokenised iris scans), a digital coin, and a means of payment, into one utility. Altman predicts that, in the future, AI will displace so many waged jobs that citizens will instead require a Universal Basic Income to survive. This payment will be issued through the Worldcoin app. To prevent fraud, the token will be tied to identity.

In the 1990s, the Cypherpunk community experimented with decentralised alternatives to government identity in the form of what they called 'identity tokens'. The system would replace traditional credentials like a driver's licence or social security number with an encrypted key. With digital tokens, the 'key *is* the identity', wrote Timothy May, one of the movement's founders.[44] Keys would be decoupled from the user's identity – or, in the language of the forum, their 'true names', a reference to a popular sci-fi novella by Vernor Vinge in which hackers work to keep their identities secret from a corrupt state.[45] The key would verify that somebody held a specific credential (age, disability, qualification) without revealing who that somebody was. These tokens worked both as payments and as credentials. More recently, Glen Weyl, an economist at Microsoft Research and the author of *Radical Markets*, has collaborated with Vitalik Buterin to create what they are calling 'SoulBound tokens' – a non-transferable identity credential backed by blockchain. Like the Cypherpunk's identity keys, these SoulBound tokens would be attached to a specific bearer without revealing more than was necessary about the bearer's identity.

Various tokens have also been designed to make use of reputation and social ties. Buterin's SoulBound tokens are presumably a reference to 'soul binding' in video games – a practice where virtual loot is tied to a character's in-game ID and cannot be transferred to others. Because teamwork is such an integral part of in-game quests, many communities create their own informal reputational currencies. Dragon Kill Points, or DKPs, for example, are tokens to reward participation in cooperative raids. They are a mark of social standing, and can be redeemed for virtual loot.[46]

In 1993, the Extropian community founded the Hawthorne Exchange. Users could trade units of reputation as a currency. Others, Nick Szabo and Timothy May included, explored the possibility of 'reputation capital', linking online reputational systems based on your 'actions, [and] the opinion[s] of others' to experiments in DigiCash.[47]

Cory Doctorow's Whuffie, meanwhile, described in *Down and Out in the Magic Kingdom*, is a currency that measures personal capital with friends and neighbours. SunnySide, a runner-up in the 2014 Future of Money Design Awards, imagines a token designed to stimulate social behaviour. Its exchange value varies as a function of the user's reputation: 'You are now a currency. And so are brands. And companies. With every action you take, your value fluctuates.'[48] Helping an influential neighbour move house increases your currency. Coca-Cola negotiates a transaction according to whether a particular consumer ought to be associated with their brand – not a huge leap in the context of sponcon and artificially scarce luxury goods.

Persistent Scripts

Scripts sketch both a user and a framework for action, Akrich writes. Most of these scripts contain the possibility for refusal – the big refusals, but also the small, the winks and nudges: Noel accepting the butter voucher under the counter and handing over a box of cigarettes. But programmable money writes, as Buterin acknowledged, a 'persistent script'. Unlike external laws or norms, which nudge behaviours in one direction or another, these tokens *prescribe* action, an action that sticks around even when the humans who thought it up are no longer present. By giving agency to the token, a certain amount is taken from the user. 'In 10 years' time, my smart wallet and your smart wallet are going to be talking to each other', writes Birch confidently, 'and we won't be in the loop so much. We won't be bothered.'[49] The computer says no, but you probably can't.

'We won't be bothered', Birch writes, a little breezily. This is something I hear a lot at fintech gatherings: the privileged refrain that transacting is actually a big hassle and it would be better if our money just got on with spending itself. IBM employees might experience this programmable money as the free exercise of their heart's desires. If the average delegate is indicative, these desires run in the direction of not having to remember to buy pool filters, or only purchasing fair-trade chocolate that's free of palm oil. But still others – the elderly, say, or the poor, the migrant, or the gig worker, the groups that most often rely on cash and mutual aid and extra-legal tokens – might find they no longer have much freedom at all.

Programmable transactions are coming, Birch argues, and 'different communities will choose money that combines different elements' to tally with their personal values.[50] Lana Swartz calls this a 'transactional community' – the sense that users are bonded by their transactional media, the ones they choose and the ones they are forced to truck. Public money, for example, imagines the nation-state as one big transactional community.[51]

But Silicon Valley is creating multiple private currencies, and thereby multiple transactional communities for our online selves. 'Different communities' may indeed 'choose money that combines different elements', as Birch writes. But this does not exclude the likelihood that some communities will find that they have no choice at all.

Some will be bonded by privilege, while others will be cribbed together by shared disadvantage. One user might be an affluent early adopter who wants to patronise ethical supply chains. Another might be an asylum seeker, a welfare recipient, or a gig worker whose payments are skewed to reflect identity, religious custom, education, nutrition, or parenting style. These tokens are not designed to secure greater ease or agency. They swap out the freedom of fungible money for something with strings attached. One kind of money for you, another for me.

What happens when we create programmable money? Money with a memory, money with an API? Transactions where disparate elements like our identity, a society's norms, dictator's morals, or a platform's shareholder margins are folded into a token? Tokens not only prescribe particular actions for their users – from seemingly small acts like signing up to a Binance account to larger ones like buying particular groceries as part of a weekly shop; they also fix and automate what can happen. Tokens write value, but also *values*, into our money – values that shape users, and persist when this government party or that person is no longer around.

Such 'prescription is the moral and ethical dimension' of technology, Bruno Latour once wrote, and 'no human is as relentlessly moral as a machine'.[52] We can see a famous example of this moral script at work in the bridges built on roads connecting Long Island to New York State in the 1960s. On the one hand, a bridge is just a bridge, like money is just money, part of a benign infrastructure that moves stuff from place to place. But there is something odd about these bridges. 'They're very ... low to the ground', people venture, when confronted with a Google Images search of one of the low-slung arches. So low, in fact, that they prevented tall vehicles like buses from accessing the parkway. A 'bridge' that is more of a chokepoint. To get to these leisure areas you had to own a car, unlike the vast majority of poorer and African American people living in the area at the time.

Arguably, the bridges were part of a concerted effort to regulate access to these leisure spaces, to gate-keep the poor. A bridge was part of the script written into infrastructure by the urban planner Robert Moses.[53] Moses is dead, but the bridges remain, comically squat against the ground, still policing who or what gets through. Tokens also have a script – and, like Moses's bridges, some of these block liquidity, channelling value in particular ways. But who gets to write the script? Whose values get written into the token?

Who Writes the Script?

Who writes the script? In *The Road to Serfdom* (and later in *The Denationalisation of Money*), Hayek argued for multiple private currencies as a fetter on the state's power. In the aftermath of fascism, Hayek felt that state control of money allowed for the exercise of totalitarian economic policies. It was only through competition between private issuers that the dictator could be edged out. Instead of bad money driving out good, as in Gresham's Law, private tokens would compete to keep the system honest. Money itself could be regulated by the market.[54]

Almost eighty years after Hayek, David Birch also imagines that the future of money will be shaped by private platforms issuing multiple bespoke currencies: de Bono's IBM dollars, BA miles, or – always one for a pun – 'Facebucks'.[55] Private money is inevitable, and the state's role in money issuance will be absorbed by platforms with a legacy in processing data and programming behaviour.

Others, like the economist Hyman Minsky, argue that private innovations are only ever a testbed for state devices that follow soon after. Private tokens have cropped up at various moments in history, but sooner or later the innovations they offer are absorbed by the state.[56] IBM dollars might start life as a private token, before becoming another infrastructure for state violence. Alipay and WeChat Pay might be more interested in underwriting credit than in cultivating prudent financial behaviours in their customers (Alipay users get a bump in their credit ratings for buying on the app even though it isn't a reflection of creditworthiness); but when the government intervened to access the transactional data held on their servers, it became part of the architecture of Xi Jinping's data-driven state. In 2021, the super-app Alipay (and all of its consumer credit data) was folded into a financial holding company under the organisation of the People's Bank of China.

This is not the first time the Chinese government has intervened in a private payments system. When the Chinese gaming company Tencent first began to sell online, it made a virtual token called QQ, which users could buy in stores and use to buy virtual goods from Tencent. The balance was linked to a user's instant messaging account. Tencent allowed users to gift the tokens to their contacts, and users started to send QQ for peer-to-peer payments. Businesses opened accounts and 'friended' their clients. Because there was a limit on how many tokens could be gifted, users also began to transfer whole accounts with denominated amounts as a workaround. Vendors came forward to buy and sell the tokens from others. By 2006 QQ had become the default internet currency in China, threatening the Yuan. A game retailer had become a bank – and the People's Bank of China pushed back. In 2007 it announced that QQ coins could no longer be used to buy real-world goods.[57]

Maybe the 'super-apps' were never really the giants, threatening the power of the state to issue and regulate tokens. They were the incubators.

In June 2019, Facebook announced plans to issue its own digital currency, originally called Libra, alongside a blockchain-based wallet, Calibra. I assumed the name had something to do with libertarian freedom – free as in markets; but I learn that the Libra was an Ancient Roman token. It was a unit of measure, like the scales of the astrology sign. In what was possibly an attempt to soft-pedal Facebook's role in the initial proposal, Libra was presented as a venture involving twenty-eight investing companies that included sharing platforms, network operators, micro-lenders, and payments providers. No banks were involved in the consortium.

Facebook was attempting to position itself as another super-app, comparable to China's WeChat Pay or Alipay – a system blending social media, messaging, payments, and now, perhaps, money issuance.[58] There were a few possible business models for Libra. Despite claims in the Libra whitepaper that it would make 'no use of transactional data', many assumed Libra's revenue might draw on payments data from Facebook's 2 billion users. After all, a vast share of the platform's revenue already relied on such data. Another source might be in fees for remittances. In the guise of 'financial inclusion', Libra might become the pre-eminent payments system, and maybe even the currency of choice for 1.7 billion unbanked users – people with mobile phones but no bank account, people for whom 'Facebook' was already synonymous with 'the internet'.

A third suggestion was that Facebook might extract revenue by providing users not so much with *money* as with a portable online identity, similar to Altman's Worldcoin. This is sometimes called 'identity-as-a-service', as though who you *really* are can be brokered and sold back to you (it can). An essential piece of any payments system is what is known as 'Know Your Customer' or 'KYC'. To issue an account, in other words, the bank has to be sure that you are who you say you are.

Entering payments, Facebook would not only need to manage real money, then – it would also need to manage real identities. 'An additional goal of the association', Libra wrote in the depths of its whitepaper, 'is to develop and promote an open identity standard. We believe that decentralized and portable digital identity is a prerequisite to financial inclusion and competition.'[59] Issuing identity, like issuing money, might be managed by a platform instead of the state. As the centre of a global social graph, Facebook was in a position to issue a token tied intrinsically to online identity, replacing the state's role as an authenticator and money-issuer all in one. As legal scholar Katharina Pistor put it when interviewed by US congress, 'Facebook might become the provider of global digital identity.' 'The question before us,' Pistor continued, 'is not whether such identities need to be created, but *who* shall do so – governments that are subject to democratic control, or private actors that can insulate themselves from any accountability.'[60]

When questioned by congress about how KYC might work in Libra, Zuckerberg said there was a possibility that anti–money laundering and KYC regulations could 'be encoded at the network level and not just at the level of … wallets'.[61] Alongside their policy of linking real names to online accounts, a policy that made Facebook a gatekeeper for authentication on the web – even for users who never visit the social media site – the platform had already explored approaches to the problem of linking digital and real-world identities. Facebook's real-name system, for example, decrees that users must use their real given names on the site, not nicknames or handles.

Recent patents from the platform have experimented with open standards for identification. Others have algorithmically scored a user's trustworthiness based on their online activity. Facebook's system used AI to try and flag whether someone online was not really who they said they were, measured by an assurance value, scaled between 1 and 10. Zuckerberg claimed that Facebook would use the technology to identify and curb terrorist content on the social network.

Like reputational credentials and the Hawthorne Exchange, our online reputations, actions, and social graph might become a gateway for transaction. Tokens as credentials, or as a proxy for identity or reputation, are in our future. And who better than Facebook to manage that? 'I call it KYZ or "Known by Zuck"', Birch tells me with a twinkle. 'And really, why wouldn't your Facebook identity be more reliable to Uber or whoever? I can buy a fake passport on the dark web, but building a fake profile with a real social graph and real history takes a lot of grunt work.'[62]

The Road to Serfdom

The question before us, as Pistor argued, is not only whether programmable tokens or identities will be created, but who will do so: a government that is to some extent accountable to its citizens, a private entity beholden only to its shareholders, or, as the Cypherpunks hoped, a decentralised identity system that gives control to users.

In launching Libra, Facebook planned to exploit the network effects of being the largest social media platform to enter payments, but at the same time to bypass the regulatory conditions that normally govern commercial banking, payment, identity management, and the issuance of tokens. Facebook would exploit the regulatory limbo offered by not-really-banking and not-really-money. The platform applied for a US money transmitter licence for its wallet, but not a banking licence. Nonetheless, as David Gerard observed, 'Facebook [wanted] to do bank-like things in the background – take other people's money. And issue credit slips that they say can be used as money.'[63]

Facebook hoped not only to dodge the rules, but to write those rules going forward. In a secondary whitepaper called 'Commitment to Compliance and Protection', Facebook stated that its intent was 'to shape a regulatory environment'.[64] Facebook was hoping to be big enough to make regulators bend to its will rather than the other way around. The platform would control data, manage identity, and issue money – a token tied to its identity system, but also to Facebook's values. Like IBM, the company would use its legacy in data processing and computation – its sheer infrastructural clout – to reshape money in its own image.

Facebook's control would be so extensive that some have likened it to 'Silicon Valley Feudalism'. Far from the totalitarian state controlling money, as Hayek feared, a private platform would write the future of the global economy in its own image. This was another road to serfdom.

For a moment in the summer of 2019, Libra pointed to a future where the power of the platform might outstrip that of the state. The backlash was decisive. In Europe, the G7 established a group to explore the risks of private currencies. In the United States, members of the House Financial Services Committee created a draft bill called, transparently enough, the 'Keep Big Tech Out of Finance Act', designed 'to prohibit large platform utilities from being a financial institution', and maintain 'a firewall between commerce and banking'.

The act was designed to prevent a large platform from offering financial services or issuing a digital token. Facebook would not be able to act as or be affiliated with a large financial institution, or to 'establish, maintain, or operate a digital asset that is intended to be widely used as medium of exchange, unit of account, store of value, or any other similar function'.[65]

The People's Bank of China accelerated its plans, in place since 2014, to issue its own Central Bank Digital Currency (CBDC). Like a stablecoin, whose value is tethered to a real-world currency, the value of a CBDC, issued by a country's central bank, is tied to that of the fiat currency. Fifty-six of the sixty-five central banks worldwide are experimenting with some form of CBDC. At the time of writing, nine countries have launched their own pilot versions. Issuing a digital currency is not just a matter of transforming fiat money into a digital token. It also raises questions around how the CBDC will manage accounts and consumer due diligence.

As things stand with central and commercial banking systems, users do not hold accounts directly with the central bank. Instead, commercial banks issue accounts and manage KYC regulations – which is to say, they deal with the business of vetting and identifying users outside the money system. This may change with a CBDC. If users held an account directly with the central bank, then the central bank would also deal with such concerns directly, managing KYC and consumer due diligence. Once more, the question of digital money becomes a question of identity management.

In terms of design, the Bank for International Settlements advises that all CBDCs should be identity linked, taking the form of an account rather than a digital bearer instrument. Money and identity might be folded together not only at the point of sale, as is currently the case with online payments, but at the point of issuance. Such accounts, Simon Scorer, senior manager of the CBDC for the Bank of England argued, could also be used to add a new layer of 'programmability' to government payments, automating tax deductions and managing humanitarian aid, for example, or managing spending. Such accounts, the report goes on to suggest, might even be structured to include credit data and other personal information.[66]

In many ways, the vision of the CBDC is not so different from the vision offered by Libra. It is a stablecoin with identity, exchange, and programmable conditions rolled into one token. The key difference is that this token would be issued by the state.

Facebook was forced to downsize its proposals for Libra radically, from a central-bank-like platform issuing tokens with a reserve towards yet another payments processor sitting atop a publicly mandated system called Diem, and eventually to nothing at all. After a limping year of proposals for a stablecoin linked to the US dollar, Facebook confirmed that it was winding down plans for the digital currency altogether in January 2022. Far from failing *despite* its monolithic power, Libra failed *because* it was twinned to one of the largest platforms in the world.

Facebook's token was a catalyst for governments to push back against platform payments and imagine a state-run alternative. While buttressing strong regulation, many initiated plans to develop their own digital currencies. This seems to be a question not only of offsetting the systemic risk that a platform poses to the broader financial system, but also of pushing back against the suggestion that platforms, rather than the state, will soon be in a position to manage consumers' identity and issue currency. As Hannah Murphy and Kiran Stacey wrote for the *Financial Times*, 'Nowhere has the divide between Silicon Valley and Capitol Hill been more clearly exposed than in the tortured downfall of Diem.'[67]

The question is not only whether money will be programmable or tied to specific conditions in the future, but also who will produce and manage these scripts going forward – the state, the platform, or, as in some Web3 imaginaries, a decentralised community.

What kind of a story is this? Do we like where it's going? If not, change the script.

4

Money, but Let's Make It Social

I met Jaromil (a.k.a. Denis Roio) in No.1 Foster Place, Dublin. Foster Place was once the Royal Bank – a little piece of leftover colonialism in the heart of the city. In 2014 it housed Trinity College's Innovation Academy, a centre established to 'reclaim Ireland's ambition to create a smart economy'. The space was full of Post-its and flipcharts and other props for innovating, but also clues about its monied past, this grand, neoclassical interior that didn't really lend itself to team-building. I had invited Jaromil, a well-known hacker and the founder of a free software think-tank called Dyne.org, to Dublin for a few days, alongside other financial activists (groups campaigning for a basic income, communities issuing their own local currencies, hackers trying to game financial algorithms for social good). Somebody had thrown a few bean bags in a corner of the austere hall – like this was a Google campus – and we flopped down awkwardly in them to talk.

If the space we sat in was the shell of a once powerful institution, Jaromil believed that money had also lost its power. The financial crash and the resulting bailout had made everyday people aware of the bogus nature of the monetary system. People like me. It had, in Jaromil's words, 'broken the taboo on money'.[1] This was why I was in this rotten bank. If money was a token of our imaginations, then surely it could be imagined differently.

In 2013 I was a teaching fellow in a Computer Science Department. Jaromil's writings on Bitcoin, shared on hacker listservs, had urged me to rethink the financial system, to roll money into other discussions I was more used to in the aftermath of Occupy and the Arab Spring, discussions about using technology to organise and cooperate. At the same time, my friend Joan and I were attending Strike Debt meetings in community halls around Dublin. Veteran activists stood up and tried to explain by way of a flipchart what would *actually happen* if Ireland refused to repay its debts to the IMF, labouring to a room of young people that 'the money' and 'the debt' were not *real*. Did we understand? Earnest men in our breakout group vied to explain things to the beautiful Joan. And I understood that I didn't really understand money. It was around this time that I first read Satoshi Nakamoto's whitepaper, 'Bitcoin: A Peer-to-Peer Electronic Cash System'.[2] Its ideas felt more tangible than a lot of the other 'money stuff' I was grappling with. Maybe it was because the whitepaper treated money – in true computer-science fashion – as a protocol: a clear set of rules for a clear set of problems. But what, specifically, was the problem with money?

Classic economic theory defines something as money if it can be used as a means of exchange, a store of value, and a unit of account. If it doesn't meet all of these three functions, then it's something else.

Money is, first and foremost, a means of exchange. Usually, it is a means of *direct* exchange. Most transactions are designed to settle instantly – *this* for *this* and now ... we're quits. While gifts have no direct equivalent, money helps to fix and qualify the terms of an exchange – and in doing so, some critics argue that it edges out friendship. Think about the difference between asking a neighbour to keep an eye on your two-year-old with the vague expectation that you will (probably) do (much) the same for him (at some time in the future), versus the experience of hiring and paying for a babysitter at the going rate, plus a taxi fare. Give-and-take between friends has roots and offshoots. There is no direct equivalent for a gift, no sense that things have been squared tidily away. Real money undercuts these ties. Real money severs the lingering attachments of the gift.

Money as a means of exchange also raises the question of who oversees these exchanges. Who mints the token? Who processes the payment? Governments profit from the creation of money by generating a revenue called seigniorage – the difference between the face value of a coin or note and its cost of production. Platforms also issue tokens and process payments, profiting from the fees and data they can extract at the point of sale. These intermediaries have the power to reroute transactions, or shut them down entirely. Jaromil mentions PayPal's decision to freeze the account of WikiLeaks in 2010, made on the grounds that disclosing US embassy documents was illegal.

Money is a store of value. We are all familiar with the concept of the super-rich 1 per cent. But during the pandemic, the world's ten richest men doubled their combined income from $700 billion to $1.5 trillion. In the same period, a further 160 million people fell below the poverty line. The trend is so exaggerated that journalist Peter S. Goodman recently coined the term 'Davos Man' to describe the uber-rich tier of billionaires who profited while others struggled to access basic relief.[3] Money's ability to hold value allows some people to stockpile wealth in excess of what they can practically use or spend by themselves. This leads to vast – let's face it, obscene – inequality, with some having too much and others too little. This trend also makes the hoarder less reliant on others.

Money is also a unit of account – a standard by which other forms of value are measured. In the Bible, a virtuous woman has a price 'far above rubies'. Anthropologist David Graeber, on the other hand, mentions that slave girls ('bond maids') were the standard unit of account in medieval Ireland. Virtuous women were hard to come by, but bond maids were so plentiful they could be subdivided into units of dairy cattle.[4] Just maybe, critics of money argue, there is something in this process that crowds out other ways of measuring worth, accounting for the wrong things. It turns everything it touches – livestock, land, sex, people – into a commodity, distinguishable only by price.

One approach to the problem of money has been to abolish it altogether. Stefan and Ralph Heidenreich make the case for a moneyless economy in which tokens are abolished and replaced with algorithms matching haves with wants.[5] (The elaborate systems used to match organ donors to recipients offer an idea of how this might work.) Another approach is to design money differently, in a way that feels more equitable or fosters different social relationships, or that values things – care, the environment – that are doorstepped by the economy. With the rise of cryptocurrencies and artificial intelligence, as Jaromil suggested, there's a sense that we now have the tools to rethink how money works. Money, still, but let's make it social.

A Means of Exchange: Mutualism

Most Bitcoin evangelists believe that money is valuable because it is underpinned by some intrinsically valuable good, like gold or energy. Others argue that money is nothing more than collective trust. As Hyman Minsky famously said, 'Everyone can create money; the problem is to get it accepted.'[6] Instead of money bearing value because it is scarce, or tied to a commodity, then, money is valuable because we all know and use it. Its power is *our* power, reflected back to us. But when that money is controlled and issued by someone else, this shared power can be difficult to see.

At the time I spoke to Jaromil, Bitcoin was popular with left-leaning hackers who wanted to build peer-to-peer networks where users could cooperate free from government or commercial oversight. The word 'peer' evoked something that happened between equals, a flat hierarchy with no figurehead. These hackers wanted – in the language of network engineering – to 'decentralise' the power of money, taking it out of the hands of the banks and delivering it instead to everyday people. Jaromil was part of this cohort, arguing that 'Bitcoin makes it possible for money to become a common[s] and no longer a top-down convention imposed by a sovereign and its liturgy of power.'[7]

What does it mean for money to be a 'commons', in this sense? The term 'common' or 'commons' harks back to the practice of shared land and use rights in medieval England and Ireland, eroded during the early-modern period of enclosures, when these commons were fenced off and turned into private property. Today the term has been resurrected to describe collective ways of managing and sharing resources beyond the state or the market. Examples include shared natural resources such as fisheries, forests, and community water schemes, or shared knowledge such as Indigenous medicine and language. While libertarians such as Ronald Coase and Garrett Hardin argued that these commons were destined for ruin because people are naturally too selfish to cooperate, economist Elinor Ostrom published a study in 1990 that observed numerous examples of successful commons in action.[8] This enabled her to develop an algorithm that gave individuals an 'incentive' to contribute to a shared good – a set of rules for 'governing the commons'.[9] Like Hardin and Coase, Ostrom began from the assumption that individuals are inherently self-interested, and set out guidelines to establish a balance between individual and collective interest.

With the rise in the late nineties of a particular brand of sharing online, internet commentators like Yochai Benkler, Richard Barbrook, and Kevin Kelly began to point to a 'digital commons', where 'peers' donated their knowledge to Wikipedia or rigged up their own WiFi networks between London squats. Benkler wrote about SETI@home, a proto-mining rig that pooled users' computing power to trawl the universe for signs of extra-terrestrial life.[10] Barbrook predicted the end of private property with the rise of open-source software.[11] Meanwhile, in an article called 'Digital Socialism is Coming Online', *Wired* editor Kevin Kelly sketched a timeline from the publication of Thomas More's *Utopia* in 1519 through to the dominance by

2009 of YouTube, where users voluntarily shared homemade videos of their pets.[12]

Bitcoin enabled money itself to become another digital commons, wrote Jaromil. The Bitcoin whitepaper described a decentralised accounting system where no one individual or authority had control. Instead, a network of individual peers all collaborated to verify and record the transfer of funds in a shared ledger. An algorithm called proof-of-work prevented these peers from falsifying their accounts. In accordance with Ostrom's vision, the prospect of being rewarded with bitcoins, rather than any guarantee of high-minded socialist principles, encouraged peers to verify and witness transactions for others.[13] Despite the fact that new middlemen – wallets, exchanges, mining rigs – quickly emerged, dreams of Bitcoin and dreams of power dissolved – the power of the state, or commercial banks, or the platform – were chained together in many people's imaginations. Like the internet itself, Bitcoin has always been an ideological junction where free culture meets the free market – a strange kludge of 'free as in freedom' and 'free as in beer'. And it's not always clear if these ideals are anti-capitalist, or anarchist, or simply a newly refined capitalism where 'the commons' and 'the peer' play shadow roles. Jaromil, for his part, imagined bitcoin as a token that would form the basis for local currencies.

Bill Maurer once told me about a trip to Money20/20, not long after the Bitcoin whitepaper was first published, in 2008. Maurer, an economic anthropologist, attends the conference annually to conduct fieldwork. In that year, the newly minted crypto community lurked at the margins like surly goths. Among the expensive booths that Chase Bank had hired, there were small handwritten signs on photocopier paper for Coinbase sign-ups: '1 free bitcoin to anyone who registers!' 'Shoulda taken that free bitcoin when I had the chance,' Bill says.[14] But when I attended Money20/20 a few years later, the handmade signs had been put away. There were whole panels dedicated to Bitcoin for the unbanked and Bitcoin for the banking sector.

At night, the crypto-wealthy were hiring venues in the Venetian and throwing private parties in nearby strip clubs. The token had matured, and all of that transgression had ebbed away. By the time mainstream banks were experimenting with blockchain as a clearance and settlement tool, nobody was linking Bitcoin with the lefty internet, just as nobody in their right mind was linking YouTube with Utopia.

Then, in 2021, I start to read about 'Web3' everywhere. The decentred internet that had been re-centred by platforms and mining rigs was to be decentred once more – and there would be a blockchain in there somewhere. Tired of the middlemen – the banks post 2008, the internet complex post Snowden and Cambridge Analytica? We're *so tired* of the middlemen. 'But *this* new technology will decentralise power.' Each time I hear this claim, I feel a strange *déjà vu*. Claims of decentralisation surfaced with the World Wide Web, and then again with Web 2.0, and then, once more, with Bitcoin and something called 'Decentralised Finance' (DeFi). The claim is strangely ahistorical, as though each version will remake the world anew. Each time, it failed to disrupt the status quo. At most, it switched out one middleman for another. Instead of destroying power, it was as if the token blurred the margins between, on the one hand, decentralisation, openness, and sharing and, on the other, power, profit, and private property, so that these two sets of ideals were no longer opposed. In Silicon Valley, they somehow worked together. Maybe they always had.

Histories of monetary reform also blend socialism with the free market, a kind of 'Californian ideology' in play when Silicon Valley was still a bucolic region known as 'The Valley of the Heart's Delight'. Long before Bitcoin or Web3, so-called 'mutualists' were experimenting with tokens that did away with the middlemen. Mutualists saw surplus value (the excess and, in their eyes, *unearned* profit capitalists skimmed from owning assets, lending money, or hiking prices in vast excess of costs) as a kind of rent on society. But unlike communists, they had no major issues with private property or the market per se. Instead of working to abolish these, as communists did, they wanted to re-engineer the market for collective good. The right token would set the people free.

Mutualists drew inspiration from the ideas of Pierre-Joseph Proudhon. Proudhon was a socialist, a philosopher, an economist, and the first self-proclaimed anarchist. Who controls credit? Proudhon asked. Credit was a product of the people, but it was not controlled *by* the people. Credit was controlled by intermediaries, the agents of circulation. This idea resonates today: is there a better description of a platform than an 'intermediary', an 'agent of circulation'?[15] Instead of credit being used to help the workers, Proudhon argued, access to money was controlled in such a way as to make more. *The Solution of the Social Problem* is full of acrid descriptions of the 'parasitic middleman, usurping, like the State, the rights of the laborer', of the monetary 'parasites that suck the sap of humanity'.[16] Credit, Proudhon argued, should be shared, built on the principle of 'mutualism'. Credit was a commons. He put forward two institutions to bring this about: the Bank of Exchange and the People's Bank – incorporated under 'P. J. Proudhon and Co'.

In *Radical Markets*, Glen Weyl and Eric Posner argue that the solution to the social problem in the wake of 2008 is not a withdrawal of markets, but their drastic *intensification*. The pair want to tokenise all contemporary assets (land, housing, water, property, the book you're reading right now). Static ownership would be replaced with ongoing auctions in which citizens would be asked to bid for resources from moment to moment. Only by *intensifying* exchange – making it an ongoing calculation on use – can we eliminate unfair speculation. *Radical Markets* arguably anticipates the token economy of NFTs, where everything is an asset and a blockchain facilitates ongoing trades in their latent value. Weyl and Posner's proposal is that we might use the fullest expression of the market to combat social inequality. Economics, taken to its radical conclusion, becomes politics.[17]

Proudhon's Bank of Exchange also tokenised property. These tokens were like credit notes: promises of redemption in a good or property that circulated like currency. Proudhon describes the process as follows: A citizen shows up at a bank with the title to an asset. The title is exchanged for tokens representing fractions of the asset. Each token 'becomes a bank note; it is money'.[18] After a set time, the loan must be repaid to the bank. If the owner defaults, then the asset is repossessed and sold, with the profits going to the last holder of the note. Otherwise, it circulates in the community. Like tokenised assets, the Bank of Exchange allows for the tokenisation of property, but not for speculative purposes. It lets users borrow against their assets without paying interest. The token is a credit note that circulates at face value. If access to credit was free, then there would be 'no market for interest-bearing capital'.[19]

But mutualism is not communism. In fact, mutualists were critical of state intervention, and, like Weyl and Posner, critical of theories of communal property. In fact, they were fully behind private property, but they placed a slightly different emphasis on the various rights bundled into that term. Where modern understandings of private property draw on the formation of bourgeois property rights in the seventeenth century (when common lands were done away with), and include the right to use, sell, and, crucially, exclude others from using a good, mutualists placed greater emphasis on the right to profit from the use of an asset, and downplayed rights to profit from renting or speculating on it. Mutualists experimented with policies in which property would have to be surrendered if it was not in use. Proudhon described his exchange notes as tokens 'invested with social character', designed to foster trust and equality rather than edge it out.[20]

Proudhon's second proposal was mutual credit, a system where workers would 'mutually pledge each other their respective products, on the sole condition of equality in exchange'.[21] In a traditional credit system, the individual lender leverages their idle capital – their stockpiled money – to extract returns from an individual borrower. In mutual credit, members of a community agree to go into credit or debt with a broader community – giving to or receiving from a pool of users.

A member of the community's account might be in credit through growing vegetables or giving haircuts or legal services, or debited by accessing these. Debts incurred from one member of a community can be repaid to another. Instead of property drawing undeserved profit through interest, each credit is matched to a corresponding debt. All goods and services are traded at face value. Money, as an interest-bearing token, is replaced by a giant community ledger. Today local exchange trading systems (LETS) and time banks are both examples of mutual credit systems in action.

Local exchange trading systems operate worldwide. In Ireland, the best known was a LETS operating out of West Cork, an affluent counter-cultural community where members traded eggs for organic leaves for handwoven baskets. Different members had different motivations for participating, among them a desire for self-sufficiency, environmental concerns, and a fear of global economic collapse. Most common was a desire to keep wealth in the community and out of circulation with multinational companies or banks.[22] These were middle-class aspirations, and the LETS was almost exclusively made up of what locals called 'blow-ins' to the region: English, German, and Dutch ex-patriates who had come to the rugged Beara Peninsula to escape capitalism (but perhaps worked remotely for one of the many tech companies located on the island). Almost no local Irish participated in the system.[23] Described as an attempt to smooth class or cultural frictions, the LETS shored these up.

Time banks and time-based currencies make time itself the unit of account for goods and services. An hour of work – whatever the task and product – is equal to any other. Babysitting, cleaning, accounting, or legal advice are all 'worth' the same. Time banks draw on the 'labour theory of value' – the principle, held by Marx (and tirelessly championed by Marxist theorists at every academic conference I have ever attended), that the value of a commodity derives from the labour expended to produce it. Labour – any kind of labour – is a fungible token. Giving your time earns a credit. Taking someone else's incurs a debt. Where goods are concerned, these are sometimes priced according to the time taken to produce them, but most often reverse-engineered against the market value of that good relative to an average living wage.

I first encountered time banks at a Bitcoin meet-up in Amsterdam in 2013, and presumed – anachronistically – that they were a fuzzy offshoot of the sharing economy. In fact, these communities were shilling an old idea. The first time bank was the Cincinnati Time Store. It existed from 1827 to 1830, and was founded by Josiah Warren. Today we would probably call Warren a social entrepreneur. His store was a testbed for time-based currencies and, in particular, the labour theory of value. Warren wanted to show the principle at work by establishing a 'labor for labor' shop, in which goods would be priced according to the work required to produce them (with a 7 per cent mark-up to account for the cost of bringing them to market that went up the longer the customer spent with the shopkeeper. This was measured using a complicated time dial in the store.) Corn was used as a standard unit of account, and twelve pounds of corn was equal to one hour of work.

Like other mutualists, Warren believed that money should not yield any unearned surplus. He was a firm believer in a free market, but based on a medium of exchange that was tweaked to dispense with all advantages beyond the user's physical labour. By pricing goods according to labour time, no undue profit could be skimmed off the top. Everyone would be quits. Interestingly, Warren made small adjustments according to how difficult or demeaning some forms of work were, so that time was not always the only factor taken into consideration. Noticeboards on the wall of the Cincinnati featured advertisements for services offered or sought, so that customers could trade between themselves using the 'labor notes'. The store soon became the most popular in the region.

Warren's ideas were seeded when he spent time in a commune called New Harmony in the 1820s. Intrigued by the commune, the businessman uprooted his family and moved there for a few years to see how it worked in practice. Did his family get any say in the relocation, I wonder? New Harmony was less than harmonious. The commune was a failure – largely, Warren thought, because communal interests and the conformity they demanded 'were directly at war with the individualities of persons and circumstances and the instinct of self-preservation'.[24] Warren was critical of communal property ownership and what he saw as the authoritarianism at New Harmony. It was, he felt, a system that demanded members subvert their individual desires for the good of the collective. This was its downfall: 'Those who advocated any type of communism with connected property, interests, and responsibilities were doomed to failure because of the individuality of the persons involved in such an experiment.'[25] For Warren, individual sovereignty had to include economic freedom. Warren outlined some of his theories in a thesis called 'Equitable Commerce'. Like other mutualists, Warren believed that markets and institutions needed to conform to individual freedoms and wants and not the other way around. Fix social problems with a free market.

Following the success of the Cincinnati Time Store, Warren left to set up his own commune using the labour-for-cost principle. In 1844, Utopia was established thirty miles upstream, on the banks of the Ohio River, on the principles of mutualism, libertarianism, and private property. It was shortly after washed away by a biblical-style flood when the river burst its banks. In 1850 Warren left Utopia to establish 'Modern Times', in what is now Brentwood, New York. It was to be a whole town founded on the labour-for-cost principle. Individual sovereignty was paramount. There was no formal government or police.

Described as a forerunner of American anarchism, mutualism took many of the principles of communism – the labour theory of value, a critique of rent and unearned surplus – and combined them with the free market, dispensing with state intervention or communal property. In this sense, mutualism was closer to Silicon Valley libertarianism, with its strange blend of laissez-faire economics and strict macrobiotic diets, than other experiments taking place in Europe at the time with communism or common property. It built on a desire to exercise your will free from intervention by an authoritarian state: free as in markets rather than free as in democracy.

In accounts of mutual-aid systems in African-American communities at the time, a different picture emerges. Nashoba was a cooperative community inspired by New Harmony, the authoritarian commune Warren uprooted his family to in the 1820s. Established by Francis Wright, a twenty-nine-year-old social reformer, Nashoba was designed to be a cooperative community for enslaved African Americans, where collective work would pay for their eventual freedom and relocation outside the United States. If anarchist communities like New Harmony were positioned in relation to the problems faced by waged workers, Wright worked to apply the same principles to chattel slavery.

Two other differences were key. First, cooperation in Nashoba was not the product of anyone's high-minded rejection of the economy; it largely came about because of that economy's rejection of the people. It is a distinction that reminds me that, while affluent bohemians in West Cork or Brixton might romanticise mutual aid – cooperative child care, the growing and sharing of food – this is how half the world's population still gets by in a substandard wage economy. According to James DeFilippis, African American cooperativism established the 'roots for the emergence of community ownership' in the United States.[26] If, for a particular brand of white, affluent mutualists, experimental tokens meant the perfect exercise of their 'freedom from' the state, for others mutualism was essential because of their *lack* of freedom: their invisibility to the same institution. When the state does not see you, you need others to see you through.

Second, the story of Nashoba highlights that while mutualism – from Modern Times to Web3 – spoke of togetherness, the 'we' it brought together in mutual solidarity was typically a white, colonising, male subject. Nashoba was also a mutual community, but it wasn't particularly egalitarian. Black members could not occupy positions of office or decision-making power. Not everyone got to be among the 'we'.

Who Are 'We'?

Who are 'we'? Who gets to be a 'peer'? These questions floated in the margins of every meet-up I attended in the early years of fintech. Gaming Money, for example, was an event hosted by the Centre for Innovation Technology in University College Dublin. It was 2015, and the delegation was an awkward intersection of men from the Business School (for the audience that day was almost entirely men) and invited money theorists. Among a selection of guest speakers, all white and European, all cis-gendered men besides myself, was a Danish professor of business. He had recently published an anarchist monetary theory with a left-leaning press. (He has since turned to writing about men's rights.) In the morning session, the money-turned-men's-rights professor – let's call him Bjorn – spoke vigorously and at length on Heidegger and Žižek as they related to a commodity theory of Bitcoin. He argued for the adoption of Bitcoin by the Palestinian government. In the afternoon session I convened a workshop called 'money and the commons', debating whether blockchain might foster grassroots currencies or be used to protect fisheries from commercial exploitation.

The workshop took place in a classroom that was vacated for the summer. Grown men in suits who normally occupied the lectern, and probably didn't subcribe to the flipped-classroom model, squeezed their girths into narrow plastic chairs with little attached tables. At some point in a rowdy but also very boring debate that I was doing very little to facilitate, on the topic of what the commons actually was and whether my session should be about the commons at all or needed to be renamed by popular vote, Bjorn slunk into the room and folded his long legs into a chair directly to my right. I remember I was a little flattered that he'd decided to come.

It was around this moment that the only other woman in the room raised her hand to speak. She was also in business attire, and looked to be in her early forties. 'I'm guessing maybe the commons has something to do with gender?' she said to me, her voice rising at the end like a question. I nodded at her to go on, but Bjorn cut in suddenly. His voice was unnaturally loud in the small, dampened space. 'Have you ever thought,' he said, scowling between me and the woman in the skirt suit, 'that actually it is *men* who do all the work in these commons – all the coding and soldering and so on – while women just come into these spaces and take and *take*? That *men* made Wikipedia and *men* made Bitcoin, and now *women* get to enjoy it?'

'Ah now …' mumbled a man with a Cork accent into his chest. The conference organiser was suddenly very interested in his printed programme. I think I must have gaped at Bjorn, waiting for a punch line, because he went on: 'I mean, perhaps there are other kinds of commons that are more for women or that women dominate. For example,' he elaborated, with a wave around the unlovely space, 'my mother chooses all the furniture in my parents' house.'

At first blush, imaginaries of a peer-to-peer electronic cash system with no states and no banks were enough to make left-leaning communities take notice. In Bitcoin though, the 'peers' in the network are not individual people, but *nodes* – concentrated units of computational power that can be evenly or unevenly distributed. Touted as a radical disintermediary, new middlemen quickly emerged, from wallets to clearing houses to giant mining rigs chaining nodes together in rural China. This is to say nothing of the kinds of politics that tend to circulate around the dreams of crypto, and now Web3. The notion of the 'peer' or 'decentralisation' floated an image of New Harmony or utopia, but without any real disruption of the status quo. The 'we' in Bitcoin was mining power, then, but it was also social capital, almost exclusively white, male, tech-savvy – men like Bjorn, men like the start-up bros tipping strippers in Vegas with wads of dollar bills. Transgression, economic disruption, maybe, but still business as usual.

If, on a surface level, mutualism preached a level playing field, with no intermediaries and nobody in charge, in practice it allowed all sorts of implicit power structures to thrive, untethered. Writing of activism in the 1960s, Jo Freeman called this dynamic 'the tyranny of structurelessness' – the sense that, by declaring hierarchies 'over', we push existing ones into spaces where they cannot easily be talked about or even pointed to.[27] Power does not die in these spaces. It flourishes, unchecked.

A Store of Value: Rotting Money

'I store meat in the belly of my brother'.[28]

In *Sacred Economics*, Charles Eisenstein describes a hunter-gatherer tribe that lives hand-to-mouth on the day's kill. Instead of curing their meat with salt or storing it in a coolhouse somewhere, they store it in their ties in the community (if you share your food with me today, I'll share mine with you tomorrow). They store their meat in the bellies of their brothers. Nobody hoards, and nobody goes hungry. Social bonds are a kind of insurance. Money is another kind of security. But what if we removed the 'store of value' element from our money entirely? What kind of society would we be left with? Maybe one where users would have to invest and store good faith in one another rather than in a token.

Demurrage is a tax associated with hoarding paper money. The German Argentinian economist Silvio Gesell proposed it as a way to encourage economic activity in the inter-war years. In *The Natural Economic Order*, he described a rotting token called 'Freigeld'. Money, Gesell argued, should age over time, just like commodities do. 'Our goods rot, decay, break, rust'; our tokens should do the same. 'Only money that goes out of date like a newspaper, rots like potatoes, rusts like iron, evaporates like ether, is capable of standing the test as an instrument for the exchange of potatoes, newspapers, iron and ether.'[29] The tax would be collected by way of stamps purchased from the local authorities. Over time, these would have to be fixed to notes if they were to remain legal tender. Everyone would presumably try to avoid the tax by spending the money, repaying debts, or immediately lending it out.

Gesell was born in Malmedy, Germany (now Belgium), in 1862, the seventh of nine children. His father was a protestant civil servant for the Prussian state. His mother was a teacher in a Catholic school. He attended private school, but had to leave early when his parents could no longer afford the fees. In 1887, he emigrated to Buenos Aires and set up a dental supplies company. In Argentina, Gesell saw first-hand the fallout of the financial crash known as the Baring Crisis (after Baring Bros, a London bank that had sunk investment into the country). The experience seems to have spurred his criticism of money. But the focus of his hostility was not money itself, or money as a general concept – for Gesell was, after all, an entrepreneur – but money as it was currently designed. In his debut treatise on the topic, *Die Reformation im Münzwesen als Brücke zum*

Sozialen Staat (The reformation of coinage as a bridge to the social state), Gesell outlined his critique of the monetary system and his proposal for negative interest rates on token money.[30]

After stints between Germany, Switzerland, and Argentina, including a residency in the vegetarian commune Obstbausiedlung Eden ('Fruit-bearing residency, Eden'), north of Berlin, he relocated to Germany in 1919. In the inter-war period, he was briefly appointed a *Volksbeauftragter* (people's commissioner) for finances in the Bavarian Soviet Republic. He only held the position for a week before the government was deposed by an incoming communist regime. But, in that week alone, Gesell announced plans for a thorough monetary reform. This included the introduction of stamped money, a land reform, and an annuity for mothers. Gesell believed in female reproductive rights, and also in a wage for women's work – a token he saw as a means of bolstering women's economic independence.[31] A prototype of wages for housework, maybe.

Like Bitcoin evangelists, Gesell shared a strong belief in the token value of money and the wisdom of the free market, and a strong suspicion of the state. I found this confusing at first, because many of Gesell's policies seem to rely on strong state intervention and because, at first glance, demurrage feels inherently socialist. As with many money reformists, there seemed to be a blend of the principles of social reform with those of the free market.

In Gesell's case, the impulse was not socialist; instead, he believed that the interest-bearing nature of physical tokens hampered the growth (and liquidity) of the free economy. Money, congealed, stalled economic progress. These ideas are given free rein in *The Natural Economic Order*. I read it, braced for a boring, technical account of monetary theory, and find instead a polemic on natural selection. Men are naturally competitive, writes Gesell, but, owing to 'the impulse of race preservation', that competition needs to be limited to the unique genetic gifts conferred upon each man by nature (to the exclusion of any privileges from, say, having a rich uncle).[32] Money was a tether on natural selection. It gave unfair advantage to some men, and it forced women to prioritise economic security over their natural instincts when choosing a mate. Progressive wages for women started to make more sense. 'The freedom to marry for love is a freedom based on the whole selective activity of nature', Gesell wrote. Eugenics, not equality. 'Only when we exclude all excess privilege', he continued, 'do we create the conditions necessary for a truly free play of economic forces.'[33]

I'm reminded of a passage in Bruno Latour's *Reassembling the Social*, itself a riff on anthropologist Shirley Strum's encounters with a troop of baboons called the Pumphouse Gang in the 1970s. Strum lived with and observed the troop. She thought they seemed 'nice' – nicer than humans, at any rate. Latour argued that the baboons were only nicer to each other because their power structures were simpler. The Pumphouse Gang were limited to the power that they could store up in social ties alone, Latour argued, in acts of aggression or affectionate nit-picking – a force that could vanish with sleep or illness or taking your eye off the ball for even a second. The real power in human society, Latour concluded, resides outside of the social, in forces that don't sleep, in ties that don't break down. It lies in the tools we use to widen our influence in the world. If you can store up your power, you don't have to be 'nice' to others.[34] Money is one such tool. Money is power, stored for the future.

Bitcoin took the opposite approach to demurrage – what has been described as digital 'metallism', after an economic school of thought that associates money with some valuable underlying commodity.[35] Bitcoin, though virtual, is made to be scarce; coins are mined using real energy, and the overall supply is limited to 21 million bitcoins (18.77 million of which have already been mined at the time of writing). Because of the limited supply of the token and its consequently rising market value, Bitcoin is subject to strong deflationary tendencies. The infamous pizza ordered and paid for with 10,000 bitcoins in 2010 is worth $500 million in 2022. Bitcoin is a better store of value than a means of exchange; instead of spending it, people stockpile the token, hoarding it away for an uncertain future. It is the opposite of rotting money: a token designed to hold its own worth above all else. Other cryptocurrencies have tried to institute demurrage. Circles UBI (for Universal Basic Income) in Germany, for example, is a token designed to be worth less to its users in a year than it is today. Users are urged to invest their wealth in the Circles community rather than in a speculative token. Freicoin, too – an offshoot of Bitcoin – is a token that falls in value by 4.9 per cent each year, encouraging consumers to spend or invest it, thereby driving up GDP.

Gesell recognised that money hoarding produced an unfair advantage, making, say, a SpaceX billionaire objectively more attractive than he might otherwise be to the opposite sex. By removing the hoarding function of money – the ability to accumulate excess – Gesell hoped to ground the token back in everyday ties and relations. We are all just primates again, 'aping' into the economy.[36] Like many money reformists who followed, Gesell looked on the economy as a design problem. The perfect economy was not, as Hayek suggested, one with perfect information, but one that reflected a perfect expression of nature, where men were free to be apes.[37]

A Unit of Account: Other Values

So far, I have explored the idea that tokens could be designed to cut out middlemen or to prevent users from storing up value. But what about tokens that value things differently, that try to bring care for others or the planet into the economy?

Rene Almeling, an associate professor of sociology and public health at Yale University, spent time researching the multibillion-dollar market economy of sperm and egg donation. Specifically, she has explored how monetary compensation for both types of donation has been framed. How did money come into it? Was it centred or pushed to the side? Was the donation framed as a 'gift' or a 'job'?[38] Almeling turned to advertisements to find out. One poster, aimed at people with viable sperm, suggested that the donation could finance a fun spring break. Another, aimed at those with healthy eggs, centred the incredible gift of helping a would-be family become pregnant. The monetary compensation ($10,000 – significantly more than for sperm donation, at $100–$150 per deposit) was floated in the fine print. Now, donating eggs and donating sperm are different processes, involving different degrees of medical intervention and personal investment. (One is about as invasive as blowing your nose into a petri dish, while another means hormone injections and minor surgery.) And yet, both are intimate procedures with the potential to make life. Why were they framed so differently? Was there a gendered aspect to the differences in how the two acts were conveyed – one as a precious gift, the other as a transaction to bankroll a lost weekend? Also of interest was the effect that rendering the act as 'for the money' or 'a labour of love' had on the donor's experience of the exchange. Sperm donors felt a bit empty afterwards, Almeling noticed, while egg donors were more likely to speak with pride about the huge gift they had given.[39]

Almeling's study is one of several that trouble the boundaries between markets and morals, suggesting that money crowds out values, or somehow assigns value to the wrong things. Sociologist Georg Simmel, who is known for making this argument, claimed that money fosters a certain kind of economic subject, the *Homo economicus*, who walks upright with the market economy.[40] When interviewed about their experiences, the LETS community in West Cork observed that, in contrast to more informal exchanges ('this is my round'), the ledgers measured individual contributions a little *too* closely ('What exactly have *you* done for *me* lately?').[41]

Eisenstein wrote of the horrors of 'fungible' tokens. Because 'each dollar is identical', he argued, the dollar makes everything it touches identical in all except price.[42] The token, like the cynic, costs everything and values nothing. In *What Money Can't Buy*, Michael Sandel explores the moral conundrum of selling 'goods' such as superior healthcare, the right to pollute, college admission, green cards, blood, and organs, and the right to shoot an endangered rhino – which is to say, he debates the morality of turning these things into an economic good in the first place. Sandel asks how markets crowd out morals. Is it okay, for example, to purchase a viatical – a share in a life insurance policy that yields a profit when the claimant dies? The sooner this happens, the better for the investor.[43] Surely there's something a little too morbid about this calculation on life and death? (In the late nineties, as the AIDS pandemic shifted from a fatal disease to a chronic illness, survivors were plagued by calls from brokers who had bought their life insurance for a killing, asking, as politely as possible, why they weren't dead yet.) Through the lens of trading instruments, the viatical is just another bet. It doesn't matter if it wagers on the future cost of oil, or war, or the death of a father of four children, a global pandemic, or an environmental catastrophe. All speculation contains a germ of this calculation.

Many money reformists grapple with this question of the right and wrong sorts of value. How can we make space for more socially or environmentally orientated values? For the presence of others in the monetary exchange? Tokens that shore up care, the commons, or the planet?[44]

Fureai Kippu was a Japanese care token. 'Fureai' loosely translates as 'the formation of emotional connections across generations', or elsewhere as 'ticket for a caring relationship'. Without a word of Japanese, I come to think of the token as 'furry' money, a softening of the hard lines of a typical transaction. Fureai Kippu was designed as a local currency in 1995. It allowed citizens to earn tokens by helping the elderly in their community. The unit of account was an hour of community service. As in a time bank, these tokens were earned through acts of care, and could be redeemed for care. Users could earn the tokens and transfer them to elderly parents or relatives living in distant parts of the country. The system accommodated a Japanese cultural objection to charity by allowing for the semblance of a transaction. But the tokens were also special, in that they carried an emblem of real feeling, even a kind of referred love. Seniors preferred to receive care services paid for in Fureai Kippu than those paid for in Yen.[45]

Economist Ann Pettifor is critical of the money form as we know it. As the Strike Debt activists laboured to explain to Joan and me, money is primarily produced by commercial banks when they issue loans to customers. The interest rates on these loans and their number are set by the central bank. Here, money emerges as a promise – a promise not only to repay our debts in total, but to pay back *more*. For Pettifor, as for many monetary reformists, this interest-based token puts untold strain on society and the planet. It demands that the economy not only stay the same, but continually grow, just to break even.[46]

It is not surprising that the deregulation of finance in the 1970s was followed by a deregulation of working hours and labour regulations to keep pace. But it was also followed by a growing reliance on what economists call 'externalities', an expansion of the economy ever further outwards into stuff that was previously 'outside' the market: free time, trend-setting, Indigenous knowledge, virtual cats, previously untapped natural resources – such externalities are 'off the ledger'. They are work done or costs borne by individuals, groups, or environments not directly involved in the market transaction. Building a hotel in a culturally vibrant neighbourhood is an example of a positive externality, a 'diversity advantage' that the hotelier reaps benefits from but does not pay for. Polluting the air or water while farming livestock would be an example of a negative externality, on the other hand – a cost produced by an industry that it outsources to the environment. Our money does not take these equations into account. It is only invested in extracting as much as possible in the present. Making the future balance is someone else's problem. But what if we designed money to make reparations for what has already been taken, or to factor in the cost of today's actions to future generations? What about a money system that rewards the hidden work of childcare, or pays to use less rather than more of our shared resources?

Richard Douthwaite, a British economist whose work blended economics with ecology, proposed an energy-backed currency unit that would be shored up through investment in the environment. Douthwaite settled in the west of Ireland in 1974, and later founded a think-tank called the Foundation for the Economics of Sustainability (or Feasta, after an Irish word for 'future'). These so-called energy-backed currency units, in Douthwaite's vision, could be energy bonds (like the railway bonds that built railways throughout the United States and Europe in the 1900s) that would finance the building of community-operated energy infrastructures. The bonds would contain a promise to pay the bearer a certain number of kWh in energy when they matured. The money would come from payments made by people purchasing the alternative energy source. Once the energy board was supplying power, the bonds would turn into money and the energy provider, in effect, into a bank.[47] Pettifor pitched something similar at a national level. Governments could apply to commercial banks for loans, she argues, and issue bonds to citizens across the short, medium, and long term. The money raised could then be used to finance a green transition from fossil fuels.[48]

On a more global scale, Olúfẹ́mi O. Táíwò makes an argument for bringing the cost of colonialism back onto the ledger. His is not a proposal for a different kind of money, but for a future economic policy that recognises the costs historically offloaded from North to South, from the effects of colonial extraction, to slavery, to ongoing flows of e-waste from developed economies into landfill in former colonies. He is seeking a refund for these – not through loans or other interest-bearing financial instruments, but through unconditional cash transfers.[49] We talk a little about the Pigouvian tax, the name – after economist Arthur C. Pigou – for a tax applied to market transactions that harm or exploit those outside of the exchange. In principle, Táíwò approves of the impulse behind the Pigouvian tax: if a negative consequence of the economy is 'outside' or unaccountable, then we need to find a way to bring it onto the ledger. But taxation is just one way to internalise a negative phenomenon, Táíwò stresses. If you lose the economist's fascination with price, then other solutions reveal themselves – in regulation, in damages, in replacing a private corporation with a public company that is at least nominally accountable to the public interest.[50]

Social tokens like Fureai Kippu and energy-backed currency units represent attempts to engineer the market to value things like care, or the air we breathe. Putting a price on a social cost is supposed to make it more valuable. But, like Almeling's donors, it runs the risk of turning something beyond price into just another economic good. Users are less likely to donate blood if they are paid, and more likely to be late collecting their children from childcare if they are charged a fee, Sandel has discovered. Meanwhile, the artist Núria Güell, whose work deals with financial activism, ponders these questions in a recent work on motherhood. *Afrodita* (2018) is an attempt to justify the time she already spends with her child as an artwork, so as to get funding to make more. But Núria also disrupts the catch-22 involved with putting a price on her care. Doesn't this economic calculation risk making love into something measurable and productive – just another economic good?[51]

How could we begin to put a price on the history of colonial violence or pollution or familial care? And *should* we? 'Money activists are more than a little obsessed with the idea that price is the solution to everything', says Táíwò when I ask him about this, when perhaps this calculation needs to happen in nonmonetary ways – beyond the token, off the ledger.[52]

A few weeks before Christmas I travel to Dublin to stay with my friend Niamh. Several years ago she converted to Buddhism. She also bought a house on Dublin's Northside, using savings from her salary as an environmental scientist and a down payment from the sale of her late father's house. This house is not just for Niamh; it's also a place for other members of the Buddhist community to live free from exorbitant rents.

I arrive in the evening, and Niamh, her housemate Sarah, and I share a Greek stew that Sarah made the night before. At some point the topic turns to the book I'm writing, and to money in general. I start to tell them a little bit about alternative currencies, particularly those that are designed to bring communities closer together. It turns out that Sarah lives on what she calls 'supports', a basic stipend paid by the Buddhist community in return for her contributions. Its official name is 'Team Based Right Livelihood'. The income covers her inexpensive rent and day-to-day living expenses, but if she needs something more, 'a wardrobe, say', she can also ask the community for it. Her income is funded by community donations, and salaries are apportioned according to people's needs – slightly more for parents or for Dublin rent. 'My mother doesn't like it', she says drily. 'She keeps asking me when I'm going to get a pay rise.'

I ask if maybe financial independence is important for Sarah's mother, because, until recently, women had so little of it in this country. Petitioning your community for a wardrobe sounds about as liberated as petitioning your husband for pin money. 'I think, on the one hand, there's a prestige,' she says carefully, 'the sense that what you do and earn is the sum of your worth.' 'Sarah is a qualified solicitor!', Niamh puts in proudly, slightly reinforcing her housemate's point. 'I think my mother wants to pretend that we're not dependent on each other', Sarah muses. 'But that's what a society is. We're not just individuals. We have to rely on other people.'

I realise that this is what I have been looking for. This is a token with other values. This is a token in which the presence of others is felt. And suddenly I'm not sure I like the sound of it. 'Supports' bind Sarah to the Buddhist community. They free her from having to pursue an income in a regular workplace. But they also limit her – they make her accountable to others in ways that don't exactly tally with contemporary freedoms (or Western ideas of what freedom is, at any rate). Raised on the tacit belief that there's no such thing as society, only individuals and, just maybe, the family, I struggle to imagine a return to an economy where we depend on and are accountable to others, where the 'we' decides if you eat meat today, or buy a new wardrobe. How can I imagine such a thing? Can I even be trusted to imagine it?[53] Or will these tokens have to come from a different 'we' altogether? A 'we' that's less like me. This is a political project, not an economic one.

The Next Buffalo

'The Future is now', the MazaCoin website read. 'Cryptographic Currency is the future of money, and for the Traditional Lakota Nation that future has arrived.'[54]

In 2013, Payu Harris was an amateur bitcoin miner and a member of the Oglala Sioux Tribe, working at a video store in the Pine Ridge mall. He would leave his laptop mining bitcoin in the back room and check on it during smoke breaks. In time, Harris came to believe that crypto could be used to give Indigenous communities their own currency. As Harris saw it, while tribal sovereignty gave the reservation the right to self-government, their reliance on the dollar, and in particular on federal subsidies, kept them tied into the US economy. Harris approached crypto 'from the sovereignty aspect ... having a currency structure of our own and a vibrant, comprehensive monetary policy is how we're going to build our economy, it is

how we're going to build our markets, and it's how we're going
to build for the future – it's how we're going to get away from
federal funding. Period.'⁵⁵ A sovereign token, Harris reasoned,
would allow the tribe to make and hold on to internal value.
It would also allow the Lakota to protect indigenous resources
that were vulnerable to extraction. Harris was already working
to tokenise 'natural resources owned by the tribe, such as
unmined gold in the Black Hills or coal reserves that could be
commoditized'.⁵⁶

In the early days of MazaCoin, there was also a suggestion
that the incoming financial regulations targeting crypto might
not apply to its use in Indigenous territories. As the Securities
and Exchange Commission (SEC) took steps to regulate cryptocurrencies in the United States, the 2015 MazaCoin website
floated the possibility of 'making tribal lands a safe haven for
cryptocurrency development, start-ups, and services'.⁵⁷ Maza-
Coin's newsletter argued: 'there's nothing better the tribes could
do today than to encourage financial services businesses to move
to the reservations, and train & employ local residents. The
right to self-govern, the same rights that allow native American
gambling that is prohibited in most states, might also apply
to the use of cryptocurrencies.'⁵⁸ Here the project focused not
only on an Indigenous cryptocurrency, but on establishing an
exchange haven and mining rigs on reservation land. 'This is a
paradigm shift for tribal economies', Harris said in an interview
at the time. 'This could be the next buffalo.'⁵⁹

MazaCoin was a fork of Zetacoin, an altcoin that used Bitcoin's proof-of-work and SHA-256 algorithm. Fifty million were
initially pre-mined and set aside for use by the Lakota community, for subsidies and grants. Unlike with Bitcoin, there was no
cap on the number that could be mined. In late February 2014
the MazaCoin blockchain was launched. An inscription was
placed in the Genesis block (the first block MazaCoin mined)
that read: 'The Black hills are not for sale. 1868 is the LAW!'

In the late 1800s, after decades of tension between Indigenous tribes and encroaching settlers, the US government signed a treaty with the native American Sioux. The 1868 Fort Laramie Treaty established the Sioux reservation, a large swathe of Indigenous land west of the Missouri River. It also recognised the Black Hills, a mountain range that stretched through Dakota and Wyoming, as unceded Native American territory. But when gold was discovered in the mountains in the 1870s, the government reneged on the treaty, redrawing the boundaries of the Sioux reservation and forcing the nomadic hunter-gatherers into an agrarian bracket. In 1980 the US Supreme Court upheld the 1868 Treaty and ordered the government to pay the Sioux people $100 million in reparations. The Sioux tribes refused the money, on the grounds that the Black Hills *were not and had never been for sale*. With interest, the settlement is now worth $1 billion. But the Black Hills have no 'price'. The Black Hills Are Not for Sale. The message in the Genesis block was put there to remind users 'that Treaties are meant to be upheld, that no one has the right to sell Lands that others steward, and that governments MUST respect the Rights of Sovereigns'.[60]

A 2014 *Forbes* article framed Harris and MazaCoin as the latest chapter in a centuries-long Indigenous struggle against the US government. The article sees Harris gazing wistfully upon the site of the Battle of Little Bighorn, pondering his legacy as the 'son of the once-mighty Oglala Lakota Tribe'.[61] MazaCoin sold itself as a symbol of resistance to settler-colonialism. The coin's logo features the Lakota symbol for money. A rounded M hovers against intersecting yellow, red, black, and white segments, against the backdrop of the Black Hills. A later iteration of the logo went further, showing the hills with a Mufasa-style overlay of the faces of legendary Sioux warriors, as though the coin was ghosted by ancestral spirits rising up through the token. It was a 'solid alt coin backed by the legacy of an ancient culture and tradition'.[62]

Through 2014 and 2015, the development team posted regular updates on the website, letting their audience (investors sometimes, and Indigenous community members) know about the progress the coin was making in global markets. In the summer of 2015, the development team gathered at the sacred Mount Shasta to debate the future of the altcoin. The team spoke of the necessity of bringing crypto culture out of the conference centre and into nature, 'around the fire, next to the River, Lake ... among the Trees, so that we can consider them all in our plans, decisions, and business. (click on the image below for tickets & more information!).'[63] As well as cultivating local wealth and local exchange, the token seemed to gesture to an economy that took 'other values' into account. The team gathered to discuss how MazaCoin might protect Indigenous land and resources – 'the forests, the water, the salmon' – from commercial development and extraction, 'from pipelines, logging, freeways and more'. How to make a coin 'that will encode the responsibility we have to protect our Mother Earth and provide for those who do the work necessary to do this?' the developers asked.[64] But also, how to balance these ambitions with the coin's use of ecologically devastating mining, or with the broader ambition to position the Indigenous reservation as a great plain, ripe for crypto colonisation? The next buffalo?

The token launched amid mainstream media coverage. Harris was invited to ring the bell at the Bitcoin Trading Centre in New York. But shortly after, a downturn in the altcoin market and a large exchange theft saw the project lose trading value and public confidence. Soon after this, an article in the *Native Sun News* claimed that the Oglala Sioux Tribe were unaware of the MazaCoin pilot: 'Man claims OST has launched its own currency. Council and president taken by surprise.'[65] In the media, Harris was presented variously as a Lakota chief, a technological wunderkind, a deadbeat who had once run the video store on the Pine Ridge reservation, a saviour, a shaman, a scam artist, an insider at one moment and an outsider the next. MazaCoin was later repackaged as a coin for 'all sovereign tribes'. Subsequent social media profiles and versions of the website removed any direct reference to the Lakota people. Harris removed himself from the project in 2022. His LinkedIn profile indicates that he is currently working on tokenised cannabis.

I think of wampum, the shells traded in what is now New York until the early eighteenth century. Before European settlers set eyes on the whelk and clam shells, wampum beads were part of a dense gift economy, used for storytelling, bonding, and remembering, for ranking and marking down important events. Through a colonial lens, the wampum looked very much like a regular means of exchange, one that could be dredged from the shore and worked with European tools. Wampum were mass-produced and used by settlers to 'buy' Indigenous land, when the land had never been for sale, just as the token had never really been money.

5

Eat the Rich

Day trading became popular during the Covid-19 pandemic. This was for a number of reasons: mobile trading apps with zero fees, like Robinhood, allowed users with little financial experience to dabble in the market. Unlike traditional hedge funds (but very much like most social media applications), these apps have a business model based on user data, not fees. Those who had passed the time betting on football turned instead to retail investing. The year 2020 also saw the rise of a new brand of influencer on Instagram and TikTok who specialised in dispensing bite-sized investment advice (Mrs Dow Jones on Instagram, TheStockGuy on Twitch – even, arguably, Elon Musk on Twitter). My friend's nine-year-old son somehow follows Elon on YouTube: 'He's really funny – and handsome.' In an era of growing economic and political uncertainty, Millennials and Gen Zs with precarious employment, in debt and with no chance of financing their futures through so-called 'legitimate' channels, were 'YOLOing' their rent money for the dream of winning a down payment.

Then 2021 saw a short squeeze driven by a meme: 'Eat the Rich'. A discussion was percolating on a Reddit forum known as r/wallstreetbets about the most commonly shorted stock options. Among them were the nostalgic giants of the digital millennium: Nokia, BlackBerry, AMC, and GameStop, a bricks-and-mortar store known for trading in used junk video games. Hedge funds were shorting GameStop, essentially buying a derivative known as a call option that represented a bet on the direction the stock would take. All bets were on down.

Hedge funds were borrowing the stock in the expectation that the price would fall in the future, when they would buy it back and recover a profit. Led in part by discussions from Keith Gill (a.k.a. Roaring Kitty) on Reddit and other channels (YouTube, TikTok, Twitch), users began a coordinated action to buy and hold GameStop call options (and in some cases GameStop stock) to drive share prices in the other direction, creating what's known as a 'short squeeze'. The hedge funds that initiated the squeeze were forced to buy back the stock to avoid losing any more money. GameStop stock went from less than $3 in 2020 to $483 on the morning of 28 January 2021. At this critical point, the Robinhood app intervened to prevent its users from buying any further call options, citing 'market volatility'.[1]

If NFTs and GameStop have taught us anything, it is that it's now possible to hedge memes in the same way as oil, or real estate, or the life expectancy of a terminally ill patient. These are so-called 'meme stocks'. Their value emerges not from any strong correlation between share price and the underlying asset, but from the hype circulating around a bet. The SEC's October 2021 report on GameStop supports this, concluding that 'it was positive sentiment, not the buying-to-cover [where hedge funds are forced to buy shares to cover those they initially borrowed], that sustained the weeks-long price appreciation of GameStop stock'.[2] The space between illegitimate gambling and legitimate investment narrowed. So did the space between taking an economic stake and posting an unsolicited opinion on the internet. Finance apps emerged as a new kind of social media.[3] And social media shaped markets.

Stocks are easy to meme. And like memes, there was a rhetorical flexibility to the 'meaning' of these millions of individual investments. For some, Max Haiven suggested, GameStop was an act of revenge on a mode of capitalism that had fucked them over.[4] Or it was a gamble – a ballsy display of diamond hands (WallStreetBets speak for users who can hold out against common sense and win big). For the subculture that lurked in Roaring Kitty's comments section, it was partly an expression of their ties to that community. And for others, GameStop was a kind of ironic opportunism – a nihilistic token, an absurdist joke, and a desperate bet all in one.

On the surface, Robinhood is about making money, but with meme stocks there is also something that leaks out beyond that ambition, where signalling you have the balls to withstand the giddy twists and turns of the market has a social value that outstrips the monetary investment. There are dedicated threads on WallStreetBets for YOLOing (extreme all-in betting), and also for 'Loss Porn' (presenting and commiserating over extreme failures and wipe-outs). The value, at some meta level, is the bet itself. Like the tokens in Twitch that are both money and friend requests, in WallStreetBets, bets hedge real money, but also connect members to their tribe.

It is not surprising that Robinhood and associated meme channels like WallStreetBets operate somewhere between invest-ment tool and social media: 'Like 4chan found a Bloomberg terminal', reads the Reddit page.[5] And like 4chan and 8chan before it, the forum positions itself in opposition to so-called 'normie' culture, defined in the investment space as anything resembling safe or mainstream financial advice that your boomer elders might dispense. The language is a toxic red pill: macho, regressive, degenerate, deliberately alienating – it's all part of the 'joke' that hides the fact that all of this is not quite a joke.

Users swap homophobic and racist slurs, misogynistic back-handers and quips about suicide. There is no solidarity here. There are 'frens' but no friends.[6] On the 'loss porn' thread, someone posts that they have invested their entire student loan in one meme stock and now have nothing. They have not slept in days. In response, someone else shares a GIF of a slice of bread being fed through a cheese grater. Someone else links to a rope for sale on Amazon and suggests that the poster buy it to hang themselves. Do it, the forum agrees. It's what evolution would want. KYS. For the good of the species. All this nihilism makes a kind of meaningless sense when the future has no perceivable value.

The forum doesn't trade on individual expertise, but on a kind of collective mindlessness that might contain within it a swarm intelligence. The retail investors of WallStreetBets were not selling themselves as experts or canny investors, or even as nice people.[7] Instead, like Gessel's natural men, they were just 'a bunch of guys', they were fellow degenerates. They were, as one meme put it, 'apes, together strong'.[8]

Throughout history, 'simianisation' was a tactic to make the case that some race or ethnic group was less than human – used against Jewish, Asian, and Irish groups, but, most notably, against black people. The Bored Ape NFT, developed by Yuga Labs, has been criticised for the use of the simian trope and accused of including Nazi dog whistles in its iconography. But here the apes were, apparently, doing it to themselves. They marked themselves out as something less than human, 'degenerate', as a point of pride. And yet, scrolling through the comments, if anything bound these investors it was basic human desire: for security, for acceptance. Many passed the lockdown dreaming of home ownership, of 'winning' enough to make a down payment.

In the immediate aftermath, the Robinhood action was framed by some as a coordinated anti-capitalist attack. It was a gesture worthy of its namesake: steal from the rich and give to the poor. Robinhood monetised a sense of collectivity at a surface level (#WAGMI or 'WE'RE ALL GONNA MAKE IT' was another popular slogan), while at the same time, just beneath, was a base self-interest. As a kind of emotional contagion on social media, the GameStop short mobilised people's hatred of a system that had fucked them over, but in a way that made gains for that same system. It was hedging and monetising the poor man's fantasy of the good life, all in the service of the rich. To remix the late Mark Fisher, nothing plays so well on Wall Street as a protest against Wall Street.[9]

In the aftermath, GameStop was spoken about as David versus Goliath. It's a feel-good meme, like scrawny kids punching bullies on the internet or a clickbait kitten squaring up to a Rottweiler. I think of Randi Zuckerberg's #WAGMI video, dancing with two other female Web3 entrepreneurs in Central Park, explaining acronyms like HODL and ATH. 'We're all gonna make it, everyone', Randi sings, giving the camera an earnest rock 'n' roll salute. Robinhood was a nice flex on the power of the swarm, but it wasn't a story about the little guy. In the long run, GameStop didn't unsettle Wall Street. Some individual retail investors made money, and some traders lost, but most of the money was made by Citadel Services, the main market maker behind the Robinhood app. GameStop did not represent a radical disintermediation of power – except maybe in pointing to the power of social media not only to meme elections, but to meme the market.[10] If anything emerged, it was once more the power of a platform to shape the future of money. If memes were driving money, then social platforms were at the wheel. The point was reinforced in 2022 and 2023, when the collapse of Futures Exchange (FTX) and Silicon Valley Bank were both precipitated by viral hysteria on Twitter. It was a vast throughput of rumours and transfer requests that traditional risk assessments were not equipped to measure and financial institutions were not built to withstand.

One response to monetary reform treats money like a design problem to be solved. Coin the perfect token, and the perfect society might follow. The time banks, demurrage, and Fureai Kippu explored in the previous chapter all fall into this category. Another approach, typified by GameStop, is more fatalistic. Rather than build anything new, it parasites on the system it claims to hate. The meme, remember, was not 'steal from the rich' but 'eat the rich'. There's a difference. The slogan asks that you take the system into yourself. We don't need to quit everything and set up a barter economy in West Cork. Don't transcend – be an ape. Don't beat the system – eat the system.

The Catalan Robinhood

The first time Enric Duran and I met was on a panel in 2016. He joined via VoIP to speak about FairCoin, an anonymous offshoot of Bitcoin he was involved in developing. The currency did not need to be mined. Instead, 50 million coins were created and given away for free to anyone who wanted to sign up. That was more fair. The token had been adopted by a Catalan social movement in 2014 with the idea that it might be used to support a global cooperative movement (FairCoop). Duran described it, a little clunkily, as '[hacking] the foreign exchange market by inserting the virus of cooperation as a tool for global economic justice'.[11] Unlike GameStop, where it was unclear if the action was a social movement or just a big joke, Duran is entirely in earnest. What he lacks in humour he makes up for with an almost pathological sense of justice.

Several years before the 2008 financial crash, Enric decided to launch an exploit against the Spanish banking system. If large financial institutions were the chief cause of global injustice, he reasoned, they might also be the solution. He set about defrauding commercial banks, applying for mostly small personal loans and turning the funds over to cooperative movements in Catalonia. Between 2005 and 2008 he was granted sixty-eight different loans with thirty-nine different financial institutions, totalling €492,000. The first loan was the largest – a mortgage for €201,000.

'I learned about holes in the system and how to move around them', Duran says. In 2022 we connected via Telegram. Most of the loans were below €6,000, Duran tells me – a threshold at which debts were centrally recorded by the bank of Spain at this time. Lots of little applications made, in the end, for almost half a million euro. This was one of a number of loopholes the activist used: apply for small loans, know your language, look professional. Another was identifying a time-lag between the approval of a large loan application and its entry into the central register. In 2008, towards the end of the project, as discovery and arrest became inevitable, Duran went all-in and applied for progressively larger amounts, exploiting the latency between when a loan was drawn down and when it was registered. He learned the structural weaknesses of the financial system and gamed them accordingly. Today it wouldn't work, he says. More is recorded. There are fewer loopholes.

Duran wanted to demonstrate a form of civil disobedience against the banks by refusing to repay his debts, but he also wanted to show others that there was an alternative – that finance could support cooperative living. He turned all the money over to social movements, though not all of them were willing to accept it out of fear of litigation.

The scheme came to an end, by chance or otherwise, at the start of the financial crisis in 2008. Duran did not need to point out the fundamental flaws in the banking system after all. The project took on a new resonance: as millions of Spanish citizens were asked to shoulder the burden of private debt, one citizen refused to repay the money he had turned over to the commons. From that moment on, Duran was a fugitive.

I ask him if the exploit made him feel anxious or vulnerable. Just thinking about it gives me a hollow feeling in my stomach. Maybe, as David Graeber once suggested, it's a Catholic, knee-jerk morality at the idea of not repaying one's debts, but I suspect the feeling has more to do with the consequences of taking such an extreme action *alone*.[12] When I ask, Enric speaks about it as an economic calculation, something he weighed up and rationalised: 'The personal risk was less', he says, 'than the potential benefits to the collective.'[13]

I read accounts of Duran's exploit at the same time as I explore artist Cassie Thornton's work on debt. Much of her practice centres on the embodiment of debt, the way it makes the indebted subject *feel* in their body – anxious or tied down, cut off, lonely, ashamed, or unsafe. She hosts group meditations where people come together in solidarity and try to release these feelings – the burdens of their mortgage or their student loans – from their bodies. Pictures show participants lying together on the floor in active wear, breathing deeply in a parody of Saturday morning yoga.[14] It strikes me suddenly that what Duran was doing was taking debt into himself. He wasn't just refusing to pay. He was shouldering a collective burden. Mortgage defaulted, he would never own a house. Cut off from credit, wanted by the legal system, he was outside of the state and entirely dependent on the solidarity of the commons for his survival going forward. Maybe that is why it scares me so much. He took the risk alone, and now he stores his meat in the belly of his brother. In the month or two directly after the action was discovered, Duran had a strong support network, he says, and for about two years after that, while he was in exile, a community ready to help him with food, or shelter, or legal advice. But fifteen years on, he admits, that solidarity has mostly drained away. He remains a fugitive. And now he is largely alone with the consequences.

I ask him, finally, about GameStop. He says he finds it inspiring, not necessarily because of the economic outcomes but because it demonstrates 'the power of collective organisation'.[15] I disagree. For GameStop, there is no such thing as the collective, only individual hustlers. We're Not Going to Make It.

The Parasite

Enric Duran is sometimes described as 'the Catalan Robin Hood', the hero who takes from the rich and gives to the poor. Historically, Robin Hood was a figure who challenged the enclosure of the commons, often through legally ambiguous means. But Robin Hood was also morally ambiguous. Was he an opportunist? A nihilistic gambler? Or was he someone who wanted to restack the balance of power by any means necessary?

Well before WallStreetBets and the Robinhood app, the Robin Hood Minor Asset Management Cooperative emerged in 2013, marketing itself as a hedge fund for everyday workers.[16] The team was mostly academics and artists (with frequent mentions of software developers and lawyers in some distant elsewhere), all of whom spoke as though ChatGPT had been trained on *A Thousand Plateaus*. Beneath this, the overall strategy was simple enough. Robinhood was a mimic fund using an algorithm patented by one of its members, Sakari Virkki. The algorithm was designed to observe market activity and follow the investment behaviours of Wall Street's most successful trading funds.[17] Virkki called it a 'method or product for analyses in respect of tradable instruments'. The team preferred 'The Parasite', in a nod to philosopher Michel Serres's famous book on resistance from within the system.

Unlike other hedge funds that require investments in the realm of half a million, the fund asked its members for a €30 buy-in. The group wanted to universalise the market, to make the financial tools of an elite available to everyday workers with insecure contracts and no nest egg for the future. The investment strategy was agnostic. In contrast to Strike Debt projects or those that preach divestment from morally questionable sources like fossil fuels, the directive of Robinhood was simply to follow the money. Arms formed a significant part of the portfolio, for example. And 50 per cent of the profits were returned to the shareholders. The other 50 per cent would be used to fund what the group called 'commonfare' – things like social centres, a basic income for community workers, or interest-free student loans.

In 2014, I pulled together some public funding and lots of university money, and asked the Robinhood collective to Dublin for an event in Trinity College's Innovation Academy. Jaromil, who was peripherally connected to the Robinhood crew, was also in attendance. So were Feasta, the Irish think-tank founded thirty years earlier by Richard Douthwaite. The office kicked off with a public talk in Dublin's Science Gallery, another space owned by Trinity College on the outskirts of the Silicon Docks. I asked the journalist Brett Scott to interview Akseli Virtanen, the team's spokesperson.

Akseli's presentation resembled how a vigorous CEO might take to the expo stage to hawk the latest smart product, a kind of sociopathic zeal that brooked no objections. 'We take a position in the financial market in order to hedge our position in the precarious labour market. Yup', Akseli explained to an audience that consisted largely of artists, flourishing a whiteboard marker. 'We are a hedge fund of the precariat.'[18] The project reacted to two conditions, Akseli said, rolling up the sleeves of his black turtleneck like the real work was about to begin. On the one hand, it responded to the exponential growth of finance (Akseli drew a little square for GDP, gestating inside an enormous square representing the derivatives market). Financial capital builds on top of workers, like a parasite, said Akseli. It uses their brains and their bodies. On the other hand, the project was responding to a precarious labour market, to the fact that, in the wake of the crash, many workers had no income or job security, and this was unlikely to change.

The Robin Hood Minor Asset Cooperative took a position of risk in the financial market in order to hedge its daily uncertainty in the labour market. 'Hedging' in finance means entering into a bet in order to protect yourself against something worse. Zero-hours contract workers would share the risk to make a shared profit. 'Would it be possible to share the means of finance for precarious workers, who –', Brett tried to interject. 'No, let me finish,' said Akseli. 'This is my favourite bit. OK: Could "We" appropriate the Power of Money?'[19]

A few days later, at the group's request, I managed to convince a financial journalist from Ireland's main broadsheet to interview Akseli. I led them both to the old boardroom on the top floor of the former bank – a mahogany stage set that should have lent the project some gravitas. The journalist came jogging down the stairs less than ten minutes later, jerking his chin towards the boardroom overhead: 'Absolute nut job!' I envied that clean response. My problem was that I kept hedging my bets. The entire experience – from planning to facilitating the Robinhood office in Dublin – was run through with the bad, squirmy feeling of being 'had'. The artist, the university, the university's money – maybe even everyday workers – were the butt of a joke.

And yet, this space between a hoax and a financial scheme and performance art is still the most compelling aspect of the project for me. As 'just art', the cooperative could be set aside; but as something vague, with real money and with more than a whiff of the scam about it, it kept me alert. As I wavered, trying to categorise a group that asked poor people for money to play the market, my searchlight travelled over money, the university, and the former bank, now turned 'innovation academy', that we found ourselves in. I was forced to draw my battle lines, between art and finance, between a hoax and a legitimate financial operation – even between a left-leaning social movement and an anarcho-capitalist Ponzi scheme. And, like most things in the crypto space, the lines were blurred. 'The great art project of our age is to entirely collapse the distinctions between "fraud" and "performance art"', writes the financial journalist Matt Levine, 'so that one day mortgage-bond traders will be able to say, "Wait, no, I wasn't lying about bond prices to increase my bonus, I was performing a metafictional narrative about bond-price negotiations in order to problematize the underlying foundations of bond trading in late capitalism."'[20]

In 2021 I come across my notes from the Dublin office, recorded, messily, on a Slack channel. My job had been to keep the minutes. I am transcribing Alina Popa, a young artist and economics graduate who attended the office in 2014. She sadly died in 2018. 'Many are troubled and say they don't want to be part of the project because it's impossible to identify it fully', Alina said, 'but it's this impossibility that made me go with it. Robinhood functions on the plane of disbelief … it's a way of not believing but still acting. Two days ago, we had a conversation about whether Robinhood was just a scam. It is. It's a scam because financialisaton is a scam. Money is a scam.'[21]

After the Robinhood office in Dublin, I withdrew from the project. Its managing director, Jan Ritsema, also resigned, disillusioned with what he called the group's 'commercial approach' and alleging the cooperative was 'hiding bad news' about its yearly investment returns.[22] The group rebranded as the Economic Space Agency, or ECSA (pronounced 'EK-Sah'), and the team rented a small house in the suburbs of Oakland, California. The space was called the 'Coding House'. The name evoked frenetic round-the-clock innovation, like something depicted in *The Social Network*, but one former resident told me there was 'lots of talk, lots of ideas … but not much was being built. It was not very hands-on.'[23]

At a moment when collectives were being singled out for lack of diversity, Robinhood was obstinately white and male in composition. Most of the publicity material styled the group in the gauze of start-up culture: vigorous young men of European descent arguing over a pile of spreadsheets. Remove the Marxist tomes from the flat-pack in the living room and you had a vignette that was indistinguishable from the many ICOs emerging from Silicon Valley at that same moment. Was that all part of the joke? 'I was photographed a lot, as in "Look! There *are* women here,"' says Laura Lotti, an artist who lived in the Coding House for six months in 2017.[24] I wondered whether her experience was similar to my own, sitting in a room full of men, all earnestly discussing how Bitcoin was going to change the world, but still being expected to make the tea and keep the minutes.

Robinhood copied the investment positions of the elite. It went so far as to mimic the language of finance, the normcore aesthetic of Zuckerberg or Jobs, the risk-taking, swaggering ego of Elon Musk. We are all hedging our bets, they seemed to be saying. We are all investors now. Becoming one with the system is supposed to give the activist the necessary resources to pull it down from the inside. There is little sense that to step inside might be finally to take root – to be, once and for all, a part of the problem. With Robinhood, it felt like the surface mimicry was masquerading for a deeper, more toxic identification at work in the office, in the university, in the activist meet-up – at work in me.

Robinhood might eat the rich, but sometimes it is hard to tell where Goliath ends and David begins. It was apes all the way down.

6

Trust in the Code

We have elected to put our money and faith in a mathematical framework that is free of politics and human error.

Tyler Winklevoss

A permanent record of all transactions is set in 'cryptographic stone' on the ledger, which means no one can rewrite or deny history. In other words, it's impossible to cheat with blockchain because everything is in the open to those involved and authorized to see. Risk is minimized in a system in which governance is truly shared. I can't think of a better definition of trust.

Arvind Krishna

Money Is Trust

A veteran programmer in his sixties came up to me after a conference in Amsterdam. He didn't stop to introduce himself – he ploughed straight in, like we were continuing a conversation after a trip to the bar. 'The problem with money', he said, without preamble, standing closer than is strictly polite and fixing me with an intense stare, 'is one of trust ... of interdependence. Take *your* people for example ...' (*My* people? Academics? Artists? Blockchain critics?) 'In Ireland in the eighteenth century you had strong kin communal networks. People shared and cooperated because that was how they survived. Self-interest didn't put food on the table.' The problem is, he said, we don't need to trust each other anymore – and maybe we can't go back.

I tell him another story. In Ireland in the late 1960s and early 1970s, the banks went on strike, but the monetary system didn't collapse. Local shopkeepers and publicans came forward and acted as de facto banks in the absence of the state. First they cashed real bank cheques, then it was just plain old IOUs scrawled on scrap paper, no more official than a spit and a handshake. They could do this, the story goes, because everyone knew everyone. If there's trust, you don't need money.

My father owned a pub at the time, now closed. 'Do you remember the bank strikes?' I ask my mother. 'What were they like?' I'm looking for tales of the old country, of a community woven together. 'Of course I remember,' she said. 'Your Dad took to carrying a gun on his way home.' 'Sorry,' I say, pulled from my reverie, 'a gun?' 'Yes,' she says simply. 'There was nowhere to deposit the float at the end of the day. Businesses were incredibly vulnerable to theft.' I picture the road that winds from the pub on the hill to the house where I grew up. It's very dark. There is nobody around. My father appears, carrying a giant hemp money sack in one hand and a .22 in the other ... No, I decide, this is not the story I am after. This is the Wild West. This is every man for himself. I disappear the gun from my story. 'In Ireland the banks were closed for months at a time, but people pulled together.'

It is easy to romanticise the moral economies of a former colony, but it is also a mistake. What looks like good will is often (also) a form of insurance, a way to manage the risks posed by others. The communal spirit that my veteran programmer admired in the Irish peasant also operates through what James C. Scott called the 'abrasive force of gossip and envy and the knowledge that the abandoned poor are likely to be a real and present danger to better-off villagers'.[1] Villagers like my father, maybe, cashing an IOU in business hours, but carrying a gun into the night.

Money is generally viewed as something that *stands in* for trust. If everyone trusted everyone else, it wouldn't be necessary.

That is what the banking strikes in Ireland seemed to suggest, even if on the ground people whispered about guns and midnight robbery. It is also what the inventors of Bitcoin believed. Money, Simmel argued, was based on two different kinds of trust: trust in the government issuing the token, and trust in the acceptability of that token to others now and in the future.[2] Tokens are promises. Their value hinges on the belief that these promises will be kept. Today, though, there is more than a whiff of a sense that we can sweep aside the messiness of trust in others (and the risk this involves) and trust instead in code.

In 2009, the Bitcoin whitepaper outlined a new form of money where users would not need to trust in one another or an institution like a bank, but would place their trust in the software underpinning all transactions: the blockchain. This belief is still shared by anarcho-libertarian groups who want to replace the state with blockchain-run smart cities in the Nevada desert, but also by governments throughout the world, many of whom argue that blockchain technologies will streamline politics and make public decisions more trustworthy and accountable.

Bitcoin: 'Trust in the Code'

Bitcoin emerged at a moment when institutional trust was at an all-time low. In the whitepaper 'Bitcoin: A Peer-to-Peer Electronic Cash System', the blockchain is famously called a 'trustless' technology – 'a system for electronic transactions without relying on trust'.[3] The perfect token, the anonymous author suggests, is one where trust is no longer necessary. Bitcoin promised a token that would dispense with the need to trust in banks or in other people – where all you had to trust was that the code worked as it should.

The whitepaper described two innovations: one was an electronic payments protocol; the other was a shared, time-stamped database called a blockchain. Users of Bitcoin download free software that allows them to send and receive money from other addresses in the network. Payments are executed by digitally signing a transaction with a private key. Each transaction is verified and recorded in an entry (or block) that is added to a chain of previous transactions in the database. The blockchain acts as a public ledger, detailing all transactions that have taken place since the launch of the currency. Following a model common to peer-to-peer networks, the data is not stored in a centralised fashion, but is shared among all members of the network.

What's more, the ledger is structured in such a way that it's easy to see the data hasn't been tampered with, but almost impossible to fake. Each block is subject to a verification process that is carried out by computers connected to the Bitcoin network. This ensures users are in possession of the value they want to exchange, using an otherwise useless, energy-intensive function called a 'proof-of-work'. While the Bitcoin software installed on the computers of every member of the community aims to *oversee* all transactions, members can also agree to contribute some computer cycles to this verification process. In exchange, the peer is awarded with bitcoins. This process – running a calculation to authenticate a transaction – is how new bitcoins are 'mined'.

The blockchain is the primary innovation of the Bitcoin protocol, a technology that allows people who do not know or trust each other to cooperate, transact, and all agree on the distribution of value in the network. Much is made of the supposed immutability of records on the blockchain – a 'permanent record', 'set in cryptographic stone on the ledger, which means no one can rewrite or deny history'.[4]

At first, the blockchain was limited to transactions. But in 2014, a start-up called Ethereum expanded the Bitcoin script so that it could execute any kind of function. Its founder, Vitalik Buterin, was not quite twenty. Ethereum created what were known as 'smart contracts' to automate a wide range of decision-making processes. They also built a new governance structure called the decentralised autonomous organisation, or the mystic-sounding 'DAO' for short, a market-based organisational structure for cooperation without the need of a government. Instead, group behaviour was programmed into the contract: investment strategy, collective ownership, spending, and donating could be voted on and automated through the underlying code.

CityDAO, in Wyoming, for example, wants to create a city run on smart contract code, where citizens vote on proposals and apply for tenders through a blockchain-run crowdsourcing platform. Friends with Benefits DAO is a group of creatives who collectively invest in and crowdfund cultural projects. With a smart contract, Ethereum states, there is no CEO making whimsical decisions or crooked CFOs fiddling the books. And once the code goes live, it cannot be modified, even by the original founders. The Ethereum DAO was created by Slock. it, and raised over $100 million from 11,000 members by 15 May 2016 in the largest crowd sale of its time. The venture capital fund was structured according to a series of smart contracts running on the Ethereum blockchain, allowing its shareholders to propose investments and vote on them in a decentralised fashion.

The DAO's decision-making practices were bets, votes, and transactions all at once. They managed to fold the business of shareholder voting into the practice of government. Theirs was a vision of politics in which trust in the code replaced trust in the institutional process. It imagined a world without rule, where government is, as Tyler Winklevoss said, 'a mathematical framework that is free of politics and human error'.[5] This was 'governance by design', where cryptographic protocols not only *have* politics, but *are* politics.[6]

'In its purest form', the CEO of Bitcoin Indonesia proclaimed in 2015, 'Blockchain *is* democracy'.[7] For believers, the blockchain was not only a tool that helped with decision-making and political wrangling – it came to stand in for the political process itself. Programmers sometimes speak of software systems as being 'human in the loop' or 'human off the loop', to describe the various levels of oversight required by a computational system. The DAO's vision of governance was very much 'human off the loop'. As Buterin put it, a corporation is 'nothing more than people and contracts all the way down. However, here a very interesting question arises: do we really need the people?'[8]

With smart contracts, the proposed uses for the blockchain extended beyond payments to other systems where accountability and trust were necessary: voting systems, supply chains, land registries, so-called 'sovereign-identity' systems, medical records and their permissions – any system where a group of people do not trust one another but still need to keep their promises. In 2015, I sat on a panel with a company that wanted to use blockchain to make a people's Airbnb. In 2016, I spoke with administrators who wanted to use blockchain to manage university credentials (never lose your diploma again!). In 2017, I took part in a workshop hosted by the Department of Defense in Irvine, California, on the possible use of blockchain in weapons supply chains. In all cases, the vision of what the blockchain 'might do' outstripped its real-world applications. The blockchain was a 'work in progress'; it was a 'proof of concept'. It was ironic, really. This was a technology to dispense with talk, but many of the proposals were all talk and no action.

In the 1990s, many of the technologies that later became Bitcoin were hashed out on two mailing lists – Cypherpunk and the Extropian.[9] The Cypherpunk list was an anarchist forum that explored technological tools for privacy and cooperation. It forecast an anarchist revolution based in 'public key encryption [a system that uses secret passwords to lock and unlock messages], zero-knowledge proofs [a system where data can be verified without being revealed] and various software protocols for interaction, verification and authentication'.[10]

The list was founded in 1992 by Tim May, John Gilmore, and Eric Hughes. May was a reclusive electronic engineer who had worked at Intel and was now living off stock options and pursuing his interests in cryptography, science fiction, and guns. Similarly, Gilmore was a programmer who had worked for Sun Microsystems and Cygnus Solutions. He left in 1985, but when the company went public a year later, Gilmore made enough to retire.[11] He was also a founder of the Electronic Frontier Foundation, a staunch libertarian, and a long-time advocate for cannabis reform. Hughes, meanwhile, was a mathematician and cryptographer who had recently returned from a stint working for David Chaum's DigiCash in Amsterdam. The three established monthly meetings at Cygnus Solutions in the Bay Area, where Gilmore worked. This evolved into a mailing list, where 'anarchists, utopians and technologists' could gather to talk about cryptography and anonymous networks.

Early members were spread throughout the Bay Area, but gradually the forum acquired a more international flavour. At its most popular, the list had 700 subscribers and thirty posts a day, ranging through issues such as cryptography, privacy, and digital value – as well as more abstract discussions about politics, anarchy, and the free market. The term 'Cypherpunks' was coined by the programmer Jude Milhon, one of the only female members of the group. Milhon wrote for *Mondo 2000*, a 1980s cyberculture magazine and precursor to *Wired*. In keeping with its anarchist principles, the group had no official moderation, but members used command-line short cuts (called kill lists) to filter out unwanted users from their inbox. Many contributors also made use of recently developed Pretty Good Privacy (PGP) encryption and anonymous 'remailers' – servers that stripped messages of identifying header content before forwarding them on to their destination.

The Cypherpunks were focused on the use of cryptography. In 1993, the trio appeared, masked, on the cover of one of the earliest issues of *Wired* magazine under the caption 'Rebels With a Cause: (Your Privacy)'. The group responded to proposed NSA legislation at the time to limit citizen use of encryption. The so-called 'Clipper Chip' debate responded to a 1993 proposal that all device manufacturers be required to turn over encryption keys to the intelligence agency. The Cypherpunks' version of privacy diverged from the more standard military use of the tool, however: not only cryptography as a tool for secrecy ('I should be able to whisper in your ear, even if you're a thousand miles away'), but cryptography as the basis for technologically mediated trust – for anarchism ('I don't need to trust you if I can trust your code').[12] In 1988, May had penned the 'Crypto Anarchist Manifesto', which claimed that encryption would herald a 'social and economic revolution and alter completely the nature of government regulation, the ability to tax and control economic interactions, the ability to keep information secret, and … even alter the nature of trust and reputation'.[13]

The Extropian list, on the other hand, was a forum dedicated to transhumanism: the belief that technology should be used for human advancement. Humans would overthrow their 'blind, unconscious, animalistic nature' and move into a 'posthuman stage where old limits, old behaviors and old institutions no longer apply'.[14] The Extropians wanted to surpass the limits of bodies and so-called 'meat space'. Humans were at the centre of the project, but the Extropians did not seem to like or trust humans very much – at least not in their beta form. Humans were weak and flawed; they were due an upgrade. The Extropians explored everything from faddish Californian diets and brain-uploading, to founding separatist colonies on Mars.

The Extropian list (and a magazine called *Extropy*) was founded by philosophy and economics graduate Max T. O'Connor (until he changed his name, appropriately enough, to Max More, to signal his desire for perpetual growth). More's doctoral dissertation used metaphysical philosophy to explore the nature of individualism. Should we replace the self with a better self if such a thing is technically possible? More is now CEO of Alcor Life Extension Foundation, a non-profit in Arizona that specialises in cryogenic freezing. For a hefty fee, Alcor will preserve your dead body in liquid nitrogen, in the hope it may be revived in the future. Looking down the list of bodies stored or promised to Alcor in the future, I recognise many of them. There is Robin Hanson, who coined Idea Futures, a system where markets are used to make policy decisions that inspired Ethereum. There is Ralph Merkle, one of the inventors of public key cryptography. PayPal's Peter Thiel is, unsurprisingly, on the list, as is the AI computer scientist Eliezer Yudkowsky and the inventor of the singularity theory, Ray Kurzweil.

Extropian discussions ranged beyond the realm of human perfectibility to explore free markets and digital economies. Some of the key contributors – including Wei Dai, Hal Finney, Nick Szabo, and Robin Hanson – also made significant contributions to the development of Bitcoin. At first blush this was a strange combination: How did debates about the existence of an immortality gene mesh with those about Austrian economics and digital cash – as they frequently did both on the Extropian forum and in *Extropy* magazine? Maybe it was in the dream of endurance that a cyborg body and an absolute gold standard both promised? Maybe it was a sense that free money could literally buy the richest among us more time – perhaps even an infinite amount of it. Or maybe the intersection was in the element of time itself. Freezing your head and hoarding value are both ways of banking the future (and bankrolling the future you want).

Both the Cypherpunks and the Extropians were staunch anarchists. 'But, I mean, what does "the state" even *look like* to these people?' my friend Lana Swartz asks. It is 2015, and I'm a guest researcher at Microsoft Research in Cambridge, Massachusetts, where Lana is currently based. A group of us are eating sandwiches in front of the glass panelling that runs floor-to-ceiling the length of the centre. Boston high-rises spread out across the river. This is a lunch area engineered for chance encounters and vibrant discussions. I'm not sure I'm up to it. I talk to the economist Glen Weyl about quadratic voting, the project he is currently working on – an approach to democracy that sees individuals attaching an economic weight to their preferences rather than just voting one way or another. I speak to a famous mathematician, and discredit myself almost immediately by pronouncing 'Laplace' the way it's spelled. Lana and I have been asked to speak at a conference at the New School about blockchain. We are part of fledgling discussions about how the technology might be used for governance beyond the state: a killer app for human cooperation – blockchain for voting, blockchain for an anti-capitalist share economy, blockchain for citizen science. 'What do they imagine government even *is*?' Lana asks again. Her fiancé, Kevin, comes over to join us. We speak about J. K. Gibson-Graham's diagram of the capitalist iceberg.[15] Waged work is visible above the surface, while the bulk of care and unpaid work is hidden underneath. The same might be said for how the crypto community imagines government, Lana argues. There's the slice of the state that's visible to Bitcoin, the bit that blockchain enthusiasts want to switch out for smart contracts, but, underneath, a tonne of invisible work keeps the bulk afloat.

For the founders of Bitcoin, this thing called government looked a lot like force. It was the 'use of force' as opposed to persuasion.[16] It was the 'unilateral exercise of coercion'.[17] Government was 'the "right" of the leaders of existing institutions to impose their will on other people'.[18] But government was also seen as something boring and sluggish. It was 'paying taxes, filling out forms for every stupid thing, waiting periods', and 'all the other crap', wrote one contributor to the Extropian list.[19] Government was stasis and stagnation. The iceberg was barely moving; it was, quite literally, a drag. '[W]hat two better words are there to describe government bureaucracy than "dull" and "sluggish"?' Chuck Hammill wrote in the first ever post to the Cypherpunk list, a 1987 essay called 'From Crossbows to Cryptography: Thwarting the State via Technology'.[20]

Jude Milhon shared a short story to the list in 1992:

... The cello resumed, an annoyed cello: 'We don't believe in takeovers. In fact, we are working to make things UNTAKEOVERABLE.'

A theremin quivered, 'And to make the world safe for anarchy. *We want the air-waves, baby.*' It snickered across many frequencies.

The Tejana saxophone chuckled, (and an eerie treat that was, too): 'Problem is, how to guarantee privacy for pseudonyms. So you can have a pseudonymous economy.'

A toad croaked: 'So, full-RSA encrypted EVERYTHING. No back doors. Secure digital money. Swiss bank accounts for the millions.'

The theremin: 'A global monetary system that makes governments obsolete. Down come the governments. Goodbye the feds.' It sang, whoopingly: 'BYE BYE, LAWWwww.' Horrible broad-band snickering.

The toad croaked: 'Er ... yes. Real freedom of speech, too. Libertech!'[21]

The Cypherpunks were influenced by books such as *The Machinery of Freedom*, by David Friedman (son of Milton), an anarcho-capitalist text arguing that law should be switched out for technological solutions, and William Rees-Mogg and James Dale Davison's *The Sovereign Individual*, which forecast a shift from the nation-state to entrepreneurial governance, in which shareholder votes and contracts (not unlike Weyl's quadratic voting, in fact) would replace the democratic process.[22] The group wanted to replace politics with a neat, automated solution. Anarchy, in the words of the Cypherpunk glossary, was 'a technological solution to the problem of too much government'.[23] Anarchy, May wrote, had a bad reputation because it was most often associated with chaos and an absence of control, but here it signified an '"absence of government" (literally, "an arch," without a chief or a head)'.[24] It was rules without rulers. Chop off the head, but replace it with the right protocol.

The Cypherpunks favoured technological solutions over human politics. 'Individual liberty can be assured by something more reliable than manmade laws,' May argued, sounding a lot like a Winklevoss twin – 'the unflinching rules of math and physics.'[25] Politics would not bring freedom, but computation might. The Cypherpunk group tended to quash political wrangling (although there was still plenty of it happening on the list). Threads on the philosophy of libertarianism were shut down with an invocation of founder Eric Hughes's maxim: 'Cypherpunks write code'. In the words of one member, 'technology … was more important and interesting than yet more gabbing about liberty and privacy'.[26] 'Cypherpunks write code' was a motto, but it was also a universal putdown when arguments got too boring or complex – a geek's variation on 'If you're so smart, why ain't you rich?' And yet, it was through this sort of debate that many of the core technical and philosophical ideas that would later become Bitcoin were first teased out.

Hal Finney shared a reusable proof-of-work – a system, initially designed to mitigate email spam, that was later repurposed to ensure the trustworthiness of a shared database. Finney suggested the creation of encrypted tokens using proof-of-work.[27] In 1994, Nick Szabo posted his seminal work on smart contracts – self-executing agreements that used cryptography rather than legal mechanisms to ensure compliance. Such contracts would work not because of the threat of external coercion by the state (as in the legal system), and not because the parties involved knew or trusted one another (as in the kin-communal systems of the Irish bank strikes), but simply because the contracting parties trusted in the technology to execute the contract.[28] 'You trust the thing because of the way it behaves, not because you trust the people who gave you access to it', wrote Robert (Bob) Hettinga to the forum.[29] It was not that these systems could complement a broader political process, but that they might replace it altogether – that technology could, in itself, remake the social. As Eric Hughes put it in his statement of purpose for the Cypherpunk list, 'cryptographic protocols make social structures'.[30]

The founders of Bitcoin did not like people very much. For the philosopher Hannah Arendt, however, there was no freedom *without* other people. In *The Human Condition*, Arendt explores the desire to switch out politics for design-based solutions. One consequence of freedom, Arendt writes, is the basic unreliability of other (free) humans. Freedom carries its own risks. For Arendt, the desire for a life 'by the code' responds to this uncertainty – what she calls 'the incalculability of the future'.[31] Technologies that try to predetermine human behaviour – like contracts, or codes of conduct between otherwise free agents – are a way to grapple with the weight of the unknown, to make living with others a little more certain. A promise gives those in power the ability 'to dispose of the future as though it were the present', Arendt writes.[32]

The problem of trust was debated by computer scientist Leslie Lamport. The Byzantine Generals Problem is a classic computer science question (as well as a classic social problem). How do we trust information from someone when we do not know them and cannot verify that they are who they say they are? In the hypothetical problem the paper describes, two separate armies want to coordinate their attack on a distant city. A valley where enemy spies lie in wait separates the two. In order to coordinate an attack, army A needs to send a message to army B. In turn, army B must send a message to army A, verifying that the message has been received. How can the two armies be sure that their messages have not been intercepted and falsified somewhere along the way?

Lamport's hypothetical problem asks how a group can reach consensus in the absence of socially established trust – how to cooperate when faced with 'a group ... some of whom may be traitors, who have to reach a common decision'?[33] 'The problem', Lamport argues, is 'to find an algorithm to ensure that the loyal generals will reach agreement' even though they cannot trust each other.[34] Lamport suggests that the only solution lies in some kind of unforgeable and time-stamped written communication, a chain of signatures that cannot be forged or manipulated after the fact – though no practicable solution was in use at the time of publication. The blockchain created, for the first time, a workable solution to Lamport's problem – which is to say it created a workable solution to the problem of trust in a trustless world. It was a combination of public key encryption, blind signatures, and proof-of-work (all technologies previously explored on the Cypherpunk list). It made consensus. It gave a little certainty. Each entry in a series would be appended to the next, allowing *just enough time* to verify that the chain of communication had not been broken or tampered with, but not enough to work backwards and falsify the data. With this solution you didn't need to trust others: you put your trust in the protocol.

Technologies of trust were an attempt to paper over the cracks in an uncertain future, to account for the unaccountable in human nature. Our promises 'create little islands of certainty in an ocean of uncertainty', Arendt writes.[35] The Cypherpunks grappled with the line between freedom and chaos. What technology could manage the risk that comes with free will? The dreams of life by the code and seemingly unbreakable promises on the blockchain grappled with the risks posed by an uncertain future. This was true in the early 1990s, as people came to accept that there was no longer any such thing as society in the neoliberal state. But it was also true in the aftermath of the financial crash, when the blockchain was part of a technological effort to reframe the problem of risk.

Long before DAOs and functioning smart contracts, the lists also debated the morality of such a system: What kind of an ethical structure would be built into a world where code was law, and who would be tasked with writing it? If something was technically possible in cyberspace, for example, did that make it morally defensible? OK? As one member ventured, was an action 'OK if you can get away with it (but we set up the system so you can't get away with it)'?[36]

But not everybody on the Cypherpunk list agreed that the messiness of government systems could be switched out for a neat technical solution. Nick Szabo, surprisingly, argued that 'crypto-anarchy in the real world [would] be messy, "nature red in tooth and claw", not all nice and clean like it says in the math books'.[37] Code or no code, Robert Woodhead wrote, anarchy would be 'very uncomfortable, unless you [had] more guns and money than anyone else'.[38] Others on the list argued that the coming 'cryptorapture' would probably just create more need for lawyers to sort out and arbitrate all the ensuing messiness, and more humans to interpret code when the technology failed – 'if the governments collapse ... lawyers will have even more work', said one.[39] 'Most computer people don't seem to understand that the law is interpreted not by a computer but by humans', wrote another.[40]

The group disintegrated in the late 1990s. Tired of endless arguments clogging his servers, Gilmore tried to introduce moderation to the list, weeding out the bad seeds and the discussion topics he deemed unsuitable. After a lot of heated exchanges and homophobic slurs, the list stagnated. Perry Metzger's cryptography list took its place. Gilmore continued his work with the Electronic Freedom Foundation until he was forced to resign after a dispute in 2021. May became ever more reclusive, retreating from the world while he took to other mailing lists, working on a novel he described, shyly, as a 'better *Atlas Shrugged*', and sharing increasingly right-wing sentiments.

The Extropic of Extropia

If we live in [*sic*] more than one island it could be called the Extropics, it would be Extropical. The Extropic of Extropia.[41]

The Cypherpunks wanted to build a bolthole against the future.

Maybe the answer to the problem of government was technology. Or maybe, some members argued, it was a rake of platforms on the open water, a city on the open sea. The legal vacuum of the high seas might allow the Extropians to declare a sovereign community. A Free Oceana.[42] Blueprint designs for seasteading in issue eight of *Extropy* magazine include submerged pods (like submarines) and surface pods – 'essentially, a type of barge, multipurpose, with redundant flotation systems, a life support "office" with communications, alarms, & safety systems, and facilities for attaching engine propeller and tug hauling systems' – as well as tethered stacks of floating platforms, a proto–Water World of untethered individuals.[43] Little islands of certainty, floating in a sea of unknowns.

In 'A Home for our Hopes', published in the same issue, the author outlines his plans for a separatist Extropia. Extropia would be a sovereign community, free from terrestrial law.[44] It would be entirely self-governed. The blueprints for anarchist islands recall early experiments with anarchism, Warren's Utopia of sovereign individuals and free markets, New Harmony, Modern Times, even Gesell's short stint in a fruit-bearing Eden. Early experiments in cyberspace would be a testbed for the conquest of the high seas. And Free Oceana would be a dress rehearsal for the final frontier, the colonisation of outer space: Extropolis.

The advantages would be a world without rule, 'the chance to live drunk on freedom; the freedom of the frontier. The chance to live as a human being, away from the smell of obedience. The chance to make fortunes.'[45] Among the drawbacks listed in *Extropy* was the threat of pirates, the ever-present possibility of drowning, rust, decay, pervasive sea sickness – the kinds of entropy that Extropians were keen to overcome, the nagging whine of a body not made for outer space, or 20,000 leagues under the sea. But they could not escape the tyranny of their bodies, any more than they could escape the tyranny of other people.

The Extropians' dreams were influenced by the anarchist philosopher Hakim Bey (a.k.a. Peter Wilson) and his writings on the temporary autonomous zone (TAZ) – a non-hierarchical social space and short-lived window of freedom from the tyranny of the state. The TAZ was an altered state of consciousness if only for a moment: a chance to live drunk on freedom. For Bey, the internet featured heavily in the creation of such autonomous zones. The vital question, Bey wrote, 'concerns the "technology" of the TAZ, i.e., the means for potentiating and manifesting it most clearly and strongly'.[46] Bey's philosophy resurfaced in the Covid-19 pandemic, when Black Lives Matter protestors occupied six blocks in the Capitol Hill neighbourhood of Seattle. The area was called the Capitol Hill Autonomous Zone or CHAZ in a nod to Bey's principles of anarchy. In the aftermath of George Floyd's murder, the protestors demanded that police funding be redirected towards community projects in historically black neighbourhoods. The zone featured political murals, screenings, talks, a vegetable garden, and a 'No Cop Co-op' for food and supplies. In the 1850s, critics of Josiah Warren's anarchist commune had led to a newspaper comment that 'the women of Modern Times dressed in men's clothes and looked hideous'.[47] In the summer of 2020, President Trump tweeted that the CHAZ was full of 'ugly anarchists' and demanded that the army take it back.[48] Others compared the vibes in CHAZ to a small Burning Man festival, only with more guns. At night, vigilante volunteers patrolled its boundaries.

Some members of the list also suggested colonising a tropical island. 'The Extropics of Extropia!' said one poster.[49] 'Money & fun in the sun', wrote another.[50] But others argued that a tropical island was too impractical. These discussions revolved around technical rather than social or political concerns. Declaring a sovereign community and having it recognised was one thing, but were the foundations going to be made out of sand or hard rock? Sand wasn't solid enough to found a new civilisation, one Extropian wrote – but what about the Alaskan and Canadian coastal islands where he had holidayed as a child, full of fresh water, timber, and seafood, and founded on some of the hardest rock in the known world?[51]

Mark O'Connell has argued that the transhumanist desire for escape is a desire for conquest. Mars is the newest Brave New World.[52] This is true: Earth was framed as a launch pad for a multiplanetary species. 'Earth is the womb of the human race,' Max More wrote in the inaugural issue of *Extropy*. 'Not only is there space, there are massive quantities of resources waiting to be exploited for the purposes of the spacers and those left on terra … the vast expanses of space offer us the opportunity to make a fresh start – or as many fresh starts as we want.'[53] And yet, it seems to me that Extropia was more about withdrawing than forcing the frontier – a dream of leaving the world behind. It was, as one Extropian put it, 'more suited to "retreat" than to colonization'.[54] Extropia was a retreat from the burdens of the flesh, but also from the burden of care – of trust in and responsibility for others. A retreat from the world and all its problems. A retreat from politics and anything like slow, incremental change. These blueprints set out a desire to be completely self-sovereign, to *have no kin*. This was what their version of freedom looked like.

The founder of PayPal, Peter Thiel, is also a fan of seasteading. As well as buying land and applying for citizenship in New Zealand as a bolthole for the apocalypse, Thiel explored the possibility of communes, both on the high seas and in outer space. These were described in his 2009 essay, 'The Education of a Libertarian'. Much like the Extropians, Thiel argued that the only path to the future was to move beyond the frontier of democratic processes. To escape from the world was also to escape from politics. 'In our time,' Thiel writes, 'the great task for libertarians is to find an escape from politics in all its forms – from the totalitarian and fundamentalist catastrophes to the unthinking demos that guides so-called "social democracy".'[55] In the essay, Thiel writes that he does not despair for the future. This is not, as we might be forgiven for thinking, because he owns a giant bunker in New Zealand and enthusiastically pursues life-extending technology. Instead, he has hopes for the future because he no longer places any hope in others, choosing to focus instead on 'new technologies that may create a new space for freedom'. 'The critical question then becomes one of means', Thiel writes, 'of how to escape not via politics but beyond it. Because there are no truly free places left in our world, I suspect that the mode for escape must involve some sort of new and hitherto untried process that leads us to some undiscovered country.'[56]

Like the Extropians, PayPal's founder was at pains to stress that his vision of freedom was in conflict with democracy, with the demos: it was a freedom from reliance on or accountability to others. Thiel abandoned the plan for a seasteading commune – not because it was socially impossible, but on the grounds that it was, as yet, 'not quite feasible from an engineering perspective'.[57] We were back to discussions of sand versus soil. It was as though the whole civilisation rested on wrangling the right protocol – Thiel's so-called 'technologies of freedom' – with very little attention paid to the kinds of social or political processes that might emerge. With the right bedrock, these would presumably fall into place.

Bonanza: Control Your Future

Storey County, Nevada, is best known for the Western TV show *Bonanza*, which ran from 1959 to 1973, following the fortunes of the Cartwright family. A 'bonanza' was the name that miners gave to the discovery of silver ore in the vast mines uncovered beneath Virginia City in 1859. After its silver, Storey County is probably best known for its legal gambling and prostitution. Lance Gilman, the owner of a number of brothels in the area, bought the land surrounding his businesses in 1998 for $20 million from Gulf Oil. The company had intended to create a luxury shooting reserve on the property, complete with imported big game, until the price of oil plummeted and the project was deemed an unnecessary luxury. Gilman had the real estate pre-approved for industrial purposes instead, and transformed it into the Tahoe Reno Industrial Center, selling the land to tech companies who were drawn to the state for its tax breaks and lenient regulation. Acres of land in the Wild West now house some of the world's best-known technology platforms. Google and eBay both have campuses there. Tesla has an enormous battery factory. Switch operates a 1.3 million-square-foot data centre. In 2018, Jeffrey Berns, the CEO of a company called Blockchains LLC, purchased sixty-seven square kilometres of land, and established its headquarters there. The company now owns about half of Storey County – acres and acres of land, arid as the surface of a desert planet.

Berns made his fortune buying ether in the 2015 crowd sale. But his background is not in financial investment, but in law – in particular, class-action lawsuits against financial companies. A look at the company's composition shows that most of the senior staff have backgrounds in law and litigation, as opposed to technology or finance.

Berns planned to transform the Nevada estate into a smart city called Painted Rock. 'The city would feature the amenities and services of a typical city – homes, schools, businesses and industry', the proposal states, 'yet it would be built with block-chain technology at its core.'[58] The city would use blockchain to provision energy and control autonomous vehicles, but also to make and enforce its laws.

Painted Rock wanted to break with surrounding government. It would be a law unto itself. Like the separatist islands imagined on the Extropian list, Blockchains LLC's city in the desert would be a place that commercial companies could assume governance over. Government, in its current guise, is a fetter on technical innovation, Berns argued. But if we created a space where these corporations could be *bigger than government*, they would be free to run with their ideas and drive innovation. The resulting area would be called an 'Innovation Zone'. The proposal likened the Innovation Zone to other corporate enclaves, such as Disney's Reedy Creek Improvement District, only with far more sweeping powers. Blockchains would operate outside the jurisdiction of pre-existing local government, and could create its own court systems, impose taxes, create schools, and even make zoning decisions. Local government decisions would be made by a three-county commission, two of which would be nominated by the Blockchains LLC company. These two would be the majority voice, and would not require any previous political qualifications. The initial proposal for a sovereign city was supported by the Nevada governor, Steve Sisolak. Sisolak touted the Innovation Zone as a possible bonanza in a state hit hard by the pandemic.

Blockchains LLC pitched a city of 36,000 at Painted Rock – eight times the population currently resident in the area. This included 15,000 homes and 33 million square feet of commercial and industrial development within seventy-five years. The project would also provide amenities like water and electricity (anything you could find on a Monopoly board). These were to be operated using smart contracts run on a blockchain. Blockchains would also be used to manage citizen data and allow citizens to determine the markets for their personal data. The whole city would be a giant incubator, a testbed for governance by design.

The architectural plans for Painted Rock were developed by EYRC Architects in California. In its mission statement, the company describes itself as taking a 'humanistic' approach to design. The team is inspired by a new Californian modernism, it says – a kind of 'architecture without architects'.[59] In the brochure, Painted Rock appears as a place without context or history – like the Metaverse, a whole city airlifted top-down into the desert. These pictures could be anywhere. They could be Mars. A walled city rises out of the wilderness. Buildings, like giant Tetris blocks, are covered with glaring solar panels. The tetrahedral shapes feel like a nod to Colorado's Drop City, designed by Buckminster Fuller – another architect of the escape from the mainstream. This was the city, not as an organism, but as code.

The brochure contains images of people of indeterminate race with cell phones pressed to their ears, or perched on outdoor seating with a laptop balanced on their knees and a coffee by their side. Mothers lead children along a wooden promenade in the blinding sun. There is one God's-eye view, with tiny stick figures pouring from the entrance of what looks like a Greek amphitheatre. Who are all of these tiny people, and where did they come from? The image is dispassionate, removed, as if depicting ants in a colony. This is not a city for real people, it seems to say. This is humanity 'off the loop'. But who would work to maintain this city in the desert? Who would clean the streets and pick up the garbage and do all the other messy stuff?[60]

Painted Rock was launched as a legislative proposal. But the government of Nevada and Storey County's law enforcement raised a number of concerns. They were worried by claims that the technology company would build its own government 'from scratch'.[61] The system seemed to have no authority in play beyond that of the blockchain technology. Where was the oversight – the 'checks and balances', as one member of the government committee put it? What did Blockchains LLC think government *was*, anyway? This was not limited government, or separatist government, said the report, this was 'no government', an arch without a chief or a head.[62] The committee also objected to the representation of government as a corporation, arguing a little primly that 'government is created for the health, safety and welfare of its citizens, not solely for economic development'.[63]

Other members of the committee raised concerns about the technological feasibility of the proposal. As with many blockchain projects, there was an array of proposed applications and far-flung aspirations, but very little in the way of a 'developed blockchain technology as of yet' that Blockchains LLC could point to.[64] There was, once again, more discussion than action.

The government in place was broadly supportive of the technological innovations – the blockchains and stablecoins and other markers of digital innovation in the plan – but opposed to separatist government in any form. In September 2021, Blockchains LLC withdrew its plans to develop Painted Rock – though it retained a commitment to experiments with blockchain, identity management, autonomous vehicles, and renewable-energy systems on its campus. In a letter to Governor Sisolak, Berns expressed disappointment with the government's short-sighted attitude to the company's proposal. Seriously, wasn't their code enough? While the corporation firmly believed that blockchain could offer 'a better future for all humans', Berns wrote, this vision could only proceed if it was fully supported by the state.[65] The problem is not sand or soil, in other words, but whether or not your community will be recognised by existing government. I click on the website to see what's happening now. A phrase flashes up in black on white, and just as quickly disappears from the screen. It says: 'Control your Future'.

Futarchy and the DAO

Futarchy, or 'Idea Futures', was first explored on both the Extropian and Cypherpunks lists. It was, in founder Robin Hanson's words, 'a fancy name for decision markets applied to government'.[66] Markets were used to decide which policies ought to be implemented. Hanson, an associate professor of economics at George Mason University, devised a mode of government in which tokens are bets, and bets are beliefs. His work built on a general interest in the community in what were known as 'Agoric systems', on the suggestion that market mechanisms could be used to divine software processes, and now perhaps democratic processes too.[67]

In everyday life, people don't have a good reason to tell the truth, Hanson argued in the Winter 1991/92 issue of *Extropy* magazine. 'They massage evidence, suppress criticism, and just plain lie.' They do so at the expense of the 'honest consensus' of experts.[68] Futarchy is a futures market in, well, futures. Price represents a general consensus about the value of a good. A futures market in oil, for example, is a consensus about the future price of that commodity. And traders have a good incentive to tell the truth, because 'you put your money where your mouth is', Hanson writes.[69] So why not shill the future? Say we created a token that would be redeemable for $1 if the first person reached Mars by 2020. The percentage of the dollar this speculative token traded at would indicate a consensus of the likelihood of that scenario coming true. If the future traded at $.023, Hanson wrote, this would represent a 23 per cent consensus that such a future might come to pass. Money links the present to the future. And so the value would not only measure the likelihood of whether such a thing might happen – it would be a measure of the collective will of the market to *make* it happen. The token could call such a future into being.

Key thinkers were called on in Issue 15 of *Extropy* to take bets on future innovations. Nick Szabo (thought by many to be the founder of Bitcoin) was asked to forecast when a vast chunk of the economy would exist off Earth (2050), when nuclear weapons would be as cheap as guns (2200), when AI intelligence would exceed human intelligence (2150), when more than a

million people would use electronic cash (1999), when the first
baby would be gestated in an artificial womb (2100), and when
more than 30 per cent of labour would telecommute to work
(2050). His forecasts are the most conservative among those of
the experts polled. Eric Drexler, a leading nanotechnologist at
the time, forecast that all of these events would have occurred
by the year 2021.[70]

Futarchy drew on William Rees-Mogg and James Dale
Davidson's *The Sovereign Individual* – from which, as we
saw, the Cypherpunks also drew inspiration. This text forecast a shift from political to corporate governance, in which
economic expressions like signing contracts, buying in, or
cashing out would replace political expression. Rees-Mogg
and Davidson – the editor of *The Times* and a private investor,
respectively – argued that customers in a market with shares and
tokens had more political clout than citizens with a democratic
vote. The book is written in the proselytising style of a utopian
manifesto – a utopia where the fullest exercise of markets would
be an exercise in freedom.[71]

'Such coupons can be thought of metaphorically as futures,
and more literally as bets, a metaphor used to describe both
investments and science,' writes Hanson.[72] Through the mechanism of price, a consensus would form around debated topics.
Idea Futures might be used to guide public spending or make
decisions. 'The money votes', wrote one poster to the Extropian list. 'That's where the democracy comes in.'[73] Hanson also
suggests that the future could be used as a way to offset risk.
Voting *against* the future you wanted could also be a way to
hedge your bets if the worst came to pass.

In Marc Stiegler's 1999 science fiction novel *Earth Web*,
Idea Futures (known as 'forecasts') are used to determine the
course taken by a crew through outer space. The trading value
of information is used to decide whether to turn left or right.
The novel is set in a future where the internet has replaced
government and forecasts are used to shape policy.

The economist Friedrich Hayek famously wrote that price was information, a signal. People speak of incentives, writes Hayek in 'Competition as a Discovery Procedure', not in terms of the monetary incentive to behave in a particular way, but because it gives them information. Price works because it signals the best route to take, not because it entices an actor to make a particular decision. The chief guiding principle, Hayek writes, 'is not so much how to act, but *what to do*'.[74]

Over twenty years later, Ethereum's founder Vitalik Buterin made direct reference to Hanson's Futarchy in the design of the DAO. Buterin was born in Russia in 1994, in the same year that Szabo published his essay on smart contracts. When he was six, his family emigrated to Canada in search of economic stability. His father, a computer scientist, introduced Buterin to Bitcoin when he was seventeen. Three years later, he received a grant from the Thiel Foundation to make Ethereum the future.

The DAO is a leaderless governance structure. Decisions are made and instituted by voting on and implementing smart contracts. Economic shareholders are voters. Tokens are used to cast your vote. As Buterin explains, the DAO uses market forces and automated contracts as the foundation for the democratic process. Tokens collapse the vote and the stake into one, just as they collapse government and commercial enterprise. Politics becomes economics.

But not everybody shared Hanson's vision of governance. Hal Finney was a core developer for PGP encryption tools and proof-of-work, and was the programmer responsible for the creation of the first anonymous remailer. (He also received the first ever Bitcoin transaction from Satoshi Nakamoto: some even speculate that Finney *is* Nakamoto, because, among other things, he once lived near to a man of that name.) Finney argued that the kinds of decisions an ideas market could make were limited. Idea Futures are good for predicting some kinds of future events, he wrote on the Extropian list. They can also provide conditional predictions – for example: What will the murder rate be if we do/do not have gun control? Should the spaceship turn left or turn right? But by itself this does not enable you to choose policies or say what is the 'right' decision in any particular situation. The choice was driven by a technical rather than a moral compass. Not how to act, in Hayek's words, but simply *what to do*. Should we raise or lower taxes? What should the criteria be? Greater income equality? Higher economic growth? Greatest average income for the poorest 20 per cent? The choice of what values should govern decisions, Finney concluded, would always be a political matter.[75]

The DAO, with its tokens representing shareholder votes and value, recalls other moments when tokens have functioned as democratic and monetary tools at the same time. I'm reminded of voting by allotment in the Athenian agora, where tokens acted both as credentials and as payment for participating in the democratic process. Symbola, as they are now known, were 'little plaques cut in half along an irregular line in such a way that any given half would join only its mate and no other'.[76] Like the medieval tally stick, which etched a debt in wood so that it was clear to see and hard to fake, symbola were designed to make the democratic process more transparent. (In *The Sovereign Individual*, Davidson and Rees-Mogg mention voting by allotment as evidence that computer technology could be used to automate representational governance.[77])

Archaeologists have drawn on written accounts from Aristotle to flesh out the allotment process. Athens was broken into what were known as demes or *demoi* – like voting constituencies or school districts. Registration in the citizen lists of a particular deme was the basic requirement for Athenian citizenship. Each of the demes were assigned a number of seats on the council, and on allotment day would send citizens to engage in the selection process. Juries were assigned to vote and adjudicate.

Allotment made use of the symbola tokens, but also a device known as a *kleroterion* (an anachronistic stone machine with rows of identical vertical slots that looked a bit like the one

Fred Flintstone used to clock in and out of the stone quarry). It was designed to automate the selection process. Citizens would insert one-half of their token into a slot. A mechanism in the back released white or black beads into each of the vertical rows. Rows that came up black were eliminated, and those with white beads were elected as councillors for the day. At this point, the councillor received the other half of the symbola as credentials and payment. The tokens and the kleroterion were pre-modern authentication devices, designed to produce transparent democratic processes and avoid vote-buying.[78] The token was a technology for transparency and trust. And yet, despite the claims that these tokens would make democracy more accountable, records suggest that the technologies themselves called up *more* need for human intervention and oversight when things did not go to plan.[79]

It is tempting to draw comparisons between the Greek agora and the use of blockchain today (several DAOs make use of the word 'agora', or references to agoric systems, in their publicity materials). But anthropologist Bill Maurer argues that this is a reductive understanding of what the agora was. The Cypherpunks waxed lyrical about the openness of the agora and the perfection of agoric systems – a tokenised politics, but they didn't really understand how the system worked. The agora was not a marketplace for votes, and the Athenian political subject was not a self-interested individual persuaded to cooperate by way of a token. The interests of the randomly chosen citizen lay not with his own self, but with the interests of the demos, with *the collective*. As Maurer explains, 'that citizen did not vote with his voice, so to speak. He tried to anticipate the voices of other free men in the deme, standing part for whole. His singularity was not that of his own incommensurable distinctiveness but that of the deme itself.'[80] Instead of exchanging the political voice for an economic process, as the DAO suggested, this was a democracy that blurred the boundaries between the individual and the collective. The Athenian interest was not self-interest or market interest, in other words. These tokens had another politics written in their clay – not the self-sovereign *Homo economicus*, but a part, standing in for the whole. The Demarchy was not a Futarchy.

Code ! = Law

For Ethereum, code was law. In June 2016, however, a bug known as a 'recursive calling vulnerability' was identified in the smart contract code structuring the DAO. Imagine that you have an account balance of €20. You go to an ATM and withdraw €20 from your account – but, due to an error, the records do not update immediately. The €20 is in your pocket, but the computer still thinks it is in your account. Theoretically you could continue to withdraw increments of €20 until the error is spotted. This was essentially what happened with the Ethereum exploit. A hacker abused this vulnerability on 16 June 2016, and proceeded to move one-third of the ether held by the DAO (roughly $50 million) into a clone DAO. Because of the way the DAO operates, however, the funds would not be released for twenty-seven days. As a number of commentators explained in the aftermath of the attack, under the terms and conditions of the DAO, what the hacker did was not illegal or forbidden from a technical standpoint. Because it was *technically feasible*, it was *technically legitimate*. As the hacker wrote in an open letter to the community, 'I have made use of this [recursive calling] feature and have rightfully claimed 3,641,694 ether, and would like to thank the DAO for this reward.'[81] Thanks for the free ether, everyone!

The exploit was a maleficent attack, and yet something about the way it was executed (not to mention the fact that the hacker could not draw down the funds for four weeks – plenty of time for the developers to come up with a counter-ploy) made it feel more like a teachable moment than a technical heist. It materialised, in a knowing way, some of the entirely hypothetical discussions the Cypherpunks had conducted in the 1990s. In life by the code, if something was technically permissible, was it morally acceptable? OK? Either way, the attack was a catastrophe for the Ethereum community. If code *was* law, then how to deal with this expression – an act that violated cultural norms while obeying the smart contract? In the twenty-seven days before the funds were released, the community gathered to debate what was to be done.

One Reddit commentator, Lefteris Karapetsas, the lead technical engineer for the Ethereum Computer project, broke the community's possible actions into four distinct futures: do nothing; counter-exploit the flaw in the code in a white-hat attack, and reclaim the appropriated ether; perform a soft fork of the code, a kind of subtle change to the blockchain that is backward compatible; or perform a hard fork, a radical upgrade that invalidates previous transactions. The latter asked that the community travel back in time, and roll back the blockchain to the day before the attack took place – a move possible if 51 per cent or more of the DAO members agreed to install an updated version of the software on their machines.[82] In this case it would be as if the hack had never occurred. If less than 51 per cent agreed to perform the update, the blockchain would be broken forever.

A 'code is law' contingent argued that any modification to the Ethereum code constituted an ideological failure of the DAO's vision of governance. As law scholar Bryant Joseph Gilot argued in the early days following the attack, 'The integrity of the Ethereum protocol is entirely intact. The DAO has confirmed that "*Code is Law*" ... Implemented on an immutable Ethereum blockchain, code can also be cruel.'[83]

For Gilot, the attack represented a failure in the human implementation of the DAO, but not in the technical system itself. The answer was to do nothing, because if some action was *technically possible* under the conditions of the smart contract, then it was also legally tenable. Alongside Gilot, the 'code is law' contingent argued that, under the conditions of the smart contract, the hacker was entitled to keep the ether they had 'won' from the system. Although a 'do no harm' Memorandum of Understanding featured on the Ethereum website's specifications, if this semantic expression was not translated into machine-executable code, then it didn't really apply.

Another contingent, including those with a vested interest in the financial success of the DAO, such as developers Vitalik Buterin, Christoph Jentzsch, Lefteris Karapetsas, and others argued for a hard fork. They claimed that human oversight was necessary to maintain the integrity of the blockchain and to reclaim the appropriated funds. Such a move relied on the democratic participation of the Ethereum members – a coordinated 51 per cent attack. As Christoph Jentzsch wrote in a public statement, 'It is part of the Ethereum protocol that a majority of the miners/community can do an upgrade/split if they think something isn't working as intended. This does not take anything away from decentralization, since no one can decide about the fork except for the miners and the community themselves – and *no one else*.'[84]

Following this debate, the majority of members elected to move to a new blockchain. A small faction of the 'code is law' crew chose to stay with the original (now called Ethereum Classic), and forfeit the money. This hard-core contingent believed that reinterpreting the contract constituted a fundamental transformation of the principles underpinning the DAO. It was a debate treading the fault line between the axiom 'code is law' and a belief that other social and judicial mechanisms needed to intervene (or 'code ! = law').

The twentieth century ushered in a new understanding of democracy. In Joseph Schumpeter's *Capitalism, Socialism and Democracy* (1942), and later in Anthony Downs's *An Economic Theory of Democracy* (1957), democracy got an upgrade from notions of a common good towards a model based on the negotiation of (personal) interests.[85] This view of democracy imagined an economic subject motivated by self-interest rather than a moral belief in what was right. It argued that political institutions should be reorganised around the aggregation of individual preferences, away from the demos of the Greek agora, in other words, and towards something resembling Weyl's quadratic voting or Hanson's future markets.

Instead of democracy as collective discussion or time-consuming debate, the DAO preached a bland 'consensus'. It was a vision of democracy based on self-interested actors, the self-sovereign individuals of the Extropian list, the rational players in Hanson's Futarchy, the faceless nodes and peers of the Bitcoin community. Chantal Mouffe argues, in contrast, that politics is not some kind of bland agreement – 'all in favour say aye' – but precisely the opposite: lots of dissenting voices, debate, disagreement. Mouffe calls this 'agonistic pluralism'. It is through the rabble – all that 'gabbing about liberty' – that social orders are made and unmade. A politics based on consensus, Mouffe says, ensures that everything will stay the same.[86] Real change does not happen alone on a tropical island with a blockchain in one hand and a gun in the other. It happens here, in the messiness of other people.

The heated discussions on the Ethereum Reddit remind me of the debates that broke out on the Cypherpunk list more than twenty years earlier. Despite the putdown 'cypherpunks write *code*' every time someone dared to mention John Locke, the online forum was where most of the politics of the anarcho-capitalist group were thrashed out. Even arguing that some kind of discussion was 'the wrong sort of politics' was itself a kind of politics. It was a vital discourse, even as the group made the case for a future of robot butlers and human 'off-the-loop' government.

While the blockchain imagined politics as a protocol, other political processes were still brought to bear. Traditional institutions continued to operate. Legal interventions were significant, but so was arbitration from the general community. The hack surfaced key debates, such as 'Who is liable in the case of a failure?', 'Who bears responsibility for restitution?', and 'Who enforces or arbitrates in the case of a dispute?' It soon became clear that these disputes needed off-chain settlement. It was not in the blockchain but in the discussion on the Ethereum sub-Reddit and slock.it that the politics of the Ethereum community were truly enacted.[87] Core developers with a vested interest in the slock.it platform, such as Vitalik Buterin and Christoph Jentzsch, took to social media and argued for a hard fork, while others in the community argued just as persuasively that code is law. And so, the online debate showed two things: not only that the community did not agree on the role the blockchain should play in its politics, but that there was still space for human debate in the off-chain infrastructures that structured and informed debate. (Cypherpunks might write code, but the politics usually happened somewhere else.)

In 2022, in a move known as 'the Merge', Ethereum moved from the proof-of-work blockchain to a system known as 'proof of stake'. Proof-of-work makes use of a computationally expensive calculation to prevent users from cheating the system; it represents trust as a function of processing power. Proof of stake, on the other hand, allows the users with a greater economic stake in the community to play a greater role in oversight. Or, as researcher Paul Ennis quipped on Twitter: 'What we really need is a consensus mechnanism where you need millions of dollars to buy equipment and keep a giant industrial warehouse with staff running. Only then will we have truly democratised!'[88] Instead of the token representing an investment in energy, it takes a financial stake in the system. Validators are required to stake capital in the form of ether. The staked token 'acts as collateral that can be destroyed if the validator behaves dishonestly or lazily'.[89] The logic, once more, is game-theoretical: it assumes that those with a stake in the system have less of an incentive to act in a way that will destroy its value. 'The money votes' – that's where the politics comes in.

The Ethereum website claims this reduced the energy consumption of the blockchain by more than 99 per cent. It also scales better. Evgeny Morozov, always quick with a hot take, coined the term 'stakeholder capitalism' – a social field where users are economically rewarded when they contribute to a system that oppresses them, where arcane notions of the citizen or the deme are reframed as 'key stakeholders and their objectives'.[90]

In the face of the pandemic, climate change, economic instability, and global political unrest, the future feels grim. Rents are higher. Social ties are weaker. We hunker down on our little islands of uncertainty, we shelter in place in our flats and houses. What's left when trust is lost? A world without a chief or a head? Guns? Crypto? There is a sense that blockchain, with its promise of promises, might be one technology for banking on an uncertain future.

Alongside a host of other tokens – kleroteria, politeia, symbola, agoric systems – the blockchain abstracted trust away, but it did not dispense with the need for other people. If anything, it created new necessities for human oversight, humans who argued in one breath that we do not need messy democracy, but were more than capable of making a case for it when their money was on the line. Ethereum and the development of the DAO were held up as oracles for 'trust in the code'. But the reality was, once more, 'messier than what it said in the math books'. In practice, politics in these systems calls for a lot of community-building on the ground in order to function. Politics still needs humans-in-the-loop.

7

Outside of Borders

Art as a store of long term wealth ... is a very good hedge against structural changes in the relative value that currencies have against each other as well as the long term loss of value that currencies have as central banks print more money to stimulate and stabilize currencies in troubled times.

Stefan Simchowitz

Ibrahim Mahama's *Outside of Borders* was a readymade installation for the 2015 Venice Biennale, made from 300 repurposed jute sacks that covered the interior of the gallery space. Mahama's artwork deals with the circulation of goods within and across borders, and the role of human bodies and human labour in these commodity chains. The sacks are woven from rough cloth, well worn, and patched with regional, patterned fabrics. The names of co-ops and government institutions are printed on the outside, along with import and export symbols – the traces of its movement in a global supply chain.

The jute sacks were initially used to transport cocoa, and later coal, in Mahama's native Ghana. They are woven from the stems of a tropical plant whose rough texture is often used for cloth or sacking. Jute, known as the 'golden fibre' because of its natural sheen, was an industrial material that was grown, milled, and traded on plantations in Bengal from the seventeenth century, prior to the development of plastics. The textile was mass-produced and sold on colonial plantations for hessian or burlap sacks. The jute sack relates the rise of global trade, the long history of colonial extraction, and the movement of goods across borders, from South to North and East to West.

The surface has traces of the goods it has carried and the hands that stitched and patched it, as well as those that packed and moved the goods in Africa. Today, the bags are made in Asia. Mahama gives workers new sacks in exchange for their old, worn-out ones.

In *Outside of Borders*, the jute sacks are taken out of one economy of circulation – a good with a specific use value in global trade – and brought inside another system of exchange, now as a readymade work of art, and maybe also a form of currency in a broader financial network. Mahama's work is the subject of another commodity chain – the movement of artworks as currency in a global marketplace.

These jute sacks were also central to a legal dispute involving LA-based dealer Stefan Simchowitz. Simchowitz is an art dealer for the internet age, a meme trader who flips work on Instagram, but nonetheless cultivates a large network of art collectors. Simchowitz, who argues that artworks provide a neat hedge for market volatility, is well known for his speculative investment practices, buying into relatively unknown artists, inflating their value on social media, and selling their work for a profit before moving on to the next promising talent. Reputations are blown up and broken. A long career characterised by sustained relationships with galleries or collectors is replaced by arbitrage: the practice of quickly exploiting information and/ or price differentials in a global marketplace.

Simchowitz acquired some of Mahama's works after meeting the artist at London's Frieze art fair (or plucking him from obscurity on the internet, if you believe the dealer). But at the time of the 2015 Venice Biennale, Simchowitz's company, Simcor LLC, and a Dublin-based dealer, Jonathan Ellis King, had filed a multi-million-dollar lawsuit against Mahama in the US federal court. The case concerned the outcome of a jute sack installation acquired by the pair and exhibited in the Ellis King Gallery in Dublin in December 2014. Mahama signed 294 of the sacks prior to the opening of the show. In the aftermath, King and

Simchowitz proceeded to dismantle the huge installation into hundreds of individual jute sack pieces, and began to sell these as individual, smaller works mounted on stretchers – like paintings: jute canvas. The two dealers would allege that they made an oral contract with the artist, agreeing to pay him $148,000 in exchange for a large part of the assembled installation.

The lawsuit was filed when the pair received correspondence from Mahama claiming that he had not authenticated the individual pieces or agreed to such explicit commercialisation of his work. Their lawsuit demanded that Mahama agree to authenticate the works they wanted to sell. 'He was using jute coal bags made by migrant laborers for pennies', said a furious Simchowitz. 'We assisted him in repurposing them and now they hang on gallery walls as valuable artworks.'[1] Presumably he was annoyed because, in the dealer's eyes, it is the walls of the institution that manage this neat alchemy, from the rags the artist trades with migrant workers, to art-market riches. Arjun Appadurai calls this process 'commodification by diversion': through some mysterious sleight of hand, an object can be diverted from its everyday use to become a valuable work of art – and, as Mahama shows, put back again. Such things attain their value not through the normal routes, says Appadurai, but through an 'aesthetics of diversion' where commodities are knocked off their usual path into some unlikely context. Aesthetic and entrepreneurial impulses are brought together.[2] For Simchowitz, this is where the real artistry lies.

Tokenised Things

AS NFTs have already shown us, tokens can be used to market insubstantial things – famous people's farts, virtual kittens, skins in *Fortnite* – to make ephemeral things solid enough to enter the economy. For most of history, however, tokens were used to do the exact opposite: to make solid things liquid enough to circulate in a global market. Tokens dilute solid (or, in the language of the market, 'illiquid') things – things like gold bullion, grain or cocoa stored in a warehouse, land, cars, and houses. Tokens turn use value into exchange value; they let value flow and circulate.

For much of history, tokens have been used to overcome the frictions associated with securing and transferring real assets stored in real places. Instead of buying the thing itself, you might buy a token that represents a claim to some or all of it. There are several advantages to this: you don't have to store and guard the thing yourself; you can move the token around much more easily; you can easily exchange it for other things; and, in the meantime, you might also benefit from tax or regulatory advantages based on where the underlying thing is located. You can sometimes even access lines of credit based on your ownership of the distant thing. The downside of possessing a token and not a thing is that all you have now is a stream of value – exchange without use; but for many investors this detail is immaterial.

Such tokens are value contracts, a codified representation of an object that exists in the real world. In ancient Mesopotamia, grain harvests were collectively housed in state warehouses. Clay tokens were used to represent an individual share in the store. When the grain token was used as collateral in a debt, the token was stored in a hollow clay ball, and the transacting parties put their signatures on the outside. Things, and records of things, and promises were rolled together.

Rai stones were huge granite monuments that acted as ceremonial gifts for the native inhabitants of the Yap islands in Micronesia. They were not money exactly, in the way that a lot of objects that change hands in gift economies look like money to the colonial gaze. The stones were heavy; the largest weighed more than the average car. Maybe because of this, ownership of a stone was transferred not by moving the artefact from place to place, but simply by observing that the stone now belonged to someone else. For the stone to 'change hands', another entry was made into collective memory, an invisible ledger held in trust by the Yapese community. Ownership was not determined by possession or location, in other words, but by an entry in an oral ledger. A transfer was effected by adding a new name to the oral history attached to the stone. The stone stayed in the same place, but it still changed hands. Rai stones were sometimes manufactured off the island. On one occasion, a work crew was bringing a large stone to the island by canoe when a storm blew up. The rai fell overboard in the swell and sank to the bottom of the ocean. Everyone agreed that while the stone was no longer visible, it was still there somewhere, and so they continued to use it to transact.[3] Yap now has paper money, but the rai stones continue to be used in official ceremonies such as marriages, political deals, and treaties.

In a 1991 paper, the economist Milton Friedman argued that while the Yap system of immobile money might seem bizarre at first glance, it is not actually that different from the operation of bullion in the Federal Reserve of New York, which can move gold from one government to another without its ever leaving the vault.[4] In the inter-war period, the Bretton Woods system set out rules of exchange between North America, Canada, developed Europe, Australia, and Japan. Foreign currencies were to be convertible to the US dollar, and the dollar in turn was convertible to bullion held in the Federal Reserve. In 1971, the United States ceased issuing the dollar according to a fixed reserve.[5] This was a move to promote global trade by making markets more flexible. From that moment on, state money ceased to be standard, and became fiat money – no longer backed by gold or silver, but by the declaration that it was legal tender. 'Fiat', as in *fiat lux*, or 'Let there be light' – it is because I say so. The stone was sunk. In economic terms, 1971 was a watershed – the moment when exchange value parted company with commodities and entered into the realm of financial speculation.

In seventeenth-century Britain, the Goldsmith's Receipt tallied deposits. People who were suspicious of depositing money in the mint because of sovereign corruption (Charles I was said to be dipping into the country's money supply) began depositing their gold with private goldsmiths. In return, they received a paper token that tallied their deposit. Over time, gold increasingly stayed in the safe, and only the tokens moved from hand to hand. The receipt shifted from a record of a stored asset, to a transaction, to an anonymous bearer instrument whose value was underwritten by the promise of a good stored in some distant elsewhere.

Proudhon's Bank of the People was also an experiment in tokenisation. Notes were issued to users as a bill of exchange backed by property deeds. They traded at face value. The purpose of the token was to reduce usury and credit speculation; but it was also, in Proudhon's words, to 'convert property itself into money; to free it, to mobilize it, to make it circulable like money'.[6]

Art, as the Mahama lawsuit suggests, is also routinely tokenised: valuable works are purchased for investment and shipped directly to tax-free spaces known as free ports. And here they stay, until the time is right for them to be sold. Like Friedman's observation of bullion in the Federal Reserve, a painting can change hands in the free port without ever leaving the building, and be used as collateral to finance future loans.

Like the rai stone or the goldsmith's deposit, in many cases the certificate or deed for the work takes precedence over the work in question, housed in some distant elsewhere. In 2002, for example, a collector lost his certificate of authenticity for a Dan Flavin sculpture in a fire. The work, which survived, was an arrangement of fluorescent light tubes like the ones you might find at a local garden centre. Without the piece of paper detailing ownership and authenticity, however, the light sculpture was no longer deemed to be a 'real' Flavin. It was made of the exact same stuff, but now it was worthless.[7]

Since 2013, blockchain companies have been exploring ways of associating physical assets like fine art or gold with cryptographic tokens. This involves coupling a physical object to a hash, recorded on a blockchain. Instead of a hash encoding the details of a transaction, it records information about the ownership and authenticity of an asset. This information can be verified by comparing a hash of the object with one stored on the blockchain to ensure they match. In some cases, smart contracts are also associated with the hash – automated pieces of code written to manage the sale and transfer of the goods in question. Companies are now linking fine art, real estate, natural assets, gold bullion, precious stones, and just about any tangible asset imaginable with cryptographic tokens. These tokens may represent full or fractional ownership of an object that exists somewhere in the real world.

Everledger was one of the earliest companies to experiment with asset tokenisation. The company lists diamonds on the blockchain. Every diamond, it turns out, has a unique signature, and diamond houses grade and certify each gem for the market. Everledger uploads this data to the blockchain, along with details of the diamond's provenance. And there it stays, 'forever', or until the ledger is abandoned – whichever comes first. The service is attractive for investors who want to unlock the liquid value in their diamond investments, but also for retailers who want to be able to trace the ethical provenance of their precious stones and prove to prospective buyers that their particular diamond was ethically sourced.

In 1999, Systemics Inc. launched DigiGold, an internet payments account 100 per cent backed by gold held in Bermuda. More recently, in the face of Bitcoin and Ethereum's volatility, Singapore-based Digix Global returned to the principles of the gold standard, tokenising gold bullion stored in the Singapore Safehouse. One DGX token is equivalent to 100 grams of stored gold. Once more, investors benefit from the advantages of having a stable, illiquid asset, while also taking advantage of the arbitrage and liquidity offered by a virtual token. Digix allows investors to acquire tokens that represent ownership of a real commodity, in other words, but trade and move assets in ways that defy the limits of physical goods and locations. 'Don't be limited by the physicality of gold in vaults', the website reads under a tab titled: 'Move gold across borders.' Such tokens are like dreams of teleportation, of real things whizzing around above our heads in thousands of bits. One way the company moves its gold is through a token that is listed on an exchange alongside other tokens. The tokens would have 'the same functionality as money, and you could transfer between ether, bitcoin and other currencies, just like money', the company's founder Kai Chng tells me. 'We want our product to be a stable point in a volatile world.'[8]

In March 2022, Santander, the Spanish banking multinational, partnered with Agrotoken, an Argentinian platform, to offer loans in Argentina backed by tokenised crops of soy, corn, and wheat. One thousand farmers received loans collateralised with tokens that were based on soybeans (SOYA), corn (CORA), and wheat (WHEA), listed by Agrotoken. One token corresponds to a ton of grain stored in a grain elevator. The company plans to expand to Brazil and the United States – thereby encompassing the three countries that together account for over 70 per cent of the world's production of these crops. In the summer of 2022, they also partnered with Visa to use the crops as a payment method; farmers were issued debit cards backed by their grain stores. The tokens were 'Agrocommodities', like 2022 was ancient Mesopotamia.

Warhol on the Blockchain

Blockchain technologies are also used as a provenance, traceability, and authentication tool for goods. Works are stored in high-security warehouses, represented by virtual tokens, and traded as equity, divided into shares, or used to secure loans. One example is Maecenas, a start-up tokenising physical works of art on the Ethereum blockchain. Maecenas allows dealers to list up to 49 per cent of the value of a painting. The company has developed its own token – provocatively named ART – a clearing and settlement token for art auctions. Investors can buy fractions of famous paintings, not to stick them on their wall, obviously, but as part of a broader portfolio of investments. The Maecenas whitepaper gives a description of this process:

> Maecenas uses blockchain technology to create tamper-proof digital certificates linked to pieces of art … A single artwork is broken down into thousands of certificates, similar to how a public company issues shares. Investors can then purchase these certificates to own a percentage of a given artwork, and they can sell them back to other investors at any time via the Maecenas exchange. Artworks can be listed in any fiat currency (e.g. USD, EUR) or cryptocurrency (e.g. BTC, ETH).[9]

I met Jérôme Croisier, the CFO of Maecenas, in January 2018 at an art and finance event in Sotheby House, London. Croisier is an art historian based in Switzerland with a background in the fine-art auction business. He lectures in Zurich University's executive master's programme in art-market studies. He described Maecenas as 'like a Nasdaq for fine art', a platform where art owners could raise capital in a process similar to an IPO. The blockchain, as Croisier saw it, was first and foremost a tool to access the equity tied up in the work. 'Art is not *made* for investment, obviously', he told me, 'but it does have value "locked up" inside it. Stored value.'[10] Blockchain records also potentially allowed for an added layer of security and provenance.

In late 2018, Maecenas tokenised shares in an Andy Warhol work entitled '14 Small Electric Chairs' (1980), a multiple screen print of the device used to execute the alleged communists

Julius and Ethel Rosenberg in 1953. The work was broken into fractions represented by tokens on the Ethereum blockchain. Buying a token was buying the rights to a share in a collectively owned work by Warhol. The auction offered 31 per cent of the painting, valued at $5.6 million. Buyers could bid using bitcoins, ether, or ART.

In 2022, Signum, a Zurich-based crypto bank, auctioned shares in a Picasso painting, *Fillette au béret* (1964). A total of 4,000 tokens were sold, at 1,000 francs a piece, to hopeful investors and issued as art security tokens. The bank speaks fancifully of 'teleporting' the good onto the blockchain, but what are actually teleported are the legal ownership rights. The painting itself was stored in a nearby free port, awaiting sale.

It is easy to collapse the tokenisation of physical things into the NFT frenzy, but there are ostensibly differences between tokenised physical assets and non-fungible tokens. First, each of the tokens representing a fraction of the Warhol piece was fungible or interchangeable with the others, in the same way any €5 note is supposed to be interchangeable with any other. NFTs, on the other hand, are non-fungible; each one is unique. Second, the ownership rights associated with these physical goods are generally more secure. NFTs are tokens that are often loosely 'associated' or 'affiliated' with a digital good. More often, owning an NFT of a film does not give the owner any rights to the footage. But with a tokenised security, the buyer does legally *own* a ton of grain or an ounce of gold or a fraction of a Picasso – even if they never come into contact with it. The token is a share in a real thing, even if there is no way to possess or use the thing in question, and even if the thing is locked up in a grain house or a free port at some distant location, or buried at the bottom of the ocean. Legally, there is a difference; practically, I am still unsure if there's much of a difference at all.

Sharing Nicely

Tokenisation represents an attempt to account for things, though largely as a means of making those things more liquid, accessing the equity tied up in illiquid assets like paintings and gold bullion. In 2019, economist Glen Weyl and legal scholar Eric Posner prescribed 'radical markets' as a cure-all for the stagnant economy: every asset, from spare time to rental homes, bikes, and umbrellas could be represented as a token and auctioned on an ongoing basis. In 2001, legal scholar Yochai Benkler outlined a similar concept. He called it 'sharing nicely'. In a proposal that anticipated the business model of Zipcar and Airbnb by almost a decade, Benkler bemoaned the excess value locked up in everyday goods, from cars and houses to radio spectrum. Wouldn't it be much better, Benkler mused, if, instead of exclusive private property that we guarded jealously, we had a really granular economic system for allocating and auctioning this leftover value. Here the invocation to 'share' is less about altruistic giving and more about turning solid things into equity tokens. More shares, less sharing. Tokens imagine that things might shake off their material trappings and whatever it is that makes them lumpy and unwieldy, and become instead pure value or information, an on-demand economy with a price for everything and everything for purchase: Yap stones, paintings, and diamonds whizzing around above our heads like Mike Teavee.

This ambition to make things more liquid is at the heart of crypto. Timothy May, founder of the Cypherpunk mailing list, observed in 1992 that 'crypto anarchy will create a liquid market for any and all material which can be put into words and pictures'.[11] Tokens could make a liquid market for any 'thing' or non-thing that could be represented by a piece of code: tokens to move past the constraints of bodies, physics, or geography, to unlock equity and onboard real value into the metaverse. As a Money20/20 panellist put it twenty-five years later: 'We might trade equity in just about any *thing* for anything else!' I don't remember his name, or even the panel, but he was telling a story about the future internet of things; but instead of those things talking to each other, they were busy transacting – a smart car bidding for parking space, an umbrella trading shares in itself when it rained.

With tokenisation, Kai Ren and Zakie Twainy observe, 'any asset can move almost instantly'.[12] Tokens are a kind of geospatial arbitrage, a way to push aside the frictions and messiness of the 'what' and the 'where'. And yet, just as it works to forget where things are located, the blockchain has also been suggested as a tool for tracing the provenance of assets like diamonds and fine art. The art world takes this business of provenance very seriously. It has to. When I worked as an invigilator in the Irish Museum of Modern Art, a Marlboro Red cigarette was stolen from an installation piece one summer. The damaged work was cordoned off and eventually sent away for restoration. A formal enquiry was launched. The invigilator on duty in the room at the time nearly lost his job. Two foreign exchange students shared a cigarette worth thousands of euro. Sending a technician to the nearby shops for a totally identical cigarette would have been a quick material fix for the damage, but one that would destroy the transmutations of value at play in the work of art – the 'creative diversions' that Appadurai refers to.[13] It would poke a hole in the shared consensus. It would be like printing your own money.

'It was a Jack Pierson,' a former colleague says when I ask her if she remembers the incident, 'and we don't know for sure [redacted] was asleep.' Alongside enigmatic drawings and paintings, Pierson's work features arrangements of found furniture and miscellaneous objects. In art history, these are known as readymades, because the artist does not make anything new, but simply designates an existing mass-produced object as 'art'. Dan Flavin's light bulbs, Pierson's crumpled pack of Marlboros, and Mahama's jute sacks all trouble the relationship between art, representation, and intrinsic value.

But maybe our first mistake is in thinking that diamonds or gold or cigarettes are *intrinsically* valuable goods, that value can ever be found in the thing 'in its own right', as opposed to in the legitimating stamp of social and institutional consensus. *Outside of Borders* treats the circulation of goods in a global economy; but, at the same time, it points, a little slyly, to the circulation of value in a globalised art market: the institutional walls and signatures and paper trails that see an old jute sack or a primed canvas turn into a valuable asset. Like fiat money, readymade artworks come to suggest that value emerges from the extrinsic structures surrounding the object rather than from the intrinsic 'thinginess' of the thing itself.

Art Is an Asset Class

In the aftermath of the Brexit vote, LA dealer Stefan Simchowitz maintained that art was a store of wealth, a means of exchange, and a hedge. 'Art will effectively continue its structural function as an alternative currency that hedges against inflation and currency depreciation', he claimed. As Simchowitz argues, investors are encouraged to buy art as a way of diversifying and managing risk in the face of market volatility. Art investment is not exactly the safest bet, but trends in this market do not always follow the ups and downs of the overall economy. This makes art a good 'hedge' in a portfolio, potentially offsetting losses from an unexpected downturn while keeping the door open to an unexpected windfall. The recent pandemic seems to support this theory: while galleries initially struggled to remain afloat during the pandemic, the sale of art increased overall. The market was thriving in the midst of all that uncertainty.

Deloitte's report, 'Why Should Art Be Treated as an Asset Class?', argues that while art has always been an investment, opportunities are growing due to low interest rates in other investments and the sense that technologies like the blockchain might solve extant issues with authenticity, risk, high transaction costs, market transparency, and market regulation. Deloitte's 'Art and Finance' reports (published approximately every two years) also mention an increase in what are called 'High Net Worth Individuals' (or simply HNWIs – 'han-wees') looking to invest their capital in 'passion assets' such as cars, fine wine, and fine art.[14] Despite the name, the value of these goods is usually divorced from pleasure. In a keynote at the Talking Galleries Symposium in Barcelona in 2015, Marc Spiegler, the global director of Art Basel, described the death of what he called the 'connoisseur collector' – a buyer intimately acquainted with the art world. Spiegler described the emergence instead of a new breed of plutocrat collectors who buy 'with their ears, not with their eyes'.[15] Banks and boutique lenders are developing new financial instruments specifically for this market. Art investment funds, in which buyers club together to invest in a portfolio of works, are one example. Another is art securitisation, where collectors use works in their portfolio as equity to raise capital and secure future loans.

Collective art ownership is not exactly new. André Level, the secretary of the Board of Docks and Warehouses and director of the French Society of Transport and Refrigerated Warehouses, established the first art investment fund in Paris in 1904. It was called La Peau de l'Ours (The skin of the bear), after a Jean de la Fontaine story in which two enterprising hunters sell the hide of an animal they have yet to capture and shoot. Level was responsible for managing and acquiring the artworks, and his background in supply-chain logistics shaped his approach to the paintings as an investable commodity.

The British Rail Pension Fund (BRPF) art investment programme was established in 1974, in the period after the termination of Bretton Woods and the oil crisis. The fund was designed to hedge against the inflationary risks of the period by investing in collectibles: mostly Impressionist paintings, but also

books, manuscripts, prints, and *objets d'art*. While many were
outraged at the decision to invest railway workers' pensions in
elitist artworks, the fund explained that the decision was driven
by the lack of good investment options at the time: the London
stock market had fallen and the property market had collapsed,
while exchange-control regulations and a high dollar premium
made it difficult to invest abroad.[16] The works were sold in a
series of auctions through the 1980s and 1990s, generating an
overall 13 per cent return on investment. Profits were boosted
by selling at the height of a Japanese-driven speculative boom
in Impressionist paintings.[17]

A solution to falling profit margins from the 1970s onwards
was to utilise financial products as a means of maintaining
and expanding monetary assets, placing the money in financial
activities remote from the production of material goods. Then,
as now, these assets were a way of making money not by producing and selling new *things*, but by staking a position with
respect to illiquid assets like real estate and art.

Alongside the growth of art investment funds, art-backed
lending – whereby owners can use works of art in their collections as security on future loans – is on the rise. Banks
and large auction houses like Christie's and Sotheby's, new
boutique lenders with a particular focus on art lending have
entered the market. Some believe tokens could ease the frictions involved in selling and securitising the work. Croisier
described Maecenas, the company tokenising fine art on a
blockchain, as less an asset fund than a securitisation vehicle,
with a marketplace for shares and a secondary marketplace
for bonds. Collectors could access the latent equity tied
up in a Warhol in the same way they might remortgage a
property.

The Free Port

Free ports – high-security warehouses located in offshore enclaves – have emerged as veritable 'banks' for the collections of wealthy individuals and art funds eager to exploit their duty-free storage conditions. Even more recently, blockchain companies such as Maecenas and Codex have partnered with free ports. These companies are developing strategies for recording the provenance and circulation of art sales on the blockchain; for creating new tokens that can be associated with artworks and traded as shares; and for facilitating the securitisation of flows of capital on the back of artworks registered on their blockchain.

Historically, free ports are places where goods extracted from elsewhere – tea and opium from China, cocoa from Africa, grain from Germany – were stored before being shipped out again. Because the goods in question were only passing through, no duty was applied – it was as if they were never there at all. These spaces still exist today, where they are routinely exploited for their duty-free status.

Like tokens, free ports are part of the infrastructure that makes solid goods more liquid in a global marketplace. When an artwork enters the free port, it allows a buyer to hold it there indefinitely without paying tax, while they await the right conditions for resale. In the meantime, the free port also provides a secure base to list the work as collateral for a loan. A buyer can potentially use the work, or even sell shares to finance the purchase of other works, for example, often without having to surrender the work itself to the bank, depending on the jurisdiction. The art is fiscally 'in transit' from one place to another, even if it is going nowhere anytime soon. In turn, the free port acts as a kind of 'bank' for art, and the works in question are assets, resting indefinitely in high-security vaults, even changing hands without changing location.

Free ports form part of a broader offshore global infrastructure.

From a legal standpoint, these places are extraterritorial – many are located in the transit zones of airports or in historically tax-free areas. They are outside of borders. A kind of geospatial arbitrage, these fluid geographies are also well established in offshore spaces and asset-protection trusts – extra-legal contortions designed to exploit arbitrage and avoid the tax regime of a specific jurisdiction. A hotel might be present in New York but fiscally located in the Cayman Islands; a company might have all its infrastructure located in one jurisdiction but be officially registered in another, with more favourable tax breaks.

In place of the public museum, vast collections are now housed in these high-security non-spaces. The purpose of the artwork, these spaces suggest, is not to be possessed or traded as a commodity, let alone put on public or private view, but to function as a pure financial instrument. The asset is physically in the free port, but fiscally in transit from one zone to another, evading the specific duties and regulations of any single nation-state. Meanwhile, the token encrypts the asset value so that it can enter the market.

Free ports are a legacy of colonialism, goods and bodies flowing from south to north and from east to west. Free ports in Switzerland, in combination with the country's involvement in slavery and colonialism, contributed to making it one of the world's richest countries. While the Swiss had no colonies themselves, they were heavily involved in speculation, investing in the operations of colonialism elsewhere – particularly in the shipping companies that moved nearly 200,000 Africans to America. Berne and Zurich both had significant shares in the British slave-trading firm the South Sea Company. Swiss banks were involved in the slave trade – though not as directly as those in the United States, where banks routinely counted people as assets and accepted slaves as collateral for loans. Today, special economic zones are still spaces of exploitation: non-places with extra-legal working conditions, where the normal rules don't apply, where migrant workers can be paid less, where costs and bodies can disappear and the state can turn a blind eye.[18]

Free ports are a source of fascination for the artist Hito Steyerl, who sees them as emblematic of an institutional shift from the public museum – and from the artwork as a public good – to a globalised art market where art is just another asset class. In the age of the free port, art functions as a financial instrument without duties or obligations to the people or the nation-state. In turn, the state acts as a para-corporation whose main job is to shore up the market. The free port is a kind of blind spot in the supply chain, a place where regulators and states can, as Steyerl puts it, 'selectively [lose] control'.[19]

Because of the secretive nature of free ports, it can be difficult to account for exactly how many works of art are permanently housed in them. A *New York Times* article claims that the number in Le Freeport, Geneva, is close to 1.2 million, including some 1,000 Picassos. More recently designed free port spaces resemble museums more than warehouses. The Singapore free port, for example, has even commissioned a vast sculptural piece in its foyer, unironically entitled *Cage sans Frontieres* ('Cage without Borders').

In 2018, while giving a talk about blockchain in Geneva, I decide to visit the free port on the outskirts of the city, boarding the number 15 tram from Cornavin station and disembarking at Carouge, GE. Ports Francs et Entrepôts, in Geneva, occupies parts of an old freight station and an industrial storage building. The free-trade zone occupies the back of the old storage building, so that various jurisdictions run through one and the same construction.[20] It is a space that manages to be innocuous and imposing at the same time. The sense is of something deferred – from the logistical setting to my conversation with the security guard, who appears almost as soon as I cross the barrier into the entrance. The guard seems bemused about why a student of arts management (my bad cover story) would visit a space like this when I could surely visit a museum. Or he acts bemused, at any rate. 'Why would you want to look?' he asks. 'You can't even see the Picassos, right?' 'But they're there,' I venture, in my terrible French, waving my hand vaguely at the palettes and crates and the miles of brutalist architecture right behind us, 'er … inside. And that's of interest to me.' 'But that doesn't really matter when you can't see them,' he says – or something to that effect. 'It's so boring.' 'And besides,' he finishes, a little bluntly, 'it's private. "Visiting" is forbidden.'

Fractional ownership is sometimes framed as democratising access to a good, or more accurately as democratising access to speculative financial instruments: now the 99 per cent can own fractional shares of Manhattan real estate, or Picassos housed in a free port in Geneva. But this is misleading. It increases access to speculative financial instruments that are usually the purview of the mega-rich, but in doing so it often decreases public access to the artworks themselves. In *Duty Free Art*, Steyerl questions the morality of such an action. The 'duty' in the title references the offshore nature of the art market, of course, but also the question of whether culture has a duty to be seen and shared and viewed by the public, and whether the state still has a duty to make this happen.

No Longer Art, but …

Mahama's jute sacks bear a kind of material witness to where they have been in their weft, the thread used to sew and repair the fabric, the stamps of companies and exports on the bag's exterior. They are almost like the back of museum paintings, I think, with their legitimating stamps and seals that trace a history of auctions, institutional loans, and acquisitions. In China, such seal stamps form part of the artwork, Byung-Chul Han tells us. 'They are not a paratext but belong to the text itself.'[21]

'Certificates are highly secure and impossible to forge thanks to the cryptographic properties of blockchains', the Maecenas whitepaper states. Enthusiasts argued that records on the blockchain provide a good way to expedite the transfer and ownership of works of art, but also to keep track of the authenticity and provenance of a work – where it has been and where it is going to. Like the Chinese seal stamps, these traces become part of the value of the work of art. And yet, the issue that always seems to be pushed to one side when speaking of these tokenised goods is that of representation: How are a virtual token and a physical commodity tied together? How do I know somebody hasn't come along and switched out my painting for a replica after the record was placed on the blockchain? How do I even know that the information stored on the blockchain is accurate in the first place?

Everledger, the diamond company, deals with the problem through a digitised signature: even if a diamond is subsequently cut, the data points stored on the blockchain can help to recognise that it is *this particular* diamond in the future. Digix approaches it through detailed chains of custody and independent audits of its gold reserves. There are no fractional reserves, but simply a one-to-one relationship between their tokens and their assets. A similar approach is usually taken with so-called 'stable coins' tied to 'real-world' currencies: there is a supposed guarantee that the token is backed by real currency, and not just the idea of a real currency. Tokenised grain, meanwhile, uses what is called a proof-of-grain reserve, or POGR – an acronym that mimics the technical language of proof-of-work but ultimately amounts to the usual auditing processes, certificates, and paper trails. Art funds speak of fanciful and mostly unrealised solutions: digital watermarks; QR codes stuck to the back of a canvas; stickers; or 'smart dust', a special kind of spray that might coat physical things in indelible information. But ultimately it is very difficult to keep the physical thing out there in the real world coupled to its digital twin. The solutions get more and more convoluted, but ultimately what it comes down to in all cases, as Digix Global's CEO puts it, is 'trusting [that] the data is the truth'.[22]

Value Is in the Token

Tokens can represent a share in something, or a membership certificate; or they can be a codified representation of something that exists in the real world. But what happens to the value of my token if my artwork is damaged in a fire, or my grain gets spoiled, or my stone sinks to the bottom of the ocean? *And does it even matter?*

The term 'token' is sometimes used in English to refer to an object that stands in for a gesture or a feeling. The lover's token, the money-like keepsake inscribed with a message from a loved one, points to real feeling or affection, and is used to bring someone or something to mind: 'Look at this and think of me.' The token represents a real bond to something absent. But we might also describe words, actions, or gestures as being 'tokenistic' – a 'token apology' for empty words; a 'token marriage' for a relationship with no genuine feeling. The token points to some 'thing' – but the relationship between the two can be murky. Sometimes what we are pointing to is really there. And sometimes, it isn't.

During the Bretton Woods period, from 1944 to 1971, international currencies were stabilised by the convertibility of the US dollar to gold. All notes in circulation were a representation of gold in the Federal Reserve. But from 1910 until the postwar period, and from 1971 until today, that link was severed. With the end of Bretton Woods and the abolition of the gold standard, these monetary tokens were decoupled from any real-world referent. Like fiat currency, the state of what the token actually refers back to may no longer matter.

The financialisation of goods is not just a matter of allowing new kinds of things to enter the market. In facilitating new markets, the physical asset and its token, or instrument, begin to part company. In the transformation from commodity to exchange, the value of the token is decoupled from the underlying good itself and becomes a function of the information and confidence that swarms around it. 'Value' is no longer in possession of the good, but in possession of the token.

The flipside of this schism between owning and possessing occurs in Yves Klein's *Zones of Immaterial Pictorial Sensibility* (1962). Klein is an artist known for his performance works (and for patenting his own colour – a vivid shade known as International Klein Blue). In his 1962 work, Klein sold seven invisible zones of the river Seine in Paris for a pre-specified weight in gold. To purchase the work, the buyer had to meet Klein, and, in the presence of an expert witness of some sort (a museum director, curator, or gallery expert) and two other witnesses, transferred the gold to the artist. Klein would then throw half of the gold into the Seine, where it would be irretrievable – not unlike the rai stone that sank without a trace on the way to the island of stone money. The buyer would now be presented with a certificate of ownership for the immaterial zone. The catch was in the following clause: in order to *truly possess* the work in question, Klein specified, the buyer now had to burn the deed. Only then would he *truly* be its owner. From this point on, the work was no longer transferable. To accept the token was to relinquish ownership. To own it was to relinquish all possibility of future exchange. What remains of value when exchange is lost? What remains of art when exchange is all there is?

These are questions also posed by the Salvage Art Institute. The objects here are on display, but not in any way you're likely to confuse with a gallery exhibition; paintings rest on pallets, sometimes with the remnants of the packaging they were delivered in; sculptures and drawings lie flat on dollies.

An oil painting rests at an angle on a trolley. It is a realist pastoral scene – a harvest – only there's not much harvesting going on. The hay is stacked in the cart, ready for storage. The workers stand around in the sun, chatting, resting in the cut grass. In the foreground, a large tear runs directly through the withers of a cart horse, which continues to graze, unbothered. The canvas sort of flops open to reveal a section of the board underneath. The legend reads: 'SAI 0016: materials: oil, canvas; size 52'×35'; damage: 03/16/2010, torn in transit; claim 03/23/2010; total loss 03/2010; production 1850; artist: Alexandre Dubuisson; title: *La Moisson*.'

The term 'salvage art' draws from the insurance lexicon, describing works demoted from their status as fine art due to accidental damage. From a curious insurance perspective, salvage art objects are no-longer-art. Once the work is declared a 'total loss' and indemnity is paid, it is stripped of all exchange value and usually put into storage. The Salvage Art Institute takes these zombie-like objects and puts them on display.

SAI 0015 is a small aluminium-and-porcelain sculpture of a red balloon dog. Without reading the label, it is easily recognisable as a Jeff Koons. The poodle rests on its side on a dolly, its nose and part of its hind leg broken away. Beside it is a small, crumpled parcel with the word 'broken' scrawled across it in biro. The label says that the sculpture was 'shattered in a fall' in 2008. Now that the Salvage Art Institute has rescued it from an Axa warehouse, we can look at it once more. Like the luxury goods that defined the 1980s, Koons's sculptures are the ultimate Veblen good: a Möbius strip in value theory, where the object is worth something precisely *because* it is so expensive. If we are drawn to the little balloon dog, it is likely that we are here to feel a shiver of that deflated value. The work is materially much the same, but is no longer worth anything.

In her introduction to *The Picasso Papers*, critic Rosalind Krauss drew a connection between the rise of modernism – and, in particular, the readymade – and the death of the gold standard in 1910. From that moment on, as Tina Rivers Ryan observes, 'representation is arbitrary'.[23] This ontological instability was reflected in the art of the time. The link between representation and thing reared its head when Western countries abandoned the gold standard, and again when artists started to designate mass-produced objects as art. It was only a few years before Duchamp's first readymade, *Bicycle Wheel* (1913).

This tie between a representation and a thing is not only the biggest question surrounding the nature of money; arguably, it's the biggest question surrounding how cultures make value and meaning. This link between a representation and the thing it represents is what questions of language, art, and money distil to. Tokens become a map in search of a territory. This question appears when we encounter tokens that have no underlying asset at all: fiat money, conceptual artworks, tokens of authenticity for paintings encrypted in a free port. But it is also visible when we consider art assets that have had their value destroyed in some banal way – works of salvage art that have been officially written off against indemnity, Mahama's uncertified readymades, or newly discovered forgeries and fakes that were worth billions the day before they lost their token of authenticity.

In the *Grundrisse*, Marx diagrammed the relationship between commodities and money that he developed in Volume I of *Capital*. Money, Marx says, is backed by a commodity, a process whereby the exchange value of the good takes on a life of its own, independent from the underlying thing. This exchange value, represented by price, isn't in direct relationship with the material qualities of the thing, or with what kind of labour, skill, or materials went into making it, but rather in how exchangeable the thing is for other money, in who believes in it and who accepts it. This value exists separately from 'its matter, its substance'. 'In money', Marx writes, 'the *medium of exchange* becomes a thing, or, the exchange value of the thing achieves an independent existence apart from the thing. Since the commodity is a medium of exchange of limited potency compared with money, it can cease to be a medium of exchange as against money.'[24]

Marx argues that it is this splitting-off that makes complex finance possible: hoarding, stockpiling, speculating. The market walks a tightrope between abstract money and concrete commodities, and so too between fungibility and non-fungibility – too abstract and the money is worthless as a source of value; too concrete and the object is worthless as a means of exchange.

If the industrial economy perfected the material commodity – bringing together materials from distant places to make a toaster, for example – then the economy of finance runs this process in reverse, carving into the heft of things, making them more liquid.[25] But is there a limit to how far this process can go? How abstract can we get before we are once more forced to confront the matter of things? A third year of drought in Argentina threatens its 2022 grain exports. Meanwhile, the US government is building temporary grain silos on the border of Ukraine in an attempt to counteract a worldwide food shortage caused by problems with real borders in real places. Commodity tokens are attempts to make these material inconveniences disappear, to hide them in a vault or bury them beneath the ocean. 'All that is solid melts into air.' But in the end, we might not be able for much longer to overlook the real frictions between physical things in physical places, of physical bodies and climates and wars and borders, energy shortages and blockades. And most likely we shouldn't try.

Put It Back Where You Found It

Mahama's work explores how materials take on meaning as commodities. I discuss the Simchowitz lawsuit with my students every year in a class on economies of culture. I want us to think about the curious exchanges between art and money. Art and money are entwined; but as a society we retain the sense that culture should be somehow 'outside' the market. Presumably this is why people expect artists but not doctors to do stuff for free, and why some artists themselves feel a little funny about asking to be paid properly for their work. Presumably this is also why most people instinctively dislike the idea of free ports: it feels as if there might be something not only excessive, but also a little immoral about keeping a work of art locked away in a steel vault, unseen, just waiting to accrue in value.

Simchowitz destroys young artists' careers by buying and inflating their work, then selling it on at the opportune moment. Nobody expects anything different from an art dealer. But, for an artist, being seen as too mercenary is damaging to their reputation. Take, for example, a work like the British artist Banksy's *Girl with Balloon*. Banksy is a guerrilla graffiti artist whose career rests on his anti-commercial appeal. In the style of artists like Martha Rosler and Barbara Kruger, who remix the language of advertisement to assail capitalism, Banksy adopts the visual language of street advertising to attack consumer culture. *Morons* (2007) depicts the auction of Van Gogh's *Sunflowers*. The painting is replaced by a canvas bearing the slogan: 'I can't believe you morons actually buy this shit.' In 2018, a Banksy painting entitled *Girl with Balloon* was sold for £1 million at Sotheby's. Moments after the gavel dropped, a shredder hidden in the ornate frame whirred to life and partially destroyed the work.

Selling a work at auction for millions was surely a step too far. And so Banksy shredded the painting in an outward protest against capitalism. In the immediate aftermath, Max Haiven wrote about the event as a rousing blow against the assetisation of the artwork.[26] I couldn't disagree more. By only partially shredding the work ('a mistake', Banksy claimed), the artist worked to deny his complicity with the market, while, in denying it, also boosting his own cultural capital. Seeming to decry the market can be a necessary step to being taken seriously as an artist. The intact work sold for £1 million, but the partially shredded remains, retitled *Love Is in the Bin*, were sold by Sotheby's for more than £18.5 million.

For Mahama, I initially thought, the barefaced commodification of his jute sacks was possibly a step too far – damaging for his reputation as an observer and critic of global capitalism. Maybe the artist risked looking like a sell-out, signing away penny jute sacks to be flogged to wealthy collectors. But unlike artists like Banksy and Hirst, who appear at one level to deny the market while also reaping its rewards, Mahama funnels his profits back into the community. He seemed genuinely disturbed by what had taken place in the Jonathan Ellis King Gallery.

Prior to independence, Ghana was called the 'Gold Coast', both because of its rich natural resources and because of the gold sourced and traded there. The country remains the largest producer of cocoa. After independence in the early 1960s, President Kwame Nkrumah hired Eastern Bloc architects to build large towers. The brutalist structures were built to store maize, grain, and cocoa. The aim was to support the Ghanaian economy by tokenising these commodities in a global market. The plan was unsuccessful; the silos are now abandoned. But for Mahama, there is a poetics to these siloed buildings. Infrastructures are built to do things, like store grain; but they are also a way for the state to tell a story about itself, and ask citizens to take that story for the truth.[27] The decayed towers speak of self-determination and lingering hope.

In 2019, Mahama managed to acquire one of the abandoned grain silos to create the Savannah Centre for Contemporary Art, in Tamale, Ghana. Using profits from the sale of his art-works, Mahama transformed the building into an exhibition space, educational facilities, and artist residencies. These days, there are many calls for the repatriation of African artworks looted during the colonial era, but most contemporary African art that gets sold still ends up in Western institutions, free ports, and private collections, 'because that's where capital has accumulated'.[28] In 2020, Mahama opened a second space, Red Clay, with artist studios, outdoor play areas, and recording and editing suites for audio and film. This part of Mahama's practice is based around 'resurrection', the artist says. The 're' of reparations, and redistribution, and refunding embodies a kind of anti–free port logic – a belief that, sometimes, things need to be returned to their rightful place.

8

A Celestial Cyberdimension

Giving a little more thought to the idea of buying and selling digital cash, I thought of a way to present it. We're buying and setting 'cryptographic trading cards'. Fans of cryptography will love these fascinating examples of the cryptographic arts. Notice the fine way the bit patterns fit together – a mix of one-way functions and digital signatures, along with random blinding. What a perfect conversation piece to be treasured and shown to your friends and family. Plus, your friends will undoubtedly love these cryptographic trading cards just as much. They'll be eager to trade for them. Collect a whole set! They come in all kinds of varieties, from the common 1's, to the rarer 50's, all the way up to the seldom-seen 1000's. Hours of fun can be had for all. Your friendly cryptographic trading card dealer wants to join the fun, too. He'll be as interested in buying your trading cards back as in selling them. Try this fascinating and timely new hobby today!

Hal Finney (1993)

The Ethereal Summit in New York took place in May 2018. It featured a live-art auction of blockchain artworks hosted by Codex, a company dedicated to building a registry for unique assets, and the RARE art platform, a start-up keen to make digital works of art scarce and saleable. The works auctioned were 'crypto-art' NFTs – rare digital artworks associated with unique tokens on the Ethereum blockchain. Pieces included a Twitter whale, a watercolour of the Ethereum logo by Terry Cook, and a painting of a whitepaper by Andy Boot. Nothing ground-breaking aesthetically, but that was beside the point.

Most of the works sold for between $3,000 and $10,000, until the final lot of the evening, the *Celestial Cyber Dimension* cryptokitty, was brought to the stage. *Celestial Cyber Dimension* is a cryptokitty designed by the company's head of art, Guile Gaspar. Unlike most NFTs, this cryptokitty has a physical and a cryptographic element. The lot includes the ERC-721 token, but also a custom-made hardware wallet. The wallet contains the private key and a small Tamagochi-style animation of the cartoon cat. The auctioneer's voice catches in her throat as the bids reach $140,000, sold to an online bidder.

The cryptokitty phenomenon hangs somewhere between gacha (games where players pay to win rare characters), procedural art, and rare collectibles. It uses the Ethereum blockchain to produce a kind of digital scarcity, allowing consumers to buy, sell, and trade JPEGs as though they had a physical, rival dimension. Cryptokitties started life as a game in which players could run smart contracts to acquire, breed, and trade virtual cats. The smart contract contains a genetic algorithm to determine the details of each cat's characteristics (called – what else – 'cattributes'), including background, patterns, fur stripes, spots, colour, and facial expressions. The output is a gamble: a non-fungible token that is associated with a genetically unique cat.

Players can store the genomic data and perform various operations using the smart contracts, including making new kitties, renting their cats out for breeding with others, and auctioning their kitties to the highest bidder. In 2018, most of these cats traded for around $25, but a few were auctioned for more than $100,000. In 2018, these virtual pets had more market stability than many new cryptocurrencies, and their value had, as one commentator put it, 'risen (and fallen) at a far faster rate than just about everything in the analogue art world'.[1]

In 2021, an NFT of Nyan Cat, an adorable 2011 meme of a cat with a Pop-Tart for its body, sold for 300 ether, the equivalent of about $590,000 at the time. (The original animated

GIF was based on artist Chris Torres's cat Marty, who died of feline coronavirus in 2012.) Between 2018 and 2020, companies emerged specialising in minting NFTs, including OpenSea, Mintable, and Ramble. To create an NFT, all an artist needed to do was download a wallet supporting the ERC-721 standard, and buy some ether to pay the gas (processing) fees.

NFTs exploded in 2021, alongside widespread investment in cryptocurrencies. In the face of another economic catastrophe, investors and everyday users were hedging their bets, and the price of Bitcoin and Ethereum shot up. Swarm activism on Reddit destabilised financial markets, and a cryptocurrency based on a Shiba Inu internet meme spiralled when Elon Musk bought some for his newborn child. NFTs suddenly became mainstream news. As one of my students, a hard-core crypto-enthusiast, observed, even his most 'basic' friends suddenly wanted to buy ether.

What followed was a series of giddy auctions for digital artworks that peaked with the sale of Beeple's *Everydays: The First 5,000 Days* for $69 million, making it the third-most-expensive artwork ever auctioned. The buyer, MetaKovan, planned to build a monument to the work in the metaverse. Established digital artists were watching YouTube tutorials to learn how to mint NFTs of their work, but NFTs were latching onto all kinds of intangible value. The National Basketball Association released NFTs of Top Shots – choice video highlights from games. Beeple established a company called WENEW, dedicated to tokens of 'iconic moments in time'. A bot called @tokenisedtweets was minting NFTs of famous people's pithy observations faster than they could delete them. Yuga Labs shilled images of wealthy primates; EtheRock shilled clipart pictures of stones; and luxury fashion houses shilled virtual clothing on Decentraland's wearables market.

How did it feel? It felt like everyone who hated contemporary art was, and always had been, absolutely right. It felt that, as the future looked dark, culture became a farce, a meme of a joke. The joke evolved to the point where the punchline wasn't funny. The joke was no longer a cat with a Pop-Tart for its body; the 'funny thing' was now that so many people were taking part in something so meaningless and dumb. You are the joke – and so is capitalism.

But what exactly is an NFT? The previous chapter explored 'tokenisation' – how the ownership of all or part of a good such as fine art, gold bullion, diamonds, or carbon credits could be recorded on the blockchain and transferred using a smart contract. Non-fungible tokens fall into this category. They are cryptographic tokens whose value is tied to a unique digital item. This could be a rare skin in a computer game, a song, a virtual pair of Gucci Marmont loafers, a GIF of an athlete, or a popular meme.

In 1993, Cypherpunk Hal Finney playfully suggested that cryptography might be used as the basis for trading cards – 'the cryptographic arts!'[2] As early as 2012, developers were experimenting with linking cryptographic tokens to the ownership of digital assets. While Bitcoin tokens are all identical – or 'fungible', in the language of economics – Israeli entrepreneur Yoni Assia speculated that a token could be marked up to distinguish it from others. The 'Coloured Coin', as the initiative was called, was tied to ownership of an asset.[3] (Assia went on to collaborate with Vitalik Buterin on asset ownership using blockchain.)

In 2017, Ethereum developed what was called the ERC-721 standard for non-fungible tokens, allowing a token to represent the ownership of a good. Unlike standard coins that are, at least in theory, 'fungible', meaning that they can be exchanged for each other, NFTs are associated with a unique asset. 'Think of them like rare, one-of-a-kind collectables', the Ethereum page advises. The protocol takes an everyday token and turns it into a smart contract for the exchange of a one-of-a-kind token – something a little bit like a collector's item or a centenary coin.

In 1913 and 1914, suffragettes etched the slogan 'Votes for Women' across the image of Queen Victoria on the 1897 penny coin. The countermarking of coins was an act of protest, but also a type of viral marketing. The 'Votes' coins were singled out from others in circulation. The political motif lent them a weight and significance beyond their exchange value. Today, a suffragette token is worth a lot more than an ordinary Victorian penny. They tell a story. They capture a moment. What's more, while pennies are worth pennies and normal Ethereum tokens are worth their current exchange value, non-fungible tokens are worth whatever someone is willing to pay for them.

These non-fungible tokens could be used to record and automate the ownership and transfer of digital items, and to treat these digital items – things that can be copied many times at the click of a mouse – as though they had a scarce or rival dimension. But unlike tokenised assets, which mark an ownership stake in a real asset like land, diamonds, or an Andy Warhol piece, an NFT's claim or stake is less certain. In most cases, NFTs are 'associated' with a digital asset. Having an NFT of a cryptokitty or a famous Top Shot does not usually give the owner any exclusive rights to the image or the footage, any more than having an 1897 penny gives the bearer rights to Queen Victoria's likeness.

Information Wants to Be Free?

In 1989, Tim Berners-Lee developed the World Wide Web. He had been working on it in his free time in CERN, a research institution that straddles the French–Swiss border in Geneva. The Web was an information-management system – it consisted of documents hosted on servers and retrieved and connected by URL hyperlinks. The network was decentralised – any server was able to link to any other server. The links went in one direction: you could follow the chain forward, but not back to its origins.

Berners-Lee emphasised openness and flexibility in his Web – not as a political project exactly, but as a design strategy that allowed the network to scale with as little friction as possible.

In June 2021, at the height of the NFT craze, Berners-Lee auctioned 10,000 lines of source code for the World Wide Web at Sotheby's as a token stored on the Ethereum blockchain. The lot sold for £3.9 million.

Tim Berners-Lee's World Wide Web was not the only experiment with hyperlinks taking place in 1989. Another was Xanadu, a project the computer scientist Ted Nelson began in 1964. Nelson described his vision in a self-published book, *Literary Machines*.[4] He dedicated the manuscript to Eric Blair, an author better known by his pen-name, George Orwell.

Like the World Wide Web, Xanadu was a system for the storage and retrieval of digitised content. At first blush, Xanadu looks like just another version of hypertext, but it was, in fact, a different economic vision of the internet. Instead of Berners-Lee's one-way links, Nelson's links were two-way. You could link forward, but you could also backtrack to the original source. This version of hypertext allowed anyone to publish information, but if someone wanted to *use* that information and link to it, a micropayment system delivered small royalty fees to the owner's bank account. Royalty fees were denominated in units called 'nibs' – an owner's reserve charged per byte of information. Open-source materials accrued nibs to an 'author's fund' to sponsor future scholarship and creativity.

As well as anticipating the World Wide Web, a system where all information is 'clearly and instantly available to use, in a great interconnected web of writings and ideas', Xanadu also imagined a system for the *ownership* of that information, where changes are logged and filed chronologically. Like the blockchain twenty years later, it was sold as 'a linking system for keeping track of anything', and 'a grand address space for everything, parts of which can be in different places at once'.[5] Nelson's links made it possible to own and monetise information in a new way. Referencing and using another text meant linking to it in memory, a process that also set in motion a monetary transfer to the author's account: links for nibs.

Nelson and Berners-Lee met in the summer of 1992 for lunch at the Xanadu offices in San Francisco. In his biography, Berners-Lee remembers he was nervous because a cheque sent to Nelson for a copy of *Literary Machines* had bounced, and he wanted to be sure to give him the funds as soon as possible. As fate would have it, project Xanadu had had its funding pulled that very morning. They shared lunch; Nelson paid. Berners-Lee photographed his mentor with a 35mm camera for his scrap book. Nelson took a video of the inventor of the World Wide Web for a detailed life log he was keeping for posterity.[6] When it came to it, Tim Berners-Lee was critical of Nelson's micropayment system, feeling that it added a layer of unnecessary friction to the system of information retrieval. Information wants to be free, after all.

For a long time, the cultural industries were based on making things that are not naturally subject to scarcity *artificially* scarce: things like ideas, songs, prints, photographs, recipes, and know-how.

Digital technologies tore artificial scarcity to the ground. Consumer electronics have made it cheap to copy digital content; compression and high-bandwidth networks have made it easy to store and circulate that content via the internet; and the architecture of the World Wide Web makes it difficult to trace pathways of dissemination. Napster was born. Copying and sharing are the same thing on the contemporary (which is to say Berners-Lee's) internet. As the National Research Council wrote at the height of Napster, 'Digital copies are also perfect replicas, each a seed for further perfect copies.'

Every time you choose to share a digital file – of a book or a Word document or a photo – you are making a fungible copy. These copies do not degrade through successive reproduction: each one is freshly minted.

In response, the industry tried various things, from changing the norms around copying digital content – 'You wouldn't steal a purse ...' – to lobbying governments to make copyright law and practice more extensive, as with the Digital Millennium Copyright Act. Another strategy was to develop new technologies to prevent users from copying or sharing digital files. Digital rights management (DRM), as this technology is called, included the design of region-specific codecs, embedded watermarks, security codes, and algorithmic copy protection.

An early approach used what were known as 'rootkits' – auto-executable programs that acted on a system as though they were an administrator (or 'root') user. In 2005, Sony embedded rootkit software on all of its music CDs. The software gained administrative privileges on a user's machine without their knowledge. From there, it prevented copying software from accessing the CD. It also prevented any installation of copying software on the user's computer.[7]

Other companies gradually shifted to a model where digital files were streamed or leased from a cloud-based server. In an early controversy surrounding Amazon's Kindle, a book found to be in breach of copyright after it was sold was automatically removed from thousands of consumer devices without their knowledge or consent. The book was George Orwell's *Nineteen Eighty-Four*.

Limited Editions

Before NFTs, there was thought to be no real market for digital art, though online games, artists, and gallerists had experimented with ways of making digital images more scarce or 'collectible'. Mt Gox, the first Bitcoin exchange, started life as an online trading portal where virtual 'Magic: The Gathering' cards were traded like stocks. Online games scripted virtual loot on a central server and, to the best of their ability, controlled how and when items were released into the game. Others used embedded watermarks to try to deter users from right-click saving their images. In 2014, a 4chan thread discussed watermarking and selling rare Pepe memes: 'I have 10 mint condition rare pepe pics on my flashdrive that's inside my safe and I could buy and sell your whole family if it was on the open market.'[8]

Daata Editions and Framed looked to market digital art as if it was something in an IKEA showroom, turning a GIF into a giant flat screen installed on the buyer's living room wall. Ephemeral video works and installations were sold with caveats as to where and when they could be screened: Christian Marclay's video montage, 'The Clock' (2010), was to be viewed in real-time in a gallery context (though this didn't stop hedge-fund manager Stephen A. Cohen from using his edition as a screensaver).[9] Others suggested that file metadata might be used to create a kind of indexical trace for digital objects – a value attached to where a digital file had been and who it had encountered.

Some digital artists sold their code. In 2001, Rafël Rozendaal auctioned the source code behind his website-based artworks. The website ifnoyes.com, sold in 2013, features a queasy geometric pattern that flexes and folds as a cursor rolls over the image. The open tab states that the website is part of the collection of Benjamin Palmer. Palmer, who purchased the work for $3,500 at the Phillips auction house in New York, did what many NFT buyers would do next. He didn't hang it on his wall – he posted a picture of the artwork to his Twitter profile.[10]

In 2015 artist Lorna Mills invited other well-known internet artists to make works for a video piece called *Ways of Something*. The work, a mash-up of GIFs, drawings, and archival footage, is a remix of the John Berger documentary *Ways of Seeing*, itself a response to Walter Benjamin's 1935 essay, 'The Work of Art in the Age of Mechanical Reproduction'. In this essay, which every undergraduate art student reads at some point, Benjamin argues that photography potentially destroys what he refers to as the 'aura' of the original work of art: 'its presence in time and space, its unique existence in the place where it happens to be' – what crypto-enthusiasts might today call its 'nonfungibility'.[11]

The original is not a universal concept. Benjamin's 'aura' is a product of Western philosophy and aesthetics. Western culture's rejection of mimesis can be traced back to Plato's concept of being. It equates beauty with the unique, allowing for no reproduction or facsimile. In every copy, the Korean-born philosopher Byung-Chul Han writes, 'this [Western] notion of being sees something demonic that destroys original identity and purity'.[12] Far Eastern culture, on the other hand, draws no hard distinction between the copy and the original. Instead of objects being 'things', with 'a unique position in time and space', as Benjamin puts it, objects are traces and paths that are constantly evolving. Copies are not inferior to originals, because originals are always also copies of some sort or other. There is no 'aura' to the work of art.

A decade after Benjamin published his essay, Han van Meegeren's forgery of Vermeer's *Christ and the Adulteress* landed him in jail in Nazi Germany. At first the work was so technically precise that people refused to believe it *was* a copy. Van Meegeren had to paint another forged Vermeer – *Jesus among the Doctors* – in court before everyone believed the 'fake' was 'real'. During the proceedings, Van Meegeren questioned the fetish of the authentic work of art. Surely his indistinguishable copies demonstrated that the aura was not something inherent to the material qualities of the painting itself, but to some external consensus – a token of authenticity? 'Yesterday this picture [Van Meegeren's copy of *Christ and the Adulteress*] was worth millions. Experts and art lovers from all over the world came to see it. Today it's worth nothing and nobody would even cross the road to see it for free. But the picture hasn't changed. What's different?'[13]

In *Ways of Something*, Mills retains the soundtrack and some of the video stills from John Berger's original documentary. As the art historian speaks over Brueghel's *The Procession to Calvary*, one of the invited artists, Joe McKay, joyfully Photoshops a cartoon Santa Claus shouldering the crucifix at the summit, replacing the dirt track of the Via Dolorosa winding through the painting with a JPEG of a motorway. In the background, a small, brightly coloured hot-air balloon hovers above the scene. The image abruptly pixelates, revealing itself to be displayed on the artist's own computer screen.

It is, by Mills's description, 'art about art about television about the internet'. It is also a tongue-out commentary on the remix, the internet-old claim that mashing up someone else's art is also art. In 2015, when a few start-ups were beginning to experiment with using the blockchain to record the ownership and provenance of digital artworks, Mills's New York gallerist, Kelani Nichole, used a company called Ascribe to sell tokenised high-definition stills of the video. The 113 artists who contributed to the work were all paid equally. If *Ways of Something* reflects remix culture, the idea that photography and then television, and finally the internet, have completely destroyed the concept of 'original' works, Mills's gallerist had just used the blockchain to create a marketable aura for digital art. The work was sold, Mills told me at the time in a Facebook chat, 'but when they offered me dollars or bitcoin, LOL, I took the cash $$$'.

Bitcoin was one of the first digital currencies, but it is also a type of digital scarcity, because it solved what was known as the 'double spend' problem. Double spending is an issue as old as digital cash: if I 'spend' a digital token, how do you, the recipient, know I haven't made and kept a copy for myself? Banks solve this by acting as a go-between for the transfer of value from Ann to Bob; sending the money means updating entries in a central ledger. Bitcoin, a decentralised currency with no middleman, solves this problem with cryptographic proof. A shared ledger (called a blockchain) tracks tokens so that they cannot be copied. (Or, to be specific, the ledger entries *are* the tokens.) But instead of an entry encoding who owns or transfers digital tokens, it might also record the ownership and transfer of digital artworks, ideas, music, or source code.

When the Ethereum blockchain emerged in 2014, it developed what are known as 'smart contracts'.[14] Think of them as digital vending machines, said Nick Szabo, who coined the term in the 1990s. Ethereum's smart contracts can record the ownership and provenance of digital and physical goods, or facilitate their transfer between different owners. They can allow for fine-grained rentals, micropayments, royalties, secondary royalties, and payments to multiple parties. Theoretically, any value can be linked and staked – digital art, memes, trees, carbon tokens, or plots of virtual real estate.

Smart contracts and non-fungible tokens offered a new business model to the cultural industries. This was not only a way to mint and sell 'unique' works of art in a purely digital form, and to keep track of their ownership and provenance like rare Pokémon animals; the tokens could also be used to attach conditions to their sale and transfer. Smart contracts could specify not only what kinds of ownership and use rights came attached to a work; they might also immediately remunerate multiple people, or factor in resale rights in situations where, if a digital image was resold in the future, a percentage of these profits would be returned to the original maker. As such, many creatives were drawn to it as a technology that could potentially 'cut out the middleman', allowing artists to release and license their own work and directly receive any fees for its sale, broadcast, or use.

In 2015, Rhizome gallery in New York hosted an event called 'Blockchain Horizons', imagining the future of the blockchain for the creative and cultural industries. Among the presenters was artist Kevin McCoy, who had developed a blockchain start-up called Monegraph. Previously, McCoy was best known for his self-referential internet artworks ('art about art about the internet', as Mills puts it). Monegraph was a departure – at the vanguard of developments in blockchain and the creative industries. It used the Bitcoin blockchain to record the owner-ship of digital images, be they works of art or stock photos. A proprietor, such as the artist or dealer, could use cryptography to authenticate a work and sign it with their private key. This would inscribe ownership details on the blockchain, producing an 'unbreakable chain of custody'.

Ownership could then be transferred in the same way that Bitcoin tokens are transferred from one wallet address to another. McCoy went so far as to make a user-friendly open-source layer on top of the system, through which artists could build smart contracts by choosing from a range of images representing rights to sell, use, or remix the work. As is often the case with blockchain, what began as an art project quickly became a business enterprise. In 2016, McCoy and his business partner Chris Tse filed numerous patents for blockchain appli-cations relating to the ownership and transfer of digital files.

Ascribe, the company that sold high-definition stills of Lorna Mills's work, was another enterprise that emerged at this time. Unlike Monegraph, which simply designated a particular file as 'the original', Ascribe fashioned itself as an 'ownership layer for the internet'. It offered a business model that made direct reference to Ted Nelson's failed visions for Xanadu. Digital files were designated 'the real one' using a blockchain in one layer, while, in another layer, an AI database trawled the internet to identify illegal 'copies'. The company struggled technically to realise such a far-reaching system. Internet-wide ownership was the end-goal, rather than the system as it worked in 2015. In practice, Ascribe countermarked one file as the original and, like Monegraph, did nothing actively to deter others from making inauthentic copies.

In 2015, I asked Lorna Mills how she felt about the sale of her work on Ascribe. If someone wanted to purchase a still of

Ways of Something, Mills answered, that was fine with her. Someone might 'own' a token of a screengrab, but the work was still available for free – anyone with a decent internet connection could watch it and make their own identical copies. So what kind of ownership *was* this? What kind of economy? What was the motivation to own a piece of something that is not quite a thing? And what do you 'get' when you own it, from bets to bragging rights and prestige, from standing out from the crowd to a greater sense of belonging?

Bragging Rights

Art Basel Miami's director Noah Horowitz describes some of the motivations for purchasing art in *Art of the Deal*. These impulses can overlap, and might not even be clear to the buyer themselves, but alongside those that come from recognising the aesthetic value of the work, or indeed from the sense that patronage of the arts is somehow a 'good thing to do', there are complicated forms of hedging at play.[15] For example, a buyer might purchase a work as an asset in the hope that its market value will increase in the future, or even make a purchase to prevent the bottom from falling out of a market they have already invested in. Damien Hirst and his dealer Jay Jopling, for example, have anonymously bought Damien Hirst artworks, and Beeple was allegedly part of the anonymous consortium that purchased *Everydays*.

But a buyer might also purchase a work of art because of what the act of purchasing says about them – culturally, socially, and economically. 'Signalling' plays a role in the acquisition of collectible coins and of virtual loot in online games. And signalling has always played a role in art markets. Buyers do not just buy a beautiful object or an asset they hope will grow in value; buying art is a self-investment in a world where social capital predicts economic returns. Using this framework, the purchase of the *Celestial Cyber Dimension* cryptokitty might have had several different motivations: the desire to possess an artwork that the buyer finds meaningful, to make a strategic investment in a niche market – or to acquire 'bragging rights', as a strategic investment in the buyer's own social and economic reputation going forward. Useless goods can be markers of social distinction. Their very lack of use can be a way of signalling that the buyer does not need to be productive. Here comes someone who is *stupidly* rich. Here, digital art might be the ultimate Veblen good – valuable, in a curious reversal, *because* it is so expensive, valuable because it brags.[16]

When we spoke about the mood of the auction itself, curator Ruth Catlow suggested that the purchase was also about the social or economic status of the buyer: 'In that moment the buyer was purchasing a souvenir of a moment – a moment he himself created by buying the token', she mused aloud.[17] Witnessing the giddy hype of the crypto-auction, Ruth was convinced that purchasing the token was also an act of 'signalling', designed to say something about the status of the buyer to the crypto community.

This chimed with the view offered by the auction's organiser, Jess Houlgrave. Houlgrave is a graduate of Sotheby's master's in art sales and founder of the Codex Protocol – a blockchain registry for what are sometimes called 'passion assets': art, wine, jewellery – but especially art. Houlgrave and her company featured in Forbes '30 under 30' list in 2019. Over breakfast in a London café in 2018, Houlgrave acknowledged that the prices fetched for art on the blockchain were often driven by a degree of bravado and ostentation on the part of the newly crypto-wealthy.[18] Here the work of 'art' isn't the cryptokitty, necessarily – maybe it is the auction of a token.

What gets purchased at an art auction? The buyer's own sense of self-worth? Their standing in the community? A token of a moment they helped to make happen? In the art auction, Jean Baudrillard writes, money (exchange value) gets turned into prestige (sign value). The art auction is unique for Baudrillard because it is an act of consumption where money (a sign) is exchanged for art (another sign).[19] In this sense, the label 'art' is the ideal ideological mechanism – a licence to print your own money. And in this moment of consumption, 'exchange' and 'use' value are no longer economically correlated. Use value is put out of play. Money is turned into a sign of prestige (a.k.a. a bragging right) that might be wagered in the future for greater financial returns. The sale of art becomes less about the material properties of a work, as we saw with the sale of works by Dan Flavin and Ibrahim Mahama in the previous chapter. Its material properties, its location in time and space – these are not so important. What matters more is the degree of information – call it vibes, bragging, hype, buzz, spectacle – that can be generated around it.

Friends with Benefits (FWB) is a decentralised autonomous organisation or DAO, an artist collective that uses blockchain tokens to unlock access, manage payments, and collectively vote on group investments. It emerged during the Covid lockdown in 2020, created by Trevor McFedries, one of the creators of the virtual Instagram influencer Lil Miquela. Friends with Benefits is not the first artist DAO; some of the earliest examples were built around art collectives. Just as Bitcoin ostensibly cut out the middleman from monetary issuance, these collectives hoped that a blockchain might be used to cut out the middleman in the cultural industries – the record companies, streaming services, gallerists, collecting agents, and auction houses – that take a significant slice of the artist's revenue.

In 2012, *Plantoid*, by the Okhaos collective, used Bitcoin tokens to commission a self-generating sculpture. Members of the public could 'feed' the plant by sending money to its public address. Once enough funds had accrued, Okhaos would collectively vote on a new commission for the work using smart contracts. Most of the results looked like steam-punk flowers. DAOWO (Distributed Autonomous Organisation With Others), founded in 2017 by the Furtherfield Collective in London (a.k.a. Ruth Catlow and Marc Garrett), wants to use blockchain to build collective art spaces. It has sought to find ways to sustain art beyond public or private funding.

And yet, while it is often framed as a radical disintermediator, in practice most NFT art leans heavily on the reputation of blue-chip galleries and institutions to make what would otherwise be 'scammy' deals feel more legitimate. Established auction houses like Christie's and Sotheby's help to elevate the sale of an ugly GIF to the status of fine art through the auction system. This is the special allure of the event – 'the magic', as Baudrillard writes, 'of an elective and selective community, fused together by the same rules of the game and the same system of signs'.[20]

Friends with Benefits is not the first example of its kind, then, but it received the most mainstream attention, with over 6,000 members including musicians Azealia Banks and Erykah Badu. It was like a virtual art club – a Soho House for the metaverse. Only, instead of premises, the collective runs on multiple Discord channels dedicated to fashion, music, art, and live-streamed event content. Users must buy into the FWB token to become a member of the collective. Like medieval tokens that conferred access to exclusive orgies and feasts, the FWB tokens unlock access to select gatherings and parties. Five FWB tokens makes someone a local member, giving them access to the group's Discord. Global membership costs seventy-five FWB tokens, plus a formal application and interviews with the FWB Host Committee. If membership is approved, this buy-in gives the member access to an NFT gallery and to special 'token-gated' events.

For the Friends with Benefits DAO, the benefit is in what sociologist Pierre Bourdieu called 'social capital' and 'cultural capital', to put a name to the economic clout of amorphous connections, good vibes, and good taste.[21] And, like the art auction, the DAO works to seize the floating value of these benefits and turn them into economic capital. Founder Alex Zhang compares the FWB DAO to the merchant class of Venice in Renaissance

Europe (the heads of state were even called doges). With Friends with Benefits, 'what you're getting is vibes', he says: 'This token is starting to reflect some of the value of those vibes':

> $FWB is a cryptocurrency that's tied to the Friends With Benefits DAO. Having our own tokens enables us to incentivize community participation and generate value collectively. While $FWB tokens can be purchased in any amount by anyone, and everyone who holds $FWB can have a voice in the DAO's governance, only official FWB members can earn $FWB as a reward for participation. This is a way of bolstering the value we provide to each other as an engaged and close-knit community.[22]

The token traded on vibes. The vibe is distinctly Burning Man: self-congratulatory counter-culture meets extreme libertarian economic privilege. Like Burning Man, the group also had the ambition to create their own exclusive gatherings. One of these events was a three-day festival in the grounds of Idyllwild Arts Academy, a private boarding school two hours' drive from Los Angeles. Among the attractions were a digital gallery hosted by OpenSea, a natural wine garden, sound baths with mushroom tea, pool parties, and star-gazing sessions.[23] Anthropologist Kelsie Nabben was among the attendees invited to an intimate acoustic concert by musician James Blake in the middle of a forest. She listened to Blake play the piano and she heard earnest discussions about how to save crypto before the assholes come in and ruin it.[24]

The Friends with Benefits DAO wanted to redefine the cultural industries. In 2021, it received a $10 million investment from the venture capital firm Andreessen Horowitz, which valued the DAO at $100 million. Along with minting its own NFTs, the DAO went on to collectively invest in a yerba-maté drink, which would be served at their events. I immediately think of Club-Mate, the cult beverage of late-night hackers that is stocked in maker spaces throughout Germany. The drink was imported to Berlin in the 1990s and became the fuel of choice for Chaos Computer Club meet-ups and all-night raves. Zhang, who describes the group as a 'headless media community lifestyle brand', predicts that members will eventually release dozens of products under the Friends with Benefits umbrella, including magazines, music festivals, and clothing lines. 'We're talking to everyone from Reebok to Hennessey', he said. 'We're able to help cross those bridges and explain what the potential of crypto and web3 could do to these spaces.'[25]

Friends with Benefits did not just tokenise art – it tokenised prestige, vibes, bragging rights, membership with the in-crowd. People were buying in in the hope that they would belong, but also make money. Kind of like art, honestly.

NFT tokens were monetising the social graph, too. Bored Ape, an NFT collection that emerged at the very height of the NFT craze, was an 'artwork' – a speculative token that buyers hoped would appreciate in value – but it was also an access token. Like the FWB buy-in, ownership of a Bored Ape NFT gave the user access to the token-gated Bored Ape club, and to exclusive events. If you had the token, you were in. It also allowed the user to post the image to their Twitter profile.

Bored Ape Yacht Club NFTs, created by the blockchain company Yuga Labs, are stoned-looking apes wearing clothes. 'Apes' is a nod to the crypto expression 'aping in', describing a primal impulse to act now and think later. The meme imagines a future where crypto-wealthy investors are rich beyond their wildest dreams; but now they are bored and degenerate, devolved to something less than human. What do they do next but 'hang out in a swamp club with a bunch of [other] apes and get weird'.[26] Unlike with many other NFTs, the creators of the Bored Ape series handed over full IP rights to buyers, reasoning that 'anything people create with their apes [thus far, a craft beer, skateboard line, and cartoon] only grows the brand'.[27]

Yuga Labs, currently valued at $4 billion, were not pretending that what they were doing was art, in good taste, or even all that interesting. The joke was that apes were clearly dumb – 'bored, emptied out, wrecked, and proud of it' – and yet people were *still* buying the token.[28] Yuga Labs were called out for alleged 'Nazi dog whistles' in the iconography of the Apes series. The joke was that they were shilling something so stupid – so in bad taste – and people were *still* aping in. It is the kind of joke that can make you feel a bit sick of culture – even a little sick with yourself for paying attention to and writing about the culture.

But maybe, in their total anti-art status, Bored Apes best reflected the culture of the moment. Dadaist art emerged a hundred years ago from a disillusioned culture: young artists with a desire to overturn bourgeois notions of what art and good taste were supposed to look like in 1920. Instead of Da Vinci's *Mona Lisa*, it was a grainy postcard of the *Mona Lisa* with a cartoon moustache drawn on and a bad joke scrawled underneath about how she has a hot arse. Marcel Duchamp's *L.H.O.O.Q.* (1919) was the original internet meme; one hundred years later it would not look out of place between a worried-looking Shiba Inu and an angry frog. Just maybe, cartoons of apes could be really stupid *and* the ultimate token of our cast-down culture.

Ruth Catlow writes in *Radical Friends* of 'a trend' among artists and theorists 'to opt for a polemics that discourage those who build more progressive cultures in this [blockchain + art] space'.[29] I recognise myself in that criticism. But I can no longer make an argument simply for 'holding the space'. In a moment of exhaustion and honesty, I email Ruth:

> I feel like I am still pretending to myself that art and the block-chain might be a good idea, but when I try to explain why, I can't. The answers I come up with – that blockchain is a way to ask ourselves what kind of cooperation we *do* want, or that if blockchain is the future of organisation then *somebody* needs to be in there doing it better ... seem a little vague. Tokenistic even ... I can't help but wonder why we need to build *anything* in this space at all ...

At my most cynical, I feel as though experiments in a 'good' kind of blockchain are in danger of art-washing the problem: a little culture to legitimise what would otherwise be 'spin all the way down'.[30]

Ruth responds almost immediately. While the space is 'a battleground, not to be ceded', she adds: 'I have a growing uneasy feeling that ALL networked tech is already poisoned.'[31] Blockchain, in other words, is no better or worse than the rest of the internet.

Derivative Art

Artist Kevin Abosch is the creator of *Forever Rose*, a token called ROSE on the Ethereum blockchain that derives from Abosch's photograph of a rose. 'It doesn't exist in a physical sense', Abosch explained to me. 'It is the result of using block-chain technology to create a virtual proxy of the photographic work.'[32] Unlike Monegraph and Maecenas, then, which link works of art that exist in the digital or physical sense, the ethereal *Forever Rose* has no physical presence, or even a virtual presence, only a monetary one. Abosch's works are not tokens associated with physical or digital works of art, then, but works of art or collectibles that, like a centenary coin, consist of the tokens themselves and the smart contracts they encapsulate. The artist suggests that this work, as well as a similar project, *Potato #345*, poses crucial questions concerning the relationship between objecthood, scarcity, and value.

With cryptokitties, the art purchased also has no physical manifestation. In the vast majority of cases, in fact, the digital image file itself is not stored *on* the blockchain, because block sizes only store data up to 1MB. The ledger entry is usually just the record of provenance, the artist's name, and a URL link to the work. It is metadata – a pointer. Exceptions to this can be found at cryptograffiti.info, a website that scrolls the Bitcoin blockchain to detect human-readable messages or multimedia file formats encoded in transactions. The first image of this kind was an ASCII portrait of Nelson Mandela. Usually there are political slogans about decentralised currencies and a sprinkling of Pepe frogs. More recently, there are tonnes of photos of someone's baby, a cartoon of Scrooge McDuck, and a grainy screengrab of a tweet that says: 'Oh my goodness I didn't realize this song was this song and didn't realize this song was by her what a great feeling when you find out a song you knew was by an artist you liked.'

In most cases the buyer is essentially purchasing a 256-character string that contains a link to a file stored somewhere on the internet. The string signifies a kind of possession – something we can call ours – if not exactly full ownership.[33] 'In this instance, the artwork auctioned stands in for and is interchangeable with any valuable non-fungible asset', says Catlow.[34] The cryptokitty or the *Forever Rose* has value as a set of rights to a financial asset. The buyer does not purchase an 'image', or even an 'idea', so much as a cryptographic certificate of authenticity that can be used to speculate on the future performance of the token. The aesthetic significance of a cartoon cat or a watercolour of an Ethereum logo is not the point.

Buyers not only have no rights over the future uses of the image – they don't even have any rights to hold a lasting reproduction. Similarly, NFTs do not normally build in any mechanism to prevent other people from viewing, sharing, copying, or deleting the associated image. In the aftermath of NFT sales in 2021, many new collectors went to their wallets and found a different image altogether – or just a 404 error. Like the *Forever Rose*, some tokens were signs pointing only to themselves. And, as we saw with destroyed readymades, salvage art, and fakes and forgeries, some works of art are objects without a seal of approval – a thing without a token. But, to echo Van Meegeren, what has really changed? 'What's different?'

To answer this, we should think back to Berners-Lee. For

some, Tim Berners-Lee's decision to auction an NFT of the source code for the World Wide Web was anathema to the openness of the early internet. 'Information wants to be free' – but here was one of the founders, hawking the source code for billions. But Berners-Lee argued that his NFT auction was 'totally aligned with the values of the web'.[35]

He was right. The World Wide Web challenged a traditional economic principle that links scarcity or alienation (the right to exclude others from using or copying a good) with profit. The economic founders of the internet did not get rich by controlling access to information or by making it scarce, in other words, but through an approach that *Wired* editor Kevin Kelly would later dub 'follow the free'.[36] Instead of trying to limit information, digital content is made freely available and profits are churned through network effects. While Xanadu wanted to monetise the source, Google's huge success would come from monetising the buzz and attention that circulated around information. The page-rank algorithm, detailed in Sergey Brin and Larry Page's 1999 paper, does not control or circumscribe information as a commodity.[37] Instead, it algorithmically scores webpages according to their level of audience engagement. Google's whole business model fell into place around this idea: not controlling information, but measuring attention (and putting advertisements where it is focused).

When Berners-Lee sold his NFT, he did not police the use or circulation of the source code for the web by others – it is still available for anyone to use. The NFT simply allows Berners-Lee to monetise an original without inhibiting the circulation of many identical copies. These tokens trade on the information and hype circulating around the good rather than on exclusion or artificial scarcity. 'Information almost wants to be free,' said Stewart Brand to Steve Wozniak. Almost. The second clause is less well known: 'Information sort of also wants to be expensive because it is so valuable – the right information in the right place just changes your life.'[38]

Early discussions of NFTs often framed the technology as a new kind of digital IP, or maybe even digital rights management – a technocratic system for controlling the duplication and circulation of digital files. George Orwell 2.0. But the token economy was not scarcity-based. If anything, it was an anti-rival strategy: the tokens didn't try to exclude access to the underlying digital goods, but simply to monetise the buzz circulating around them. It was 'follow the free'. As part of a series of interviews between 2015 and 2021, I spoke to Kevin McCoy about the business models he envisioned emerging from blockchain. Clearly, he didn't see it as a system for property rights? Rather than owning, McCoy argued, blockchain was 'more appropriate for bragging rights, where it's about building community, fans, or supporters'. Could 'bragging rights' be the new business model for artists, I wondered. 'Yes', McCoy said. 'Because it fits well into the complex ecosystems of support that artists are relying on now – things like micropayments and Patreon. And it could fit really well into the work of influencers, fans, content creators, y'know – a way to build a brand, create VIPs or special relationships.'[39] Bored Ape seemed to recognise this intuitively when it speculated that any use of the content would simply grow its brand. As with other memes, exchange value would grow through virality, not scarcity.

In the 1960s there was a sense that conceptual art (an emerging school based on ideas rather than things) might challenge the commodity status of the work of art. Lucy Lippard and John Chandler's 1968 essay 'The Dematerialization of Art' framed intangible works as a challenge to the ready commodification of fine art. By removing the art *object* – the painting or sculpture for sale in a gallery – art worked to shake off its commodity status – its complicity with the market.[40] After all, who would want to buy an idea or stick it on their wall?

With the rise of conceptual art, however, the *idea* became paramount, and the commodity – its material form – secondary. But where Lippard and Chandler, at first, framed this as a challenge to the artwork's commodity status, in reality it heralded the key economic shift from material commodities to speculating on information. With the NFT, 'dematerialisation' challenges the artwork's commodity status, but only to push it into increasingly abstract markets, where material form ceases to matter. As the authors later observed, 'hopes that conceptual art would be able to avoid the general commercialization … were, for the most part, unfounded'.[41] Instead, information is now the key differential in the art market, and in the economy at large. McKenzie Wark asks us to consider

> how the very properties of spreadability that characterize digital objects can be turned to advantage to make them collectable as well … Paradoxically, an object whose image is very widely spread is a rare object, in the sense that few objects have their images spread widely. This can be exploited to create value in art objects that are not in the traditional sense rare and singular. The future of collecting may be less in owning the thing that nobody else has, and more in owning the thing that everybody else has.[42]

The artwork is not a thing, but a derivative of hype and network effects. In this sense, NFTs are not radically disrupting the art market. They are 'the market, perfected'.[43]

Your Weird Meme Coin Won't Save You

There is a meme called Disaster Girl. You've probably seen it. It shows a four-year-old girl against the soft-focus background of a burning building. She is looking back over her shoulder, throwing the camera a knowing, curiously adult smile that jars with her rosy cheeks and the disaster that appears to be unfolding behind her. The suggestion is that she might be responsible. The photograph is of a then four-year-old Zoë Roth, taken by her father Daniel in 2005. The burning building is not a neighbour's house on fire, but a controlled experiment. This is a drill. Disaster Girl is commonly underscored with messages of the child-sociopath trope: 'They said it was nap time. I agreed', or of wipe-out mayhem – the burning house labelled '2020', the smiling girl labelled 'God'.

Roth sold the meme of her four-year-old self as an NFT in 2021 for $485,000. She used the profits to pay off her student debt. Maybe NFTs were desperate bets on the future by a generation with nothing gained and nothing to lose. If you don't have any stable assets or any equity, if you're saddled with years of student debt and with no prospect of owning your own home or of stable employment, if you're staring down the barrel of climate catastrophe, a global pandemic, and the economic shockwaves that are sure to follow, why not invest your money in virtual Nikes and hope to win big?

Millennials and Gen Zs were raised to be entrepreneurs of the self, to believe that if they simply worked and studied hard enough, success and security were waiting in their futures. Failure was a personal blight for refusing to invest your time wisely, for refusing to grind hard enough. Many now feel they have been sold worthless promises. Instead of speaking about investment in their university education, my students speak to me of investing in NFTs or on retail sites to try and win a home, or of buying a little breathing space, a little time to make their art. Security isn't coming with study and safe choices, so why not go all-in on a long shot?

Viewed from this perspective, the NFT artwork is a kind of desperate bet on a joyless and jobless future. But, retail investment aside, it is unclear whether artists are really making anything from the sale of NFTs. While the odd *Nyan Cat* or *Everydays* skews the average sale value of NFTs north of $7,000, the median sale at the height of the market was closer to $100.[44] And this is the sale price *before* gas fees are even taken into the account (the cost in ether required to mint and sell an NFT) – anything from 72.5 per cent to 157.5 per cent of the cost of a sale. This is not even to begin to calculate the environmental impact of a virtual economy that eats the future one transaction at a time. Your weird meme coin won't save you.

The meme for the cryptowinter might have captioned the Burning House 'NFTs' and the Little Girl '2022'. I feel like I just have to search hard enough and somebody will have made it already …

In 2022, a tax-loss harvesting platform is building 'the world's largest collection of worthless NFTs' – a kind of digital version of the Salvage Art Institute, a group that rescues devalued artworks and puts them back on display. The art is materially the same, but economically it is now worthless. We are asked to contemplate what's left behind when the smoke has cleared, when all the hype is over. So, what's different?

9

'When You Live in a Shithole, There's Always the Metaverse'

'I already live online.' Vadim joins our Zoom call from his parents' house in Waterford, a small city on the south coast of Ireland. He wears a black sweatshirt, hood up, with 'more-dunkey' printed on the front. In the background is an unmade bed and a wall full of his colourful drawings.

Lockdown life suited Vadim. 'I got to play computer games without my dad judging me too hard.' His favourite pastimes are playing video games, drawing, hanging out on Discord, and collectibles. As we are speaking, he reaches out and flips the phone camera to reveal shelves of tiny colourful figurines, displayed at eye level above the desk. I imagine Vadim's parent's installing the shelves for his school books at some point in the past, making a dedicated study area. The figures are Pucky Babies – 'I nearly have all of the circus series' – and Sonny Angels – 'Basically little cupids with silly hats.' Vadim turns his phone camera to the open tab on his computer screen. The webpage shows a site called Artoyz where he is considering the purchase of a new Sonny Angel. The dolls cost €10 each and come in blind boxes. Like Pokémon trading cards (which Vadim also collects – proudly showing me his Blaziken Vmax), each purchase is a gamble. The dolls are cute, but the wager is what draws him in. The fun, Vadim recognises, is not only in collecting and curating the little dolls and their headwear – it's also in the hedge. On one occasion, he bought a whole crate of Pucky Babies. He was guaranteed a full set just by paying. It suddenly wasn't so much fun anymore.

Vadim calls this hobby 'gacha', in reference to 'compu gacha', the computer games he also plays, in which users spend virtual in-game currency to try and win or 'pull' rare anime characters. His favourite is Genshin Impact, an open-world role-playing game launched in 2020 by miHoYo. Genshin Impact is free to play; the company makes money through micro-transactions in the game. In exchange for tokens, the user gets a blind digital item, usually a weapon – or, if the player is lucky, a character. The process, in Vadim's own words, is like a 'digital slot machine'.

For Vadim, the characters in Genshin Impact are worth pulling for because he feels connected to them. They are cute and lovable. The word a psychologist might use is 'parasocial', naming a one-sided attachment to an anime character, streamer, or celebrity. Vadim is not alone. Genshin Impact's commercial success rests on how compelling the characters are; the money players will throw down to have them in their inventory. Diluc, for example, has a tragic background and a unique fighting style. Players like his red hair – the way he somehow manages to be handsome and pretty at the same time. Shenhe is elegant and soft-spoken, 'but she'll smack you down the moment you piss her off'. Eula is an outsider: 'It hits hard when you know she simply wants to be herself but the world doesn't want her to.'[1] In a virtuous loop, spending more on a character drives attachment, and attachment drives further spending. Players don't speak of buying or even winning characters. They speak of them 'coming home'. The game is a gamble, and failing to pull the character you want means that you are unlucky in the game, but also, somehow, unlucky in love.[2] You want Shenhe, but it's almost like she doesn't want you. These tokens speak the language of attachment.

I think of the Tamagotchi kids of the 1990s, who cared for their virtual pets and even eulogised them on the early internet: 'My beloved Kuchi died during gym class one Thursday afternoon. I was very sad. When he left he was crying. I will miss him greatly and I am so sorry I neglected him. I hope he rests in peace.'[3]

'We were asked to bring a cherished object to class recently', Vadim tells me. 'And I chose this screenshot of a time I got a really cool mount in *Final Fantasy XIV*.' The screenshot is a memento of Vadim playing the game with his friends online. He has a collection of these special moments stored away on his desktop and his phone. 'These digital items have ... sentimental value to me.' But, curiously, the screengrab is also a record of what was going on away from the keyboard. Vadim remembers that, at the same moment as this particular screenshot was captured, his dad was experiencing a health scare. The captured image is a souvenir of an online triumph, but also of the other feelings he was grappling with in that moment.

In *Final Fantasy XIV*, Vadim is interested in hunting or 'grinding' for mounts. Mounts are virtual animals that a player can ride around on. They don't provide any in-game advantage. Instead, they are valuable because the community collectively agrees that they are in some way 'cool to have'. Mounts are officially acquired by completing in-game tasks ('grinding'), but the in-channel chat in the game is also run through with links to grey-market sites where they can be purchased for real money. Vadim has no interest in this. The time he sinks into playing is not motivated by getting ahead in the game or by financial speculation outside it. 'Sure – I guess I could sell my account if someone really wanted my Raiden Shogun', he says uncertainly when I ask, but clearly this speculation is not the point. The value of the item, for Vadim, does not lie in its future exchange value but in its prestige value within the game itself. These are 'bragging rights'. Having an item in your inventory cements your reputation. It also cements your bond with other players. Vadim played around the clock with an Australian girl to get this particular mount, both of them staying up late, getting up early, taking shifts, until they got what they came for. He calls it a 'choreographed dance'; everyone's steps are important to the final result.

'What does it mean to "get" "a mount"?' I ask Vadim. 'Do you own it? Have you any rights to it? Can you sell it on?' 'Well, wait' – he shrugs in an exaggerated way – 'I don't know … what does it mean to own this … I guess it's … in my inventory? But I understand the game own my profile and tomorrow it could vanish. The company owns my item. And my account, too.'

RMTs

A new category of games are called 'play to earn'. Players run tasks and are rewarded with native tokens that can be traded for crypto or fiat currency. The best known of these is Axie Infinity. The object of the game is to gather cartoon axolotls or 'Axies', represented by NFTs, an amphibian cousin of the cryptokitty. The Axies are cute (if a little dead behind the eyes, like they've been up all night playing video games). They can be bred and battled. By trading and dogfighting, users earn SLP ('Smooth Love Potion') tokens that can be swapped for money. They also earn AXS tokens that represent a voting stake in the game's future (although these can also be cashed out). During the Covid lockdown, players in the Philippines turned to gathering Axies. Their play became work.

This seems like a convenient place to end the Axie story. But as the game grew popular, the price of the NFT Axies inflated to the point where it cost incoming players as much as $1,500 just to buy into the game. Because this was prohibitively expensive for many, a system emerged whereby existing owners rented fractional reserves of their assets to others. A second tier could work someone else's Axies and take a cut. Owners are 'managers', and workers are – somewhat euphemistically – called 'scholars'. Managers recruit scholars on message boards, set daily quotas and a profit split, usually between 30 and 50 per cent. In February 2023, Sky Mavis partnered with MetaLend, a company that allows AXS holders to borrow against their in-game NFT assets. In contrast to Vadim's dad, one Philippine father is encouraging his sons to enter the business: 'in the next 12 years, my kids won't need a college degree, they'll just need to know how to create value in virtual worlds'.[4]

Final Fantasy XIV is a massively multiplayer online (MMO) game. These are immersive worlds where thousands of players come together on the same server. Long before NFTs blurred the lines between real and virtual value, these communities had thriving economies based on the production and sale of virtual in-game goods – 'loot' and collectibles. As early as 1987, gamers informally traded cash for improvements to characters in basic multi-user dungeon games (MUDs).[5] A decade on, the development of graphical MMOs and internet resale sites gave rise to a shadow economy in virtual tokens. Today, virtual assets are worth more than $100 billion each year: things like characters, weapons, clothing, and appearance modifications ('skins'), real estate, and access passes. The most common purchases are skins and cosmetic segments, followed by seasonal and battle passes.

A game is its own world. This online world lives on a centralised server, hosted and controlled by the developers. Players are clients. They access the server from their consoles or phones, or whatever device they use to play the game. In a game economy, digital items are entries in a database on the server. The data tells us what kind of item this is – a chair, an orc, a sword – and also how it behaves or might be reproduced in the game world. Developers can script how items are made, traded, or destroyed. Sometimes players also have permission to write data to the server. 'None of these database entries are "objects"' in the truest sense, says Raph Koster, the lead designer of *Ultima Online*. They are 'rows in a spreadsheet'. 'In a typical game,' Koster goes on to say, 'you never owned anything. You paid for the right to access a server which happened to keep some records linked to your character ID.'[6]

Most of the time, these virtual goods are made to be scarce. Some are limited-edition drops, released in a fixed amount by the game. Others are seasonal – available for a set amount of time before they are discontinued. Some are tied to a specific location within the game or the real world. Others are non-transferable or 'soul-bound', tied to a character ID.[7]

Virtual loot can be acquired in various ways. Items are earned through play – by completing a quest, killing a monster, or even just logging a certain number of hours within a game environment. Sometimes they are acquired through in-game exchanges. If the game allows players to create items, they might go ahead and make the thing themselves. Another mode of acquisition involves what are known as 'real money trades', where players use real money to buy virtual loot, either in sanctioned trades inside the game environment or in shadow markets elsewhere on the internet.[8]

In 2001, the Sony MMO *EverQuest* – then the largest MMO in the United States, with a player base of 4 million – was calculated to have an average hourly wage of $3.42. The economist Edward Castronova performed an analysis of the game's functional realm, Norrath, detailing the country's money supply, exchange rate (based on data from black-market exchanges on the internet), export market (again based on secondary markets), GNP per capita, and rate of inflation. Norrath emerged in the top third of developed economies – ahead of Russia, China, and India.[9]

Meanwhile, the Azerothian gold coins of *World of Warcraft* – another MMO – traded at a rate comparable to the Russian ruble.[10] Launched in 2004, *World of Warcraft* is an open-world game where avatars complete quests, fight monsters, and generally hang out with other players. Play is open-ended; quests are optional. *World of Warcraft* has a rich economy, and players can earn gold by completing tasks in the game. These include things like foraging for herbs that can be sold to other players; mining rare minerals; crafting things to sell at auction, from jewellery to weapons – and also more niche activities such as trading unique pets to battle.

World of Warcraft is subscription-based. WoW tokens can be bought using real money from the *World of Warcraft* auction house, and redeemed for game time or used to buy the Azerothian gold coins that act as currency in the space. Players with an excess of gold can sell some of these for WoW to put towards their monthly subscription. Virtual gold and WoW tokens can be exchanged for one another. Neither can be cashed out for real money – not through legitimate channels, at least.

Online games spawned grey markets dedicated to the sale of things that were not really things. Echoing the labour arbitrage at work in Axie Infinity, workers in poorer economies played to 'mine' virtual gold to sell to players in developed economies for real money. Instead of sinking hours into the game, affluent players could skip the grind of foraging, crafting, or fighting, and 'level up' with real money alone.

In 1997, Origin Systems launched *Ultima Online*, the first MMO. At the same time, a currency crisis prompted Asian governments to invest in broadband to stimulate economic development. Many citizens who lost their jobs took to gaming. The more informal practice of trading to level up transformed into a 'gold farming' industry, where wealthy gamers outsourced their play to East Asia. They bought virtual items, and sometimes whole accounts with tokens attached. Gold farmers played in sweatshop-meets-internet-café conditions. The time these players spent was changed out for disposable income from the West on internet resale sites. A *Guardian* article reported that prison guards were forcing Chinese inmates to gold farm in twelve-hour shifts. Miners were allegedly beaten with plastic pipes if they failed to meet their daily quotas.[11]

Internet Gaming Entertainment (IGE) was a gold-farming company founded by the former child star Brock Pierce in 2001. At the time, Pierce was best known for starring in Disney's *The Mighty Ducks*. Today he is known for co-founding Blockchain Capital and the Stablecoin Tether. Recognising the willingness of players to pay real money for virtual loot, Pierce hired Chinese players to play in rotating shifts. Steve Bannon, the former chief strategist for the Trump administration and co-founder of the right-wing outlet Breitbart News, joined the company in 2007 with a $60 million investment. Despite the fact that IGE's business practices explicitly violated the end-user licence agreements (EULAs) of most online games, and labour laws besides, it was valued at $880 million. Shortly thereafter, IGE faced a class-action lawsuit from the gaming industry, and was forced to restructure.

Virtual game economies also raised concerns for the IRS, which wondered, well before Bitcoin, whether in-game tokens could front tax evasion and money laundering. Criminals were using stolen credit-card data to buy in-game currencies that they resold elsewhere for traditional currency. Payments processors like Square and PayPal were also reluctant to manage exchanges for in-game currencies, for fear of fraud or charge-backs.

Most companies, and many players, loathe real-money trading. In 2004, *EverQuest* blocked accounts with multiple IP log-ins in China. Sony changed its EULA to ban gold farming, and successfully petitioned eBay to take down resale auctions. It established its own auction house called Station Exchange instead. Sony took 10 per cent of the sale price on all secondary trades. Grey-market sales continued to flourish elsewhere.

For corporations that host these virtual worlds, secondary market trades are illicit revenue streams, leaking from the game economy into some shadowy corner of the internet. For most players, *buying* an advantage is seen as 'cheating'. Gamers sometimes call this 'pay to win', gesturing to the idea that by handing over a fistful of tokens, a player can advance within the game without questing or grinding – or really doing anything to earn their status. In a series of interviews with amateur gamers on their motivations for acquiring items, 'stock-market gaming' was listed but generally denigrated. Most players were motivated by a desire to belong and display a hard-earned status in the game. Mounts, for Vadim, mean nothing if you don't grind

252

them out yourself. For those who did engage in stock-market gaming, 'it killed a lot of the fun aspect of it as everything was suddenly viewed as this financial transaction ... I would look in the auction house for trends, buy low and sell high, rather than actually playing the game itself.'[12]

Money, as Viviana Zelizer has observed time and again, needs to be calibrated to match its social context.[13] Just as some tokens might threaten the intimacy of a romance, real money, in the context of a game, threatens the carefully constructed boundaries of play – like handing over €20 in the middle of a game of Monopoly. Game economists call this 'the magic circle' – the sense that gateways from the virtual into the real economy (or into other, conflicting virtual economies) threaten the internal logic of the game environment. All the talk of quotas or grinding does not square with the fact that a game is supposed to be just for fun. Players who 'work' in virtual worlds, then, instead of simply playing in them, ruin the fun for everyone else. Their single-minded purpose disrupts 'normal' play.

Luc Barthelet is the former CTO of EA Games, and vice president of Unity, a game engine provider that develops over 60 per cent of new game releases. Games need balance, Luc is keen to stress: the right token for the right task. If a token is not well matched to a group or a reward, the mechanics of the game are thrown into disarray. Above all, the game has to feel 'fair', where fair does not mean 'equal distribution', but rather 'equal opportunity'.[14] If the rules feel too arbitrary, the game falls apart. As such, games often have multiple currencies, all earmarked for purpose. Some, like WoW tokens, can be used to buy access passes or to pay for play-time. Others can only be earned by what Barthelet describes as 'the sweat of your gameplay'; levels, skill points, badges of achievement, and high scores cannot officially be bought, for example – but so-called 'cosmetic' goods usually can.

Other tokens measure and reward solidarity. Castronova analysed the development of these informal currencies in *World*

of Warcraft – a game in which players, like Vadim and his Australian friend, sometimes formed groups and guilds to acquire
better loot. Then they had to figure out how to share it. Players
might have offered to pay each other in gold for the right to
garner the loot, Castronova observes, but they didn't. Simply
paying for a share did not feel right, somehow. Instead, users
developed their own reputational currency – Dragon Kill Points.
DKPs were earned through participation in a raid, and could
be redeemed afterwards for a share of the loot.[15] Like Time
Dollars, these were tokens designed to foster social cohesion.
They could be spent on shared loot or kept and used to flaunt
your status in the game.

Skin in the Game

Will is a thirteen-year-old gamer. He is an outspoken, extremely
kind teenager who has endless time for my five-year-old Ted's
Pokémon obsession. As well as gaming, Will plays rugby and
'builds a lot of Lego'. A half-built *Star Wars* set lies on the
table between us, a recent Christmas gift. He shows us a giant
lightsaber, another gift. As we talk, Ted is allowed to hold it and
carefully press the buttons to make the shaft change colour, so
long as he promises not to 'swing it around'.

Will and I have been speaking about in-game loot for over
a year now, about the games he likes to play, and especially
about the things he likes to collect. Our latest chat takes place
in the Christmas holidays. It's lunchtime, and he is just getting
up, wandering the house sleepily in his pyjamas. Will, his mum
Lisa tells me, has been up until 3 a.m. most mornings playing
games online with his friends. But today he is going to meet up
with an old friend from primary school. He's a little nervous.
He hasn't seen the friend in question for four years – a long
time when you're thirteen – but they still play games together
online regularly enough.

Unlike Vadim, whose tastes run to open worlds, Will's interests are closer to the more traditional first-person-shooter genre. There's *Red Dead Redemption 2*, a Wild West open world, largely revolving around shootouts and heists and horseback riding from place to place. And then there is *Fortnite*, a last-person-standing battle royale.

Fortnite was first released in July 2017, but became popular in 2020 when the platform Epic Games released a cross-platform free-to-play version during the pandemic. In *Fortnite*, a cohort of players are parachuted onto an island where they scavenge for resources and fight to be the last gamer standing. Experienced players often engage in a kind of digital arbitrage, using servers to sniff out inexperienced players who will be easy kill targets to boost their in-game credentials.[16]

As a free-to-play game, *Fortnite* makes money not from players subscribing to the game itself, but through micro-transactions within the game environment: paying to acquire additional digital items. These items can be bought using V-Bucks, *Fortnite*'s in-game currency. V-Bucks, in turn, can be purchased on the Epic Games platform. They can also be earned through in-game questing, though this takes longer. One V-Buck is the equivalent of $0.01 dollars. An exclusive battle pass costs 950 V-Bucks, or approximately $9.50. Users spend real money to buy V-Bucks, and these in turn can be used to purchase items from within the game. Characters, weapons, battle passes to exclusive fights, and skins and wraps that change the appearance of characters or weapons are all for sale.

The derogatory name for players who do not invest in extras, Will tells me, is 'no-skins'. Skins are limited-edition drops – items are available for a short period of time, and then they're gone. Will speaks wistfully of 'the Renegade Raider' and 'the Reaper' – two skins that are no longer available, but which tell you that the player in your sights is OG or 'original gangster'. Some skins are so desirable that they work as their own currency outside the gaming platform. In a practice known as 'skin betting', valuable skins are held as tokens in a virtual wallet and used as collateral for gambling on the internet. A dragon lore skin from the game *Counter Strike: Global Offensive (CS:GO)* might be worth $61,000 dollars. Marketplaces for skins include skins.cash, a platform where an automated bot buys skins for credit that can be cashed out into money.

Players can also use their V-Bucks to buy emotes. Like the emotes in Twitch, *Fortnite* emotes are funny little dances that characters can use to troll or celebrate a victory. In 2018, the French football player Antoine Griezmann marked a goal in the World Cup Final match against Croatia by performing a well-known 'Take the L' emote dance to Croatian fans. The stunt cemented the popularity of the emote and boosted the popularity of the *Fortnite* game. Emotes, as they drifted from virtual to physical spaces and back again, were a kind of viral marketing for the metaverse.

According to the guidelines set out by Epic Games, these for-purchase items are purely 'cosmetic', and confer no in-game player advantage. They are, as Vadim observed of mounts in *Final Fantasy XIV*, just kind of 'cool to have'. Some of the items are even what's called 'pay to lose', Will tells me. While Will plays as a girl because he believes that a smaller body mass makes for a smaller kill target – 'plus, people sometimes underestimate girl avatars' – other players will deliberately choose skins that are easy to shoot. The Hulk, for example, is popular, but its large size makes it an easy target. Players still want it.

And yet, Will also describes saving to get enough V-Bucks to buy 'a really cool neck tattoo', so that more experienced players in *Fortnite* would stop blowing him up in the first few seconds. Being a 'no skins' player singled Will out as an easy target for players looking to build their standing in the game, while a rare skin would signal that he might be best left alone. The tattoo was purely cosmetic, but it was also a reputational investment – a prestige item that he hoped would indicate that he was now a serious player. Luc Barthelet agrees. In *Fortnite*, 'the "game" is mostly about reaching status when you're a noob'. The right token says you have skin in the game.

In medieval France, royalty would sometimes throw tokens to the masses on special feast days or during a coronation – a kind of old-school 'loot drop'. These *jetons royaux*, as they were known, had multiple values. There was the value of the alloy itself, which everyone understood; and then there was an iconic value, the way that the symbols on these tokens – the skin, the wrap – held meanings that the everyday masses did not fully grasp. Only OGs knew the iconography on the coin, and this made them all the more valuable. 'The ability of users to understand the "code" on the token', writes historian Clare Rowan, 'in contrast to those outside the group, likely contributed to a feeling of community.'[17]

For Vadim, digital items help to cement his connection to the game. But this desire to belong does not always tally with play. Sometimes a social investment runs counter to the assumed object of the game – to progress, or win, or avoid being killed. And yet, Will's rationale for pursuing in-game collectibles also shows that these purchases are never *only* social or *only* cosmetic, as the game sites claim. Useless items can play a powerful role in signalling social prestige. 'Just bragging rights', then – except there is no such thing as 'just' bragging rights. The brag, the hedge, the skin – the swagger wields its own worth. Even if a particular skin doesn't provide an obvious in-game utility, the token can signal that someone is an experienced (and possibly dangerous) player. As with the purchase of many so-called intangibles, sign value trumps a more obvious utility. This is the conquest of cool. This is where the brag gets staked.

Tattoos are not just 'nice to look at' – and even a virtual neck tattoo can play a role in the social field. Ornament can distinguish us. Or it can be a way of binding us to others. At other times, it is a form of self-defence that marks the threshold of the body. This is partly what the anthropologist Alfred Gell meant when he argued that 'art has agency' – it *does something*.

257

The line we draw 'between "mere" decoration and function is unwarranted. Decoration is intrinsically functional', Gell argues.[18] Otherwise, it makes no sense.

Roblox is a platform where children can build (and monetise) their own games, along with in-game items and collectibles. The official tokens, called Robucks, can be used to buy access to games and in-game items. There is a whole city dedicated to digital pets. As on Twitch, roughly 70 per cent of the profits from in-game items go to the creator, with the Roblox platform taking the other 30 per cent. While MMOs are platforms for virtual games, Roblox is slated as a platform for the 'creator economy' – a company that puts out the necessary building blocks to make new worlds.

In 2019, Tencent, the Chinese gaming company responsible for QQ Coin and WeChat Pay, invested a 49 per cent stake in the company. The platform was valued at $41 billion in 2021, but Roblox has also struggled since its inception to handle users who exploit in-game glitches to clone more than their fair share of loot. Roblox also struggles to deal with the problem of 'duping', an economics graduate and employee of the company tells me – a practice where gamers exploit bugs in the game interface to make virtual copies of in-game commodities that are supposed to be scarce. Another common practice, 'AFKing' (for 'away from keyboard'), sees players exploit hacks to log false play hours. 'Like, this one time', Will tells me enthusiastically, 'you could get, like, 500 Bucks just for walking around some square! So players were just leaving their characters looping all night long. And in the morning they'd wake up and have *so much* loot!'

The Roblox game *Islands* became very popular when it was launched in 2020. Users could create their own islands and farm virtual crops. So far, so Covid-19. But users were also exploiting flaws in the architecture of the games to make duplicate items. In January 2021, *Islands* performed a site-wide economy wipe, removing collectibles from player accounts to combat the inflation caused by duping. 'After spending months patching dozens of dupes,' the developers wrote in a public post, 'we think now is the best time to clear out all of the duped items and coins that have been inflating market prices. The *Islands* economy revolves around player trading. Leaving duped items around makes it nearly impossible for us to balance. Good luck on your race to become the new richest player.'[19]

I watch a YouTube video voiced by two brothers. The younger one sounds no more than six, and keeps interrupting. 'They took so much stuff away from us!!' he shouts over his older brother. 'I was just about to say that,' says the older-sounding one. 'But yes – yes, they did. I used to have 2 billion coins! I had a *ton* of coins. I grinded so long on this game. And they took so much away!! I know this was done to fix duping and try [to] restore the economy, but a lot of hate has been going on in the Discord. This is happening to, like, everyone. *Islands*, if you see this video: even though you just wiped everyone, the dupers are just going to become rich again. It's just going to make the people who don't dupe *really* poor.'[20]

'The bottom line is that preventing duplication is extremely difficult', says Sarah Flannery, a mathematician who builds in-game economies. 'Bits are bits, and you can copy bits, and it's very, very difficult to put any limitation on that.'[21]

Into the Metaverse

Decentraland is a virtual space where virtual land and virtual assets are underpinned by the Ethereum Blockchain. It describes itself as a 'virtual destination for digital assets', making a virtual world for all of the intangible things stored on the blockchain – a place they can call home. Each virtual plot of land does not exist in the real world. They are like Klein's *Zones of Immaterial Pictorial Sensibility*, I think – the invisible plots of land by the Seine that the artist tokenised and sold for gold: unreal estate, most stand empty.

Each one is for sale as an NFT. Most are unoccupied, speculative wagers for a future in which the metaverse replaces the mobile internet. The homepage lists plots of land denominated in MANA, Decentraland's currency of choice. As things stand, there are 90,000 of these plots for sale, propped up by cryptographic tokens. They currently sell for an average of $13,000 each. Ownership gives the bearer the right to build whatever they like on a particular 16m×16m plot. Sotheby's have built a virtual gallery in the Museum District. Atari have constructed a retro gaming casino where croupiers are paid in MANA to go to work. A firm called Am Law 200 has bought a plot, ready to arbitrate the property disputes that will surely arise.[22]

Landowners are renting out plots in the metaverse for special events. Those close to where users spawn into the world are prime real estate. All this scrambling for position reminds me of the high-frequency trading land rush of the early noughties, in which real estate close to where transatlantic cables came to ground was auctioned to companies hoping to gain a millisecond in trading advantage – proof that the internet does, in fact, live somewhere.

Some of these plots in Decentraland have evocative names, like 'Rare Plaza Side Plot!', or 'Luminous Futures', seeming to want to convey some slice of the hereafter that they offer to the right buyer. Others are called simply 'Parcel 53,132'. I wander around Decentraland on an unusually hot day in the west of Ireland. For once, the blue skies outside match the unblemished blue of the sky in Decentraland. I jump into a plot of land called 'Sailings'. Fake-looking trees and plants render as I move forward through the space. Everything is bathed in a brilliant light. At first I can't figure out what it all reminds me of, and then it comes to me: Vegas. The brilliantly clear sky, the glaring stone work. The sense of being in a giant, never-ending outdoor mall – of perpetual mediation. The sense that you could turn a corner and find all this unreality busily rendering itself, one fake Eiffel Tower at a time. When I later come to read Neal

Stephenson's *Snow Crash*, the 1992 science fiction novel that coined the term 'metaverse', I notice that this city in the desert is also his touchstone. In the metaverse, Stephenson writes, 'the Street is always garish and brilliant, like Las Vegas freed from constraints of physics and finance'.[23]

I wander into an art exhibition in a space called the MV Gallery. There's a Jean-Michel Basquiat on display, *Untitled (Pollo Frito)*. Nearby is an abstract painting, incorrectly labelled as Monet's *Meule*. My laptop begins to overheat; the fan gears up, making a humming sound that registers subliminally as a machine in distress. I move out of the door as fast as I can go, bang into a window, and set off across the plaza. There are billboards everywhere, sometimes advertising some crypto-equity venture, but more often advertising the possibilities of advertisement. At the edge of the plaza there's a small grey-green cupboard, very like the exchange points found on town and city streets – the point where buried cables surface. Behind that, a blue car rotates on a podium with the label 'Cryptomotors'. I'm taken to the webpage of a 'digital automaker', a company specialising in creating NFTs of digital cars powered by the Ethereum blockchain. I set off across the plaza to another building rising up in the distance, a race stadium for e-sports. Outside is a giant Trump statue in a MAGA cap and jeans, feet spread in a cowboy stance. A QR code accepts donations. The stance is similar to the superhero poses on the Trump Digital Trading Cards the former president mints in 2022. The future being called up is not one I want to live in. 'But that's fine', the giant statue seems to say. 'It's not really for you anyway.'

When so much looks like a pre-emptive land grab for the future of the internet, Indigenous communities are now asking for a say in how these worlds are made, folding First Nations and their rights into the foundations of the metaverse. These communities want to avoid the grabs that structured the imperial world order. In 1999, 3G radio spectrum auctions in New Zealand were halted on the grounds that 'the ether' was part of Maori heritage, and therefore subject to the Waitangi Treaty. Maori culture spoke of a space between the earth and the sky that celestial communications flowed through – a proto-metaverse. 'Wow,' says a friend when I tell him this story, 'colonialism 2.0.' First Nations people are now floating the possibility of an Indigenous cultural embassy in the metaverse, a way to hold the space – though it is not always clear what the space will be for, besides selling. 'We're putting a value on our lore so it becomes economically empowering to our nations', a representative says.[24]

Land is not the only thing for sale in Decentraland. There are wearables for avatars. NFT artist Beeple launched a company that hopes to be 'a memory palace for the metaverse', tokenising precious moments like a commercial version of Vadim's beloved screengrabs. There are rainbow pride earrings; fractal NFT hoodies that look like the tie-dyed shirts you buy at Glastonbury; wizard robes; and high-top sneakers with a *Back to the Future* flair. There are auctions for the NFTs of names in Decentraland. 'Tate' is currently auctioning for 4,000 ether. Eatshit is only worth 150.

Thirty years ago, with the publication of Stephenson's *Snow Crash*, the term 'metaverse' was a buzzword for connected virtual worlds spanning the internet. (Stephenson would go on to be chief futurist for Magic Leap, and later an advisor to Jeff Bezos's space colonisation project Blue Origin.) The Los Angeles of *Snow Crash* is a Franchise-Organised Quasi-National Entity (or FOQNE), a kind of neo-feudal separatist enclave governed by corporations. Public services have all been privatised. Hiro, the protagonist, is a pizza delivery driver by day and a hacker by night, driving dangerously to deliver pizzas on time to sixteen-year-old skate-punks. He lives with a roommate in a 20x30 storage container on the edge of the city. A bit of a loser in the real world, in the Metaverse he has made better life choices. Along with a group of likeminded hackers, Hiro bought a development in the newly emerging Metaverse. At the time it was 'just a little patch of light amid a vast blackness', but now it's much more prestigious than his real world U-Stor-It. In the Metaverse he has a nice big house. But 'real estate acumen does not always extend across universes'.[25]

Usually there is an anachronistic tang to how the past imagines the future (strains of the Cold War in the 1960s cyborg, post-war domestic aspirations in *The Jetsons*). But what strikes me about the world of *Snow Crash* is not how out of joint it now seems, thirty years on, but how familiar it feels to me. It's not just the gig workers racing targets on their smart devices and desperately trying to keep pace with the rising cost of living – it's the air of hopelessness. The sense that the future IRL has been emptied of joy or pleasure, and all that is left now is the doom-scroll. As Hiro observes, 'when you live in a shithole, there's always the Metaverse'.[26]

The best known of these metaverse spaces is *Second Life*, or 'Linden', a city that moved beyond gaming into 'everything from social lives to business plans to artistic movements'. *Second Life* was founded as a game in 2003. Unlike most gaming tokens at the time, *Second Life*'s currency, Linden dollars, was exchangeable for the US dollar. In the game it was tied to 'land ownership', Cory Ondrejka, the company's former CTO tells me, where owning virtual land is the same as paying for hosting services. The player is buying space on a server. Gradually, users set up homes in Linden, ran thriving businesses, and built careers as property developers and designers and wedding coordinators. They made virtual items to sell to other residents. They made games within games. Almost anything Richard Florida could anticipate in a thriving creative city was already happening in Linden.

'As soon as the token could be traded for US dollars, regulations started to apply', Ondrejka says. 'People built games of chance inside *Second Life* using scripting language. You get very interesting phone calls from the state attorney general saying: "It sure looks like you have gambling going on?" ... – "Noooh, no, *sir*, we certainly do not. And we will *definitely* go crack down on that through policy."' Likewise, people were building banks and issuing Linden loans. The company CEO, Philip Rosedale, was quoted in an article comparing Linden dollars to the era of wildcat banking. 'It turns out that the SEC doesn't think that's very funny, either.'[27]

One such bank, Ginkgo Financial, offered interest rates of as much as 70 per cent per annum for a personal account, denominated in Linden dollars. Some claimed that the interest returns were propped up by new entrants to what was essentially a pyramid scheme. Others believed the bank's investments lay in *Second Life*'s in-game casinos. When Linden announced a ban on in-world gambling in 2007, it halved the economy and triggered a run on Ginkgo Financial. The bank collapsed. In 2008, *Second Life* prohibited fixed-interest accounts for all banks without a real-world charter. Banks without the necessary licensing closed, or were converted to stocks. Linden Labs acquired the necessary licences to be a payment processor, jumping through the same hoops that PayPal had cleared five or six years before.

Linden was the first virtual world to give IP to creators. It invited Lawrence Lessig, a legal scholar and the founder of Creative Commons licensing, as an advisor in 2002. 'And Larry was like "You know, it's kind of stupid to ask people to create things and not allow them to *own* it."'[28] In every other EULA of the time, it was typical for the company to take ownership of everything users created on its platform. 'If you composed a love poem over chat in *World of Warcraft*?? WoW *owned* it.' It was the first time that a game-like environment had decided to treat itself as a creativity product. 'Because, obviously, Microsoft Word don't claim ownership of the text you write on their software ... although the rumours are that they considered it more than once ...'

Second Life allowed users to create their own digital items and sell them for Linden dollars. In a kind of proto–smart contract, creators would attach scripts to their objects that specified terms of sale. Clicking an item might copy it and initiate a transfer to the original creator, for example. Because users retained IP in what they made, they could issue a Digital Millennium Copyright Act takedown against someone who copied their products. Users could specify that an object was not replicable. In this case, a copy request would be denied by the central server. But a lot of people didn't bother, Ondrejka says. Many creators felt that 'uniqueness was less useful than brand value and awareness and getting things out in the world'.[29]

In 2006, some proprietary code for scripting objects was accidentally leaked. Hackers wrote a program to feed the code back into the world and duplicate items. This was Copybot, a replicating machine for things in *Second Life*. Copybot allowed citizens to copy things in the virtual world without rewarding the original creators. Shops closed. People gathered in Linden to protest. It was *Second Life*'s Napster moment. 'The bottom line is that preventing duplication is extremely difficult.'

In 2006 my brother Ross's job was to protect Linden from cyberattacks. 'I don't mind when he's home late so much right now', my sister-in-law joked at the time. 'I can say he's out saving the world.' Ross's first job out of college was working for a company that designed physics engines to sell to games. 'Picture, like, a chair in a room,' one of his colleagues told me in 2000. I was standing in the basement of an office on Merrion Square in Dublin, watching three twenty-something programmers cluster around a PC. In my memory, the image on screen is not of a chair in a room, but a ball bouncing through a matrix. 'In an animated reaction I shoot the chair and it falls over. The same way every time. With a physics engine, the chair and the gun and the bullet and the room itself are programmed to behave in accordance with the laws of physics. So, like, I hit the chair at this angle and it falls over. But if I hit it at this angle … it spins around, but doesn't fall.' With physics engines, objects are programmed to exist (and persist) in the virtual world, and to obey real physical laws. And this process, it turns out, takes a lot of real energy.

Linden went on to license the company's products for their virtual worlds. My brother worked as part of the support team to fix a series of attacks against the physics engine. Hackers were 'griefing' the system by overloading the physics engine with complex tasks, making it produce more objects than it was able to. 'For example: spawn a world with 10,000 over-lapping bodies. Each object would have to collide with every other object, creating 10 million collisions to calculate. Want it worse? Make each of those a concave object made of 500 triangles. Now you've billions of collisions to calculate, and then billions more resulting constraints to solve to try to stop them from interpenetrating.' 'Kind of like a DDoS attack on a metaverse?' I ask. 'Exactly.'

Today the same brother now works for Oculus, the VR gaming headset acquired by Facebook in 2015.

In 2022, Facebook changed its name to Meta. CEO Mark Zuckerberg announced that Facebook would now be a metaverse company, not a social media platform. The company launched its own metaversal space, called Horizon Worlds, a VR environment built for the Oculus Quest.

At home on my phone, I watch the Super Bowl ad for Meta's new Metaverse headset. A band of animatronic animals play Simple Minds' 'Don't You (Forget about Me)' in a space-themed dive. The pizza café and games arcade, called Questys, is kitted out with neon planets, a nostalgic dream of space colonisation that's going out of business. The lights go off. The band is left alone. People come and start to pack everything away. A hand-made sign in the window says 'closed forever'. The lead singer, an animatronic dog, winds up in a dumpster, packed in beside beige-coloured e-waste and broken office furniture, the props of pre-pandemic work culture. Just as the jaws of a rubbish compactor are about to close on his head, the dog is 'rescued'. In the next scene he is standing in a light-filled museum called the Bosworth Space Centre. Beautiful planets are suspended from the ceiling. One paw points the way to the café. Watching, I'm not sure how this new reality is a 'win'. But then the dog comes across a virtual headset. Suddenly he's reunited with his animatronic friends in the metaverse, where nobody is forgotten about and where nobody has a bottom half. The song continues. 'With meta you can have a second life to escape your reality,' someone has written in the YouTube comments. 'Ya, if your life sucks, put on a headset and pretend like everything's ok,' writes someone else. 'What's wrong with all you people?' a third person puts in. 'Mark is trying to bring us to the *actual oasis*.' When you live in a shithole, there's always the metaverse. A second life. A second chance. A fresh start, or as many fresh starts as you want. Spawning and respawning into the virtual world.

Facebook is also developing the pieces that go with the metaverse: social networks, virtual reality, reputation tokens, a global identity token, and a global currency (allegedly dubbed Zuck Bucks). And then, of course, there are the virtual things. Meta is backing the 'phygital' economy, in which a user can purchase a digital version of Adidas Sambas to clothe their avatar in the metaverse while buying another pair for their own feet IRL. Adidas's 'Into the Metaverse' collection produced $22 million in sales in the first few hours after its launch on OpenSea in 2021. Gucci, which has experimented with the sale of digital-only accessories, sold digital bags with a price tag that exceeded their physical offerings. Nike made $3.1 million in six minutes with a sale for phygital sneakers. The make-up brand NARS released a digital twin of its best-selling blush in 'Orgasm'. Taken to its limit, it would be a virtual economy to match the real point-for-point, like the Borges story that curators love to quote in their catalogue essays.[30] Borges writes of a map so exact that it grows as big as the world it represents. The less-quoted piece of that story happens after the huge map is rolled out. The people realise it is useless. They abandon it. The torn remnants become a home for homeless and unwanted things.

Compared to the lively economies of *Second Life* or even *Final Fantasy*, where you can earn a decent living as an interior decorator, the feeling of Decentraland is more speculative. Think of the Louvre Abu Dhabi – a culture cleaved off and dropped in the middle of a desert. Or maybe it's like Burning Man after 2015: a safe, monetised version of what was once a genuine subculture. And indeed, you too will go to Burning Man. In the metaverse.

You Will Live on the Internet

Years ago I came across a children's book called *You Will Go to the Moon*. It was first published in 1959 by Mae and Ira Freeman, ten years before the first moon landing. The book predicts a future where space travel is a leisure pursuit for a baby boomer and his parents. It shows the rocket they will use to get to the moon, the gated compounds they will live in, and the golf buggies they will use to get around. It wasn't just telling a story. The Freemans were shilling a future. The grammar of Web3 is similar. You *will* live in the metaverse. Rather than putting a name on somewhere that is already there, supporters are working hard to bring it into being – not with a game engine, but through meme-hustling. These are new realities, hewn from words. 'The advocates of Web3 are quite explicit about this', Evgeny Morozov writes: 'we've got this beautiful map on our hands – all that's missing is the territory it is supposed to refer to. Perhaps, this is the right mindset for the age of the Metaverse: if there's no reality, we'll create one by talking it into existence.'[31]

The term 'metaverse', like the term 'blockchain', is both vague and capacious, mashing together visions for the future of gaming and augmented reality with scenes from *Ready Player One*. For all its varied meanings, most agree it refers to *one* place, in the sense that the internet is one place with shared standards and multiple offerings. Each platform wants to be the monopoly – a hermetically sealed 'magic circle' where, as Mitch Zamara, a metaverse game designer for the pay-to-earn game *Million on Mars*, puts it, 'You are the central bank, you are the regulator, you are the Federal Reserve. You get to do everything.'[32]

Platforms are competing to see who will build the world and develop the standards for how items are rendered, who will manage identity, and, perhaps most crucially, act as a payment rail for processing the purchase and transfer of digital items. To that end, many with a vested interest in crypto think that blockchain is a solution. As opposed to private rails, a blockchain might be used to create a payment rail that could work across many worlds. A blockchain might also be used to tokenise and maintain a degree of persistence for digital items, Matthew Ball suggests – a permanent registry where in-game items could be recorded and transferred, and where non-fungible tokens would allow for fungibility between worlds.[33]

But, as things stand today, there are many islands and many tokens and many ways of rendering virtual things, all siloed, all competing to make the future.[34] You cannot take your Tamagotchi to *Animal Crossings*, any more than you can wear your phygital Nikes to walk from Linden to Decentraland. That kind of interoperability is at least ten years away, says Barthelet. It's not just a question of developing agreements and accounting systems between different spaces. It's also a question of the 'rendering pipeline', where a sword forged in *Zelda* might be coded differently to a sword in *Fortnite*.[35] Both virtual worlds are faithfully rendered, but this doesn't mean they are faithful to each other.

Barthelet, who has spent much of the past decade living on a boat with his wife and two children, has a theory that the metaverse might eventually be good for the real environment. 'We are at a tipping point', he says. 'Somewhere around 2050, parts of the world will be deadly heat zones. We are looking at the mass migration of 2 billion people. Where will these people live in the future? It's going to challenge the democratic system, any political system. It's potentially the beginning of World War III.' It sounds like *Fortnite*, I think. It sounds like *Battle Royale*. (I wonder if this is why the Barthelets have taken to the high seas.) 'And if we follow the rules and cut fossil fuels, we are destroying 30 per cent of the economy. We are facing a recession of sixty years, which by itself might bring World War III because no political system can handle such a thing. My hope', Luc continues, 'is we can shift from a real, material economy to virtual consumption. We are already seeing that younger generations are more and more satisfied by virtual goods.' Luc's calculation assumes that virtual goods will replace physical consumption one day soon. You will own nothing and be happy – or else.[36] Or maybe 'assumes' is too strong a word. He *hopes*. The dream of the metaverse is that someday the rendered world, with its virtual things and virtual money, will feel more real than the world of things that can't be called from the command line. But if Will is anything to go by, virtual stuff collects alongside the Lego and lightsabers littering his bedroom in the real world. And where will 2 billion migrants live in this future? Not in the metaverse.

Alan Butler is probably best known for *Down and Out in Los Santos*, a video work that uses the in-game camera to capture 3D-rendered homeless people and desolate landscapes in *Grand Theft Auto*. While the poor of Los Santos are loosely rendered, Butler argues that it is still possible to have 'real emotional experiences' when interacting with them. 'This might sound sad and geeky, but it's true. The characters are aware of my presence as I photograph them: sometimes they ignore me, other times I'm attacked and have to defend myself. They chatter to each other, they share alcohol and cigarettes, they ask for money to buy drugs. Programmed to self-identify, they congregate with those in similar social situations to themselves.'[37] Butler's work takes place in game economies, but he is drawn to the stuff around the edges that the game classes as 'worthless'.

Lately he has been looking at digital rubbish. Not the discarded phones and consoles currently crowding landfill sites in Ghana, but 3D renderings of litter in online games – though ultimately the two are intertwined. In *Grand Theft Auto V*, Butler says 'Litter is there to create realism', and 'like its real world counterpart, we're invited to think of it like shit and pretend it's not there'.[38] As Butler describes it, each solitary piece of rubbish is installed as a file in the game library, a database of every element reproduced in the game. Downloading the game moves this data through multiple servers. Playing the game sees the object loaded into RAM, and processed by the CPU and GPU. Finally, the computer outputs the image via an HDMI cable onto a monitor. If a player chooses to interact with the litter – shooting it with a gun so that it explodes to pieces – new smaller litter files and sound effects have to be loaded to go alongside it. 'If you think that every street in GTA has a hundred pieces of litter on it, so how many microprocessors does it take to render them in each instance? And a hundred million people bought this video game ... this stuff is having real world devastating effects on the environment via power consumption'.[39] The shit in the metaverse is spilling over into the shit in the real world.

In 2006, the average *Second Life* avatar consumed more electricity than the average Brazilian. In 2019, data centres surpassed air traffic in terms of carbon emissions. This is to say nothing about the energy-intensive algorithms used to mine virtual loot and mint virtual collectibles in virtual worlds. While Butler doesn't arrive at a precise figure for the cost of rendering a crumbled coke can in *Grand Theft Auto*, artist Memo Akten performed a calculation for the carbon footprint of an average NFT using proof-of-work. Minting an NFT cost approximately 142 kWh, or 83 kg of CO_2, while one transaction – an auction or a resale – consumed 87 kWh, or 51 kg of CO_2.[40]

In November 2022, Meta had a huge round of layoffs, making 11,000 staff redundant. 'They just tried to grow too fast', a friend who works there tells me, when I ask about the job losses flooding the news. 'They looked to the lockdowns when everyone was online and thought that this was how it would always be.' The metaverse, rendered forever. Instead, six months after the rebrand, the company formerly known as Facebook was nagging its employees to hang out in Horizon Worlds, Meta's primary variant. The future was over before it had even begun. A company memo from the VP of the Metaverse, Vishal Shah, read: 'Everyone in this organization should make it their mission to fall in love with Horizon Worlds … Get in there.'[41] Live on the internet – or else. This wasn't some beautiful escape from a grim reality. It seemed like a real shithole.

Acknowledgements

Tokens is the product of two years of writing and a decade of fieldwork and research. I'm afraid to start thanking people, because I'm sure to forget so many who have been a source of support, information, or advice throughout this process. The list is so long.

Much of the research in this book was supported by various funding bodies, scholarships, grants, and invited residencies. In particular I would like to thank the Irish Research Council for numerous grants and awards, but in particular for the Government of Ireland Postdoctoral Fellowship and New Horizons funding, both of which directly contributed to research in this book. It's no exaggeration to say that without this support I would have no career. Thanks for taking a chance on someone with a bad degree in fine art. Thanks also to SFI Ireland, CONNECT, Trinity College Dublin, Science Gallery Dublin, European Science Open Forum, Trinity College Dublin's Performing Arts Grants, and NCAD's Research Support Fund for supporting and funding the research that went into this book. Particular thanks to the Royal Irish Academy and Fulbright Ireland for funding research and travel on this topic.

I'd also like to thank faculty in universities including UC Irvine; the New School, New York; Microsoft Research, Cambridge; the University of Edinburgh; the University of Manchester; Trinity College Dublin; University College, Galway; NUI Maynooth; the London School of Economics; Siegen University; the University of Amsterdam; and the Institute of Network Cultures, Amsterdam. I swear I'm not just listing every university I've ever visited! There have been so many amazing researchers and brilliant conversations. These are just some that spring to mind.

Thanks to many researchers in the money and internet space, including Bernardo Batiz-Lazo, Jonathan Beller, Jaya Klara Brekke, Finn Brunton, Ruth Catlow, Ursula Dalinghaus, Primavera de Filippi, Quinn DuPont, Paul Ennis, Sarah Friend, Max Haiven, Jonathan Harris, Antonia Hernández, Josh Lauer, Laura Lotti, Geert Lovink, Nicky Marsh, Bill Maurer, Tom McDonald, Liz McFall, Taylor Nelms, Frank Pasquale, Clare Rowan, Trebor Scholz, Brett Scott, Erin Taylor, Cassie Thornton, Denise Thwaites, Nate Tkacz, and Martin Zeilinger. I know there are others. Special thanks to the late Nigel Dodd, for his wonderful work on the social life of money and for his support and encouragement. In particular, thanks go to Lana Swartz, who has been a sounding board, knowledge source, cheerleader, and unofficial counsellor.

Thanks to the various interview subjects in this book, many of whom were consulted on numerous occasions, including but not exclusively Kevin McCoy of Monegraph, members of Ascribe, Cory Ondrejka, Sarah Flannery, Luc Barthelet, Cian O'Dwyer, Vadim Taranenko, and OG gamer Will O'Dwyer.

Special thanks to financial consultant David Birch for his insight into everything from payments and the porn industry to Facebucks. With thanks to Jess Houlgrave of Codex, Jérôme Croisier of Maecenas, Kai Chng of DigixGlobal, and various members of the fintech industry who have spoken to me and agreed to be interviewed over the years.

With thanks to artists and collectives including Furtherfield Gallery (London), Rhizomatica (New York), the Salvage Art Institute, Lorna Mills, Kevin McCoy, Kevin Abosch, Núria Güell, Payu Harris of MazaCoin, Cassie Thornton, and many more artists, theorists, and practitioners working at the intersection of art and money. With thanks to festivals re:publica and transmediale, Berlin, and particular thanks to transmediale curator Nora O'Murchu.

Thanks to various activists and social movements including the P2P Foundation, Procomuns, Barcelona, Jaromil, Enric Duran, the Decode Project, Feasta, Circles UBI Berlin, the Feminist Economics Department, members of the Robin Hood Minor Asset Management Agency and ECSA, Daniel Mi Sun, Olúfémi Táíwò, and everyone working to recreate the economy, one token at a time.

Eternal gratitude goes to my supervisor and friend, Professor Linda Doyle, and all of the OMG Research Group.

Thanks also to all my colleagues in NCAD; in particular, to my head of department David Crowley and director of NCAD Sarah Glennie. Without your support there would be no book.

I want to thank the two most special people, P and Ted. I love you.

Thanks to the O'Dwyer family WhatsApp for answering weird queries relating to money, grammar, and/or computer science. Particular thanks to my brother Ross for connecting me with the gaming industry, and for my sister Jeanne for reading early drafts.

With thanks to my family and friends and the staff of St John's Ward, Crumlin, for their support at an incredibly challenging time. Thanks to the incredible Maggie Armstrong for reading my narcissistic WhatsApps, telling me I am smart and letting me be horrible.

Finally, huge thanks to my editor Leo Hollis and the team at Verso, for seeing something in the proposal, guiding the project, and providing feedback and support all the way through.

Notes

Introduction

1 Clifford Geertz, 'Thick Description: Toward an Interpretive Theory of Culture', in *The Cultural Geography Reader*, ed. Timothy Oakes and Patricia L. Price (London: Routledge, 2008), 32.
2 Denise Schmandt-Besserat, 'The Invention of Tokens', in *Tokens: Culture, Connections, Communities*, ed. Antonino Crisà, Mairi Gkikaki, and Clare Rowan (London: Royal Numismatic Society, 2019).
3 Bill Maurer, 'The Politics of Token Economics, Then and Now', in Crisà et al., *Tokens*; Mabel Lang, 'Allotment by Tokens', *Historia: Zeitschrift für Alte Geschichte* H. 1 (January 1959).
4 Satoshi Nakamoto, 'Bitcoin: A Peer-to-Peer Electronic Cash System', 2008, bitcoin.org.
5 Timothy May and Eric Hughes, 'Anarchy', in 'Crypto Glossary', compiled by Timothy May and Eric Hughes, September 1992, shared to Cypherpunk mailing list.
6 Eddie Duggan, 'Stranger Games: The Life and Times of the Spintriae', *Board Game Studies Journal* 11:1 (2017).
7 Sabrina Valin, 'How Royal Tokens Constituted an Art Medium that Participated in the Monarchical System between 1610 and 1661', in Crisà et al., *Tokens*.
8 Viviana Zelizer, *The Social Meaning of Money: Pin Money, Paychecks, Poor Relief, and Other Currencies* (New York: Basic Books, 1994).
9 Kenny Parker and Chiara Fiorillo, 'Ex-Boyfriend Puts Cash in Former Lover's Bank Account with "S**g" as Reference', *Daily Mirror*, 26 September 2022; John Weekes, 'Ex Using Bank Transfer Messages to Harass Woman Says He Wants Her to Be "Scared" of Him', *New Zealand Herald*, 13 July 2022.
10 Stamatoula Makrypodi, 'Tokens Inside and Outside Excavation Contexts: Seeking the Origin. Examples of Clay Tokens from the Collections of the Athens Numismatic Museum', in Crisà et al., *Tokens*.

11 William J. Courtenay, 'Token Coinage and the Administration of Poor Relief during the Late Middle Ages', *Journal of Interdisciplinary History* 3:2 (1972).

12 Langdon Winner, 'Do Artifacts Have Politics?', in *Computer Ethics*, ed. John Weckert (London: Routledge, 2017).

13 Antonino Crisá, Mairi Gkikaki, and Clare Rowan, 'Introduction', in Crisà et al., *Tokens*.

1. A Bit of Cheer

1 Viviana Zelizer, *The Social Meaning of Money: Pin Money, Paychecks, Poor Relief, and Other Currencies* (New York: Basic Books, 1994), 107.

2 Ibid., 16.

3 See Ran Li et al., 'Examining Gifting Behavior on Live Streaming Platforms: An Identity-Based Motivation Model', *Information and Management* 58:6 (2021); Hyosun Kwon et al., '"It's Not Yet a Gift": Understanding Digital Gifting', *Proceedings of the 2017 ACM Conference on Computer Supported Cooperative Work and Social Computing*, February 2017; Jilei Zhou et al., 'The Magic of *Danmaku*: A Social Interaction Perspective of Gift Sending on Live Streaming Platforms', *Electronic Commerce Research and Applications* 34 (March 2019); Yi-Chieh Lee et al., 'Understanding How Digital Gifting Influences Social Interaction on Live Streams', *Proceedings of the 21st International Conference on Human–Computer Interaction with Mobile Devices and Services*, October 2019; Xiaoxing Zhang, Yu Xiang, and Lei Hao, 'Virtual Gifting on China's Live Streaming Platforms: Hijacking the Online Gift Economy', *Chinese Journal of Communication* 12:3 (March 2019).

4 Marshall McLuhan, *Understanding Media: The Extensions of Man* (London: MIT Press, 1994), 136.

5 Sybille Krämer, *Medium, Messenger, Transmission: An Approach to Media Philosophy* (Amsterdam: Amsterdam University Press, 2015).

6 Suzanne Collins, *The Hunger Games: Mockingjay Trilogy* (London: HarperCollins, 2009), 316.

7 Antonia Hernández, '"There's Something Compelling about Real Life": Technologies of Security and Acceleration on Chaturbate', *Social Media + Society* 5:4 (2019).

8 Clare Rowan, in conversation with the author, June 2021.

9 Krämer, *Medium, Messenger, Transmission*, 15.

10 See Asaf Nissenbaum and Limor Shifman, 'Internet Memes as Contested Cultural Capital: The Case of 4chan's /b/ Board', *New Media*

and Society 19:4 (2017); Richard Dawkins, *The Selfish Gene*, 3rd edn (New York: Oxford University Press, 2006); and Ioana Literat and Sarah Van Den Berg, 'Buy Memes Low, Sell Memes High: Vernacular Criticism and Collective Negotiations of Value on Reddit's MemeEconomy', *Information, Communication and Society* 22:2 (2019).

11 Ziming Wu and Xiaojuan Ma, 'Money as a Social Currency to Manage Group Dynamics: Red Packet Gifting in Chinese Online Communities', *Proceedings of the 2017 CHI Conference Extended Abstracts on Human Factors in Computing Systems*, May 2017, 2244.

12 Sarah Jeong, 'Dogecoin', in *Paid: Tales of Dongles, Checks, and Other Money Stuff*, ed. Lana Swartz and Bill Maurer (London: MIT Press, 2017), 53.

13 TheTinyRose, 'Amazon Wishlist', r/onlyfansadvice, 15 January 2021, reddit.com.

14 Clare Rowan, in conversation with the author, June 2021.

15 Carly A. Kocurek, '"Good for One Screw": A History of Brothel Tokens', *Atlantic*, 27 February 2014.

16 Diane Coyle, 'In E-money We Trust, All Others Pay Cash', *Business World*, 3 April 2000.

17 Silvia Federici, *Wages against Housework* (Bristol: Falling Wall, 1975), 4.

18 Zelizer, *Social Meaning of Money*, 42, 58.

19 Ibid., 45.

20 Elizabeth Bernstein, *Temporarily Yours* (Chicago: University of Chicago Press, 2021), 127.

21 Ibid., 103.

22 Zelizer, *Social Meaning of Money*.

23 Michael J. Sandel, *What Money Can't Buy: The Moral Limits of Markets* (London: Macmillan, 2012).

24 Georg Simmel, *The Philosophy of Money* (London: Routledge, 2004).

25 Viviana Zelizer, *The Purchase of Intimacy* (Oxford: Princeton University Press, 2005).

26 Zelizer, *The Purchase of Intimacy*.

27 Ibid., 117.

28 Landon Boswell (lboswell6), 'Seriously Though', r/onlyfansadvice, reddit.com, 7 June 2021.

29 Kris Graft, '"Being Found to Be Sexy by Others Is Not Against Our Rules" – Twitch', *Game Developer*, 21 May 2021, gamedeveloper. com.

30 Mary L. Gray and Siddharth Suri, *Ghost Work: How to Stop Silicon Valley from Building a New Global Underclass* (London: Eamon Dolan, 2019), 14.

31 Michelle Slatalla, 'Thanking Websites, with Cash', *New York Times*, 15 February 2001.

32 Bill Maurer, 'Closed Loops and Private Gateways: Money, Technology and the Private Interest in Payment', MoneyLab Conference, Amsterdam, 21–2 March 2014.

33 Angela Jones, *Camming: Money, Power, and Pleasure in the Sex Work Industry* (New York: NYU Press, 2020); Crystal Abidin, 'From "Networked Publics" to "Refracted Publics": A Companion Framework for Researching "Below the Radar" Studies', *Social Media + Society* 7:1 (2021), 202.

34 KNN, 'Interview with Digitrevx (Projekt Melody)', 12 February 2020, youtube.com.

35 Ibid.

36 William Clyde Partin, 'Bit by (Twitch) Bit: "Platform Capture" and the Evolution of Digital Platforms', *Social Media + Society* 6:3 (2020).

37 Carlo Vercellone, 'The New Articulation of Wages, Rent and Profit in Cognitive Capitalism', paper presented at the Art of Rent Conference, Queen Mary University School of Business and Management, London, February 2008.

38 Antonia Hernández, 'On-Demand Intimacy: The Cost and Value of Intimate Exchanges on Chaturbate and OnlyFans' (lecture, Uncommon Economies 13, University College Dublin, 6 April 2021).

39 Eliezer Yudkowsky, 'Inertialess Cash at Last!', post to the Extropian Mailing List, 9 March 2000, diyhpl.us.

2. Money Talks, Tokens Track

1 Jean-Paul Sartre, 'Doing and Having', in *Being and Nothingness: An Essay on Phenomenological Ontology* (New York: Pocket, 1978), 609, 611, 664.

2 Arjun Appadurai, 'Introduction: Commodities and the Politics of Value', in *The Social Life of Things: Commodities in Cultural Perspective*, ed. Arjun Appadurai (London: Cambridge University Press, 1988), 18.

3 Stan Alcorn, 'A New Map of the US Created by How Our Dollar Bills Move', *FastCompany*, 13 November 2014, fastcompany.com.

4 Denise Schmandt-Besserat, 'The Origins of Writing: An Archaeologist's Perspective', *Written Communications* 3:1 (1986).

5 These clay tokens were 'stored memory'. See Jane Gleeson-White, *Double Entry: How the Merchants of Venice Shaped the Modern World – And How Their Invention Could Make or Break the Planet* (London: Allen & Unwin, 2011), 12.

6 Glyn Davies, *A History of Money: From Ancient Times to the Present Day* (Cardiff: University of Wales Press, 1994).

7 Stephanie Bell, 'The Role of the State and the Hierarchy of Money', *Cambridge Journal of Economics* 25:2 (2001); Hartmut Berghoff, Philip Scranton, and Uwe Spiekermann, 'The Origins of Marketing and Market Research: Information, Institutions, and Markets', in *The Rise of Marketing and Market Research* (New York: Palgrave Macmillan, 2012).

8 Christine Desan, *Making Money: Coin, Currency, and the Coming of Capitalism* (Oxford: Oxford University Press, 2014), 180.

9 Mary Poovey, *Genres of the Credit Economy* (Chicago: University of Chicago Press, 2008), 145.

10 Charles Johnstone, *Chrysal; Or, the Adventures of a Guinea* (London: Howlett & Brimmer, 1760–5), 7.

11 James W. Cortada, *Before the Computer: IBM, NCR, Burroughs, and Remington Rand and the Industry They Created, 1865–1956* (Princeton, NJ: Princeton University Press, 2000); David L. Stearns, *Electronic Value Exchange: Origins of the VISA Electronic Payment System* (New York: Springer, 2011); Josh Lauer, *Creditworthy: A History of Consumer Surveillance and Financial Identity in America* (New York: Columbia University Press, 2017).

12 Benedetto Cotrugli, *Della mercatura et del mercante perfetto* (Venice: all'Elefanta, 1593).

13 Alexander Malcolm, *A New Treatise of Arithmetick and Book-keeping* (Edinburgh: J. Mosman & W. Brown, 1718).

14 Iulia Ciutina, *Where Credit's Due* podcast, episode 8: 'How AI Is Changing Lending, with Zest AI CEO Mike de Vere and Informed. IQ CEO Justin Wickett', 31 August 2022.

15 Stearns, *Electronic Value Exchange*, 148–9.

16 Lauer, *Creditworthy*, 247.

17 Ibid.

18 Motherboard, 'Is Venmo a Social Network?', 29 April 2021, youtube.com.

19 Hang Do Thi Duc, 'Public by Default', *22.8miles* (blog), 2018, 22-8miles.com.

20 Alex Goldman and Emmanuel Dzotsi, *Reply All* podcast, episode 4: 'Follow the Money', 7 December 2014.

21 In 2000, the US superstore Target inadvertently notified the parents of a pregnant teenager when they sent her coupons for baby products in the post. She had yet to tell her family, the story goes, but the record of her recent purchases caused the retailer to infer correctly that she was expecting.

22 Joe Deville and Lonneke van der Velden, 'Seeing the Invisible Algorithm: The Practical Politics of Tracking the Credit Trackers', in

Algorithmic Life: Calculative Devices in the Age of Big Data, ed. Louise Amoore and Volha Piotukh (London: Routledge, 2015).

23 Lauer, *Creditworthy*, 73.

24 Ibid., 100.

25 Ibid., 188.

26 Bill Maurer, 'Re-risking in Realtime: On Possible Futures for Finance after the Blockchain', *Behemoth: A Journal on Civilisation* 9:2 (2016).

27 Quentin Hardy, 'Just the Facts. Yes, All of Them', *New York Times*, 24 March 2012.

28 Ciutina, 'How AI Is Changing Lending'.

29 Matt Flannery, 'Money 20/20', October 2015. Quoted in Lora Kolodny, 'Former Kiva.org CEO Brings New App, a "Branchless Bank" to Kenya', *Wall Street Journal*, 7 May 2015.

30 Joe Deville, 'Digital Subprime: Tracking the Credit Trackers', in *The Sociology of Debt*, ed. Mark Featherstone (Bristol: Policy, 2019), 145.

31 Flannery, 'Money 20/20'.

32 Frank Pasquale, *The Black Box Society: The Secret Algorithms that Control Money and Information* (Cambridge, MA: Harvard University Press, 2015); Cathy O'Neil, *Weapons of Math Destruction: How Big Data Increases Inequality and Threatens Democracy* (New York: Broadway, 2016).

33 Timothy May, 'Scenario for a Ban on Cash Transactions', 24 November 1992, Cypherpunk mailing list.

34 Hyun Shin, Bank of International Settlements, 'Cryptocurrencies and the Economics of Money', speech on the occasion of the bank's annual general meeting, 24 June 2018, bis.org.

35 Isabella Kaminska, 'Is Our Money about to Spout Memories?', *Financial Times*, 25 June 2020.

36 Brett Scott, *Cloudmoney: Cash, Cards, Crypto and the War for Our Wallets* (London: Penguin, 2022).

37 Peter Sunde, speech at 'Future of Money', London Web Summit, March 2012. Quoted in Michael Allan McCrae, 'Cash Starts to Disappear and Privacy Advocates Worry', mining.com, 20 March 2012.

38 Ursula Dalinghaus, 'Keeping Cash: Assessing the Arguments about Cash and Crime', *Cash Matters*, 2017, cashmatters.org.

39 Olive McCarthy, in conversation with the author, September 2022; Carol Power et al., *The Origins, Ethos and Evolution of Co-operative Credit in Ireland* (University College, Cork: IRD Duhallow Women's Forum/Centre for Co-operative Studies, 2011).

40 Nigel Dodd, *The Social Life of Money* (Princeton, NJ: Princeton University Press, 2016).

41 James Gleick, 'Dead as a Dollar', *New York Times*, 16 June 1996.

42 European Central Bank, 'The Eurosystem Cash Strategy', 2023, ecb.europa.eu.
43 David Chaum, Congressional Speech, Testimony for US House of Representatives, 'The Future of Money: Hearing before the Subcommittee on Domestic and International Monetary Policy of the Committee on Banking and Financial Services, House of Representatives, One Hundred Fourth Congress, First Session', 25 July 1995, archive.org.
44 This outlined an approach where mutually suspicious groups could establish trust over a network. In Chaum's Vault, each member of a network signs, encrypts, and publicly broadcasts their transactions. These transactions are then 'chained' together using a checksum – a technique that ensures a piece of data has not been tampered with. David Chaum, 'Computer Systems Established, Maintained and Trusted by Mutually Suspicious Groups', PhD dissertation, University of California, Berkeley, 1982; Alan T. Sherman et al., 'On the Origins and Variations of Blockchain Technologies', *IEEE Security and Privacy* 17:1 (2019).
45 David Chaum, 'Security Without Identification: Transaction Systems to Make Big Brother Obsolete', *Communications of the ACM* 28: 10 (1985).
46 Ibid., 1030.
47 Finn Brunton, interview by Rachel O'Dwyer, *Neural* 68 (Winter 2021).
48 Robert Carlson, in conversation with the author, May 2022.
49 Finn Brunton and Helen Nissenbaum, *Obfuscation: A User's Guide for Privacy and Protest* (Cambridge, MA: MIT Press, 2015).
50 Alex Berke, 'Lockers and Noise: Co-opting an e-Commerce System to Improve Privacy and Wealth Distribution', poster, api.obfuscation. karls.computer/uploads/Lockers_and_Noise_Poster_a21fe87956.pdf.
51 Jonathan Harris, in conversation with the author, 10 August 2021.
52 Noah Yuran, 'Temple Mount Burn', *Burning Issue*, 2018, burning issue.net.
53 Lana Swartz, 'Bitcoin as a Meme and a Future', *Noema*, 11 February 2021.

3. Programmable Butter

1 Oireachtas, Dáil Éireann debate, 4 March 1997.
2 Begybysback, 'Butter Vouchers': 'Not sure exactly where you were living mate, but where I lived butter vouchers had multiple purposes, everything from buying cider to insurance discs in car windows', 22 December 2020, boards.ie.

3 James C. Scott, *Weapons of the Weak: Everyday Forms of Peasant Resistance* (New Haven, CT: Yale University Press, 1985).

4 Vivienne Archbold, Pride of Place Stoneybatter Facebook Page, 11 April 2021.

5 Mary Douglas, 'Primitive Rationing: A Study in Controlled Exchange', in *In the Active Voice* (Oxford: Routledge, 2011), 57.

6 Ibid., 58.

7 Ibid.

8 Karl Polanyi, 'The Economy as Instituted Process', *Trade and Market in the Early Empires: Economies in History and Theory* (New York: Free Press, 1957).

9 Friedrich Hayek, *The Denationalisation of Money* (London: Institute of Economic Affairs, 2007 [1976]), 58.

10 Viviana Zelizer, *The Social Meaning of Money: Pin Money, Paychecks, Poor Relief, and Other Currencies* (New York: Basic Books, 1994), 121, 123.

11 Ibid., 134.

12 Ibid., 137.

13 Ibid., 138.

14 Ibid., 139.

15 Bruce G. Carruthers, 'The Meanings of Money: A Sociological Perspective', *Theoretical Inquiries in Law* 11:1 (2010), 63.

16 William J. Courtenay, 'Token Coinage and the Administration of Poor Relief during the Late Middle Ages', *Journal of Interdisciplinary History* 3:2 (1972).

17 'Food Stamp and Snap Fraud', fraudguides.com.

18 Alan Bjerga, 'Trump's Budget Proposal Swaps Food Stamps for Ready-to-Eat Meal Kits', *Time*, 13 February 2018.

19 Mike Dee, 'Welfare Surveillance, Income Management and New Paternalism in Australia', *Surveillance and Society* 11:3 (2013).

20 Ibid., 274.

21 Virginia Eubanks, *Automating Inequality: How High-Tech Tools Profile, Police, and Punish the Poor* (New York: St Martin's, 2017), 22.

22 Zelizer, *Social Meaning of Money*, 133.

23 Ibid., 173.

24 Archbold, Pride of Place Stoneybatter Facebook Page.

25 Margaret Atwood, *The Handmaid's Tale* (London: Vintage, 1996), 182.

26 Ibid.

27 Margaret Atwood, 'How to Change the World', in *Burning Questions: Essays and Occasional Pieces 2004–2021* (London: Penguin, 2022), 208.

28 'Food Stamp and Snap Fraud'.

29 Madeleine Akrich, 'The De-scription of Technical Objects', in *Shaping Technology/Building Society: Studies in Sociotechnical Change*, ed. Wiebe E. Bijker and John Law (Cambridge, MA: MIT Press, 1994).

30 Nick Szabo, 'Smart Contracts', Phonetic Sciences, University of Amsterdam, 1994, fon.hum.uva.nl; Nick Szabo, 'Formalizing and Securing Relationships on Public Networks', *First Monday* 2:9 (1997).

31 Karen Levy, 'Book-Smart, Not Street-Smart: Blockchain-Based Smart Contracts and the Social Workings of Law', *Engaging Science, Technology, and Society* 3 (2017).

32 Aaron Wright and Primavera De Filippi, 'Decentralized Blockchain Technology and the Rise of Lex Cryptographia', *SSRN* electronic journal, 10 March 2015, 26, ssrn.com.

33 Vitalik Buterin, quoted in David Birch, 'They're Not Smart and They're Not Contracts', *Forbes*, 4 September 2021.

34 Edward de Bono, *The IBM Dollar* (London: Centre for the Study of Financial Innovation, March 1994), 2.

35 Ibid., 1.

36 Ibid., 3.

37 Ibid., 7.

38 Jonathan Rosenoer, 'Bespoke Programmable Crypto Token', United States Patent 10,742,398, 11 August 2020, trea.com.

39 Ibid.

40 David Birch, *The Currency Cold War: Cash and Cryptography, Hash Rates and Hegemony* (London: London Publishing Partnership, 2020), 50.

41 Timothy May, 'Scenario for a Ban on Cash Transactions', email to Cypherpunk list, 24 November 1992.

42 Andrew Singer, 'Programmable Money: How Crypto Tokens Could Change Our Entire Experience of Value Transfer', *Coin Telegraph*, 16 September 2020.

43 'Tokens', Foundling Museum, London, foundlingmuseum.org.uk.

44 Timothy May, quoting Bill Stewart, 'True Names and Webs of Trust', Cypherpunk post, 21 August 1995.

45 Vernor Vinge, *True Names ... and Other Dangers* (Wake Forest, NC: Baen, 1987).

46 Edward Castronova and Joshua Fairfield, 'Dragon Kill Points: A Summary Whitepaper', *SSRN* electronic journal, January 2007, ssrn.com.

47 Tim May and Eric Hughes, 'Reputation', Cypherpunk Glossary, Cypherpunk Forum, 1992; Hal Finney, 'Real World DigiCash', Cypherpunk forum post, 7 November 1993.

48 Rene Verhoeven and D. Carr, 'SunnySide', 2014 Future of Money Design Award, futuremoneyaward.com.

49 David Birch, cited in Bill Maurer, 'Late to the Party: Debt and Data', *Social Anthropology* 20:4 (2012), 478.
50 Birch, *Currency Cold War*, 51.
51 Lana Swartz, *New Money* (New Haven, CT: Yale University Press, 2021).
52 Bruno Latour, 'Mixing Humans and Nonhumans Together: The Sociology of a Door-Closer', *Social Problems* 35:3 (1988), 301.
53 Langdon Winner, 'Do Artifacts Have Politics?', in *Computer Ethics*, ed. John Weckert (London: Routledge, 2017).
54 F. A. Hayek, *The Road to Serfdom* (London: Routledge, 1976); Hayek, *Denationalization of Money*; David Boyle, *The Money Changers* (London: Routledge, 2015).
55 Birch, *Currency Cold War*.
56 Hyman P. Minsky, *Stabilizing an Unstable Economy* (New Haven, CT: Yale University Press, 1986).
57 Vili Lehdonvirta and Edward Castronova, *Virtual Economies: Design and Analysis* (London: MIT Press, 2014).
58 It was not the first time the platform had tried to build its own currency. Launched in 2009, Facebook Credits, like QQ coins, could be bought in bricks-and-mortar stores, earned from advertisers, and used to buy virtual items. The token was officially launched in 2011, and phased out in 2012.
59 Libra Association Members, 'An Introduction to Libra', 23 July 2019, sls.gmu.edu/pfrt/wp-content/uploads/sites/54/2020/02/LibraWhitePaper_en_US-Rev0723.pdf.
60 Katherina Pistor, 'Examining Facebook's Proposed Cryptocurrency and Its Impact on Consumers, Investors, and the American Financial System', Hearing before the Committee on Financial Services, US House of Representatives, One Hundred Sixteenth Congress, First Session, 17 July 2019.
61 Mark Zuckerberg in conversation with Denver Riggleman, 'An Examination of Facebook and Its Impact on the Financial Services and Housing Sectors', Hearing before the Committee on Financial Services, US House of Representatives, One Hundred Sixteenth Congress, First Session, 23 October 2019.
62 David Birch, in conversation with the author, November 2019.
63 David Gerard, *Libra Shrugged: How Facebook Tried to Take Over the Money* (self-published, 2020).
64 Diem, 'Commitment to Compliance and Consumer Protection', April 2020, diem.com.
65 Keep Big Tech Out of Finance Act, HR 4813, One Hundred Sixteenth Congress (2019), congress.gov.
66 Simon Scorer, 'Beyond Blockchain: What Are the Technology Requirements for a Central Bank Digital Currency?', *Bank*

Underground (blog), 13 September 2017, bankunderground.co.uk.

67 Hannah Murphy and Kiran Stacey, 'Facebook Libra: The Inside Story of How the Company's Cryptocurrency Dream Died', *Financial Times*, 10 March 2022.

4. Money, but Let's Make It Social

1 Dennis Roio, 'Bitcoin, the End of the Taboo on Money', *Media-N*, 2013, median.newmediacaucus.org.

2 Satoshi Nakamoto, 'Bitcoin: A Peer-to-Peer Electronic Cash System', 2008, bitcoin.org.

3 Peter S. Goodman, *Davos Man: How the Billionaires Devoured the World* (London: HarperCollins, 2022).

4 David Graeber, *Debt: The First 5,000 Years* (New York: Melville House, 2011).

5 Ralph Heidenreich and Stefan Heidenreich, 'On a Post-Monetary Network Based Economy', in *Moneylab Reader: An Intervention in Digital Economy*, ed. Geert Lovink, Nathaniel Tkac, and Patricia DeVries (Amsterdam: Institute of Network Cultures, 2015).

6 Hyman Minsky, *Stabilizing an Unstable Economy* (New Haven, CT: Yale University Press, 1986), 255. These two belief systems – money as a valuable commodity and money as a social or credit relationship – constitute two competing approaches to money theory known as metallism and chartalism.

7 Roio, 'Bitcoin, the End of the Taboo on Money'.

8 Ronald H. Coase, 'The Federal Communications Commission', in *Private and Common Property*, ed. Richard A. Epstein (London: Routledge, 2000); Garrett Hardin, 'The Tragedy of the Commons', in *Green Planet Blues* (London: Routledge, 2019).

9 Elinor Ostrom, *Governing the Commons: The Evolution of Institutions for Collective Action* (Cambridge: Cambridge University Press, 1990).

10 Yochai Benkler, *The Wealth of Networks: How Social Production Transforms Markets and Freedom* (New Haven, CT: Yale University Press, 2006).

11 Richard Barbrook, 'The Hi-Tech Gift Economy', *First Monday*, 1998.

12 Kevin Kelly, 'The New Socialism: Global Collectivist Society Is Coming Online', *Wired* 17:6 (2009).

13 Nakamoto, 'Bitcoin'.

14 Bill Maurer, in conversation with the author, February 2023.

15 Pierre-Joseph Proudhon, *The Solution of the Social Problem*, [1927], excerpts, transl. Shawn P. Wilbur, revoltlib.com, 2021, 20.

16 Ibid., 35–6.
17 Eric A. Posner and Glen Weyl, *Radical Markets* (Princeton, NJ: Princeton University Press, 2018).
18 Proudhon, *Solution of the Social Problem*, 34.
19 Nigel Dodd, *The Social Life of Money* (London: Princeton University Press, 2014), 573.
20 Proudhon, *Solution of the Social Problem*, 40.
21 Ibid., 52.
22 Ethel Crowley, 'Local Exchange Trading Systems: Globalising Rural Communities', *SSRN* electronic journal, 2004, ssrn.com.
23 Ibid.
24 Josiah Warren, *Periodical Letter* II, 1856.
25 Ann Caldwell Butler, 'Josiah Warren and the Sovereignty of the Individual', *Journal of Libertarian Studies* 4:4 (Fall 1980).
26 James DeFilippis, cited in Jessica Gordon Nembhard, *Collective Courage: A History of African American Cooperative Economic Thought and Practice* (Philadelphia, PA: Pennsylvania University Press, 2014), 53.
27 Jo Freeman, 'The Tyranny of Structurelessness', *Berkeley Journal of Sociology* 17 (1972).
28 Charles Eisenstein, *Sacred Economics: Money, Gift and Society in the Age of Transition* (Berkeley, CA: North Atlantic, 2021), 168.
29 Silvio Gesell, *The Natural Economic Order*, transl. Philip Pye (London: Peter Owen, 1958), 269.
30 Silvio Gesell, *Die Reformation im Münzwesen als Brücke zum sozialen Staat* (self-published, 1891).
31 Gesell, *The Natural Economic Order*, 114.
32 Ibid., 18.
33 Ibid., 15.
34 Bruno Latour, *Reassembling the Social: An Introduction to Actor-Network-Theory* (Oxford: Oxford University Press, 2007).
35 Metallism emerges from the Austrian School of Economics, which is wary of hyperinflation and believes that the money supply should be determined by currency markets as opposed to by government policy.
36 'Aping' is a term used for mindless groupthink in online trading. See Erin Gobler, 'Stonks, Apes, YOLO: Your Guide to Meme Stock Trading Slang', *The Balance*, 19 June 2022, thebalancemoney.
37 Friedrich Hayek, 'The Use of Knowledge in Society', in *Knowledge Management and Organizational Design*, ed. Paul S. Myers (London: Routledge, 2009).
38 Rene Almeling, 'Paid to Donate: Egg Donors, Sperm Donors, and Gendered Experiences of Bodily Commodification', in *Money Talks: Explaining How Money Really Works*, ed. Nina Bandelj, Frederick F.

Wherry, and Viviana A. Zelizer (Princeton, NJ: Princeton University Press, 2017).

39 Ibid., 317.

40 Georg Simmel, *The Philosophy of Money* (London: Routledge, 2004).

41 Crowley, 'Local Exchange Trading Systems'.

42 Eisenstein, *Sacred Economics*, 88.

43 Michael J. Sandel, *What Money Can't Buy: The Moral Limits of Markets* (London: Macmillan, 2012).

44 Jonathan Beller, in conversation with the author, December 2021.

45 Mayumi Hayashi, 'Japan's Fureai Kippu Time-Banking in Elderly Care: Origins, Development, Challenges and Impact', *International Journal of Community Currency Research* 16:A (2012).

46 Ann Pettifor, *The Production of Money: How to Break the Power of Bankers* (London: Verso, 2017).

47 Richard Douthwaite, *The Ecology of Money* (Bristol: The Schumacher Society, 2006).

48 Pettifor, *Production of Money*.

49 Olúfẹ́mi O. Táíwò, *Reconsidering Reparations* (Oxford: Oxford University Press, 2022).

50 Olúfẹ́mi O. Táíwò, in conversation with the author, February 2022.

51 Núria Güell, 'An Annex to *Afrodita* (2017) for *Who Cares Festival* (2020)', nuriaguell.com.

52 Táíwò, in conversation with the author, February 2022.

53 Cassie Thornton asks this question in her recent book, *The Hologram: Feminist Peer-to-Peer Health for a Post-Pandemic Future* (London: Pluto, 2020): 'I wonder what a post-individualist feminist economy looks like, and if I can be trusted to imagine it?' (65).

54 MazaCoin website, 4 June 2014, WayBack Machine, web.archive.org.

55 Harris, quoted in Tate Ryan Mosley, 'He Created an Indigenous Digital Currency. The Dream Is Still Alive', *MIT Technology Review*, 27 April 2022.

56 Ibid.

57 'Happy 2015!!', mazacoin.org, 6 January 2015, WayBack Machine, web.archive.org.

58 Mazacoin.org screen capture, 2014, WayBack Machine, web.archive.org.

59 Alysa Landry, '9 Questions Surrounding MazaCoin, the Lakota CryptoCurrency: Answered', *ICT*, 12 September 2018, ictnews.org.

60 'About Mazacoin', mazacoin.org, February 2015, WayBack Machine, web.archive.org.

61 Jasper Hamill, 'The Battle of Little Bitcoin: Native American Tribe Launches Its Own Cryptocurrency', *Forbes*, 27 February 2014.

62   'Mazacoin: National Currency of the Traditional Lakota Nation',
     mazacoin.org, 2014, WayBack Machine, web.archive.org.
63   'StarCamp Shasta, Rainbows & Unicorns', mazacoin.org, 24 August
     2015, WayBackMachine, web.archive.org.
64   Ibid.
65   Quoted in Tekobbe and McKnight, 'Indigenous Cryptocurrency'.

5. Eat the Rich

1   'Keeping Customers Informed through Market Volatility', Robin-
     hood blog, 28 January 2012, blog.robinhood.com.
2   US Securities and Exchange Commission, 'Staff Report on Equity
     and Options Market Structure Conditions in Early 2021', 14
     October 2021, sec.gov.
3   Lana Swartz, 'Lana Swartz on the Power of Payment Platforms', 4
     February 2021, *Big Tech with Taylor Owen*, podcast.
4   Max Haiven, 'The GameStop Saga Is Not the Revenge Against
     Finance We Deserve', *Truthout*, 3 February 2021, truthout.org.
5   See r/wallstreetbets, reddit.com.
6   The slang 'Fren' is also used in crypto and Web3 communities to
     refer to fellow crypto enthusiasts. It rose to prominence on the
     message board 4cgan.
7   'They weren't saying they were experts. They were saying they were
     apes.' Swartz, 'Lana Swartz on the Power of Payment Platforms'.
8   'Apes together strong' is a catchphrase used by the WallStreetBets
     community.
9   'Nothing runs better on MTV than a protest against MTV.' Mark
     Fisher, *Capitalist Realism: Is There No Alternative?* (Winchester:
     Zero Books, 2009, 9).
10   Amy Ohlheiser, 'We Actually Elected a Meme as President: How
     4Chan Celebrated Trump's Victory', *Washington Post*, 12 November
     2016.
11   Fair.coop, quoted in David Bollier, 'Faircoin as the First Global
     Commons Currency?', P2P Foundation blog, 10 October 2014,
     blog.p2pfoundation.net.
12   David Graeber, *Debt: The First Five Thousand Years* (New York:
     Melville House, 2011).
13   Enric Duran, in conversation with the author, January 2022.
14   Cassie Thornton, 'Debt Visualisations', *Feminist Economics Depart-
     ment* (blog), 14 March 2016, feministeconomicsdepartment.com.
15   Enric Duran, in conversation with the author, January 2022.
16   This Robin Hood Minor Asset Management Agency should not be
     mistaken for the Robinhood trading app that launched in 2015.

17 Seppo Sakari Virkki, 'Methods, Systems and Program Products for Market Analysis', United States Patent 7,835,968B1, November 2010.
18 Brett Scott and Akseli Virtanen in conversation, Openhere festival, Dublin, November 2014.
19 Ibid.
20 Matt Levine, 'Hedge-Fund Pay and Trader Lies', *Bloomberg*, 16 May 2017.
21 Alina Popa, Robinhood Dublin Office, November 2014, author's transcript of the meeting.
22 Jan Ritsema, in correspondence with the author, June 2015.
23 Laura Lotti, in conversation with the author, December 2021.
24 Ibid.

6. Trust in the Code

1 James C. Scott, *The Moral Economy of the Peasant* (New Haven, CT: Yale University Press, 1977), 5.
2 Georg Simmel, *The Philosophy of Money* (London: Routledge, 2004).
3 Satoshi Nakamoto, 'Bitcoin: A Peer-to-Peer Electronic Cash System', 2008, bitcoin.org.
4 Arvind Krishna, 'The Future of Trust as Blockchain Reimagines Entire Business Ecosystems', *Forbes*, 30 June 2016.
5 Tyler Winklevoss, quoted in Nathaniel Popper and Peter Lattman, 'As Big Investors Emerge, Bitcoin Gets Ready for Its Closeup', *New York Times*, 11 April 2013.
6 Primavera De Filippi, in conversation with Rachel O'Dwyer, 2015: 'I use the term "governance by design" to describe the process of online communities increasingly relying on technology in order to organise themselves through novel governance models (designed *by* the community and *for* the community), whose rules are embedded directly into the underlying technology of the platforms they use to operate.'
7 Oscar Darmawan, in Leighton Cosseboom, 'Blockchain Tech Can Eradicate Corruption in Asia', *Tech in Asia*, 20 August 2015, techinasia.com.
8 Vitalik Buterin, 'Bootstrapping a Decentralized Autonomous Organisation', *Bitcoin Magazine*, 2013, bitcoinmagazine.com.
9 In 2010, Satoshi described Bitcoin as 'an implementation of Wei Dai's b-money proposal ... on Cypherpunks ... in 1998 [and] Nick Szabo's Bitgold proposal'. Satoshi, 'Re: They want to delete the Wikipedia article', 20 July 2010, bitcointalk.org.

10 Timothy May, 'A Crypto Anarchist Manifesto', in *High Noon on the Electronic Frontier: Conceptual Issues in Cyberspace*, ed. Peter Ludlow (Denver: Bradford, 1992).

11 Jordan Carey, 'The Story behind John Gilmore: What Is EFF Founder's Net Worth?', *24/7 Crypto*, 9 October 2022, 24-7-crypto.com.

12 Phil Zimmerman, quoted in Timothy C. May, 'True Nyms and Crypto Anarchy', in *True Names and the Opening of the Cyberspace Frontier*, ed. James Frenkel (London: Penguin, 2001), 18.

13 May, 'Crypto Anarchist Manifesto'.

14 Max More, 'From Human to Transhuman to Posthuman', *Extropy* 8 (Winter 1991–92).

15 J. K. Gibson-Graham, *A Postcapitalist Politics* (Minneapolis: University of Minnesota Press, 2006), 70.

16 Technotranscendence, 'Re: We luv the guv't', Extropian mailing list, 16 January 1998, 21:34:04, available at lucifer.com/exi-lists.

17 Tony Hollick, 'Karl Popper on "Why Government?"', Extropian mailing list, 18 January 1998, available at lucifer.com/exi-lists.

18 Technotranscendence, 'Re: Re: We luv the Guv't', 16 January 1998, available at lucifer.com/exi-lists.

19 den Otter, 'Re: Suggestion: Extropian Country', Extropian mailing list, 21 February 1998, available at lucifer.com/exi-lists.

20 Chuck Hammill, 'From Crossbows to Cryptography: Techno-Thwarting the State', presented at the Future of Freedom Conference, November 1987.

21 Jude Milhon, a.k.a. St Jude, 'The Cypherpunk Movement', in 'secretions', Cypherpunks Mailing List Archive, 25 September 1992, mailing-list-archive.cryptoanarchy.wiki.

22 David D. Friedman, *The Machinery of Freedom: Guide to a Radical Capitalism* (Chicago: Open Court, 1989); James Dale Davidson and William Rees-Mogg, *The Sovereign Individual* (London: Simon & Schuster, 1997).

23 Timothy May and Eric Hughes, 'crypto anarchy', in Timothy C. May, 'Crypto Glossary', Cypherpunks Mailing List Archive, 22 November 1992, mailing-list-archive.cryptoanarchy.wiki.

24 Timothy C. May, 'Crypto Anarchy and Virtual Communities', in *Crypto Anarchy, Cyberstates, and Pirate Utopias*, ed. Peter Ludlow (Cambridge, MA: MIT Press, 2001), 69.

25 Jamie Bartlett, 'Cypherpunks Write Code', *American Scientist* 104:2 (April 2016).

26 Timothy C. May, '"Cypherpunks Write Code" as a Putdown', Cypherpunks Mailing List Archive, 20 July 1995, mailing-list-archive.cryptoanarchy.wiki.

27 Hal Finney, 'RPOW – Reusable Proofs of Work', 15 August 2004, WayBack Machine, web.archive.org.

28 Nick Szabo, 'Smart Contracts', Department of Phonetic Sciences, University of Amsterdam, 1994, fon.hum.uva.nl.

29 Robert Hettinga, 'e$: Non-Repudiation', Cypherpunks Mailing List Archive, 22 September 1995, mailing-list-archive.cryptoanarchy. wiki.

30 Eric Hughes, 'A Statement of Purpose', Cypherpunks Mailing List Archive, 5 October 1992, mailing-list-archive.cryptoanarchy.wiki.

31 Hannah Arendt, 'Unpredictability and the Power of Promise', in *The Human Condition* (London: University of Chicago Press, 1998), 245.

32 Ibid., 245.

33 Leslie Lamport, 'My Writings', 13 August 2022, lamport.azureweb sites.net.

34 Leslie Lamport, Robert Shostak, and Marshall Pease, 'The Byzantine Generals Problem', *ACM Transactions on Programming Languages and Systems* 4:3 (July 1982), 382.

35 Arendt, 'Unpredictability and the Power of Promise', 244.

36 Hal Finney, 'Re: Force is not physical', Cypherpunks Mailing List Archive, 31 August 1994, mailing-list-archive.cryptoanarchy.wiki.

37 Nick Szabo, 'Practical security, Internet commercialization, etc.', Cypherpunks Mailing List Archive, 27 August 1993, mailing-list-archive.cryptoanarchy.wiki.

38 Robert J. Woodhead, 'Anon Bank Accounts/Imminent Demise of US Govt (Conclusion)', Cypherpunks Mailing List Archive, 20 October 1993, mailing-list-archive.cryptoanarchy.wiki.

39 James A. Donald, 'Re: cryptography eliminates lawyers?', Cypherpunks Mailing List Archive, 7 September 1995, mailing-list-archive. cryptoanarchy.wiki.

40 Perry E. Metzger, reply to Marc Horowitz, 'thoughts on digital cash', Cypherpunks Mailing List Archive, 30 November 1992, mailing-list-archive.cryptoanarchy.wiki.

41 CALYK@aol.com, 'Re: Extropia', Extropian mailing list, 18 February 1998, available at lucifer.com/exi-lists.

42 Tom W. Bell, 'Extropia: A Home for Our Hopes', *Extropy* 8 (Winter 1991–92).

43 Bill Eichman, 'Ocean Colonization: A Practical Approach', *Extropy* 12 (First Quarter 1994), 8.

44 Bell, 'Extropia: A Home for Our Hopes'.

45 Eichman, 'Ocean Colonization', 5.

46 Hakim Bey, 'Primitives and Extropians', *Anarchy* 42 (Fall 1995): 39–43.

47 William Bailie, *Josiah Warren: The First American Anarchist* (Boston: Small, Maynard & Company, 1906).

48 Donald J. Trump (@realDonaldTrump), 'This is not a game. These

ugly Anarchists must be stooped IMMEDIATELY. MOVE FAST!',
Twitter, 11 June 2020, twitter.com.
49 CALYK@aol.com, 'Re: Extropia'.
50 Den Otter, 'Re: Extropian Country', Extropian mailing list, 21
February 1998, available at lucifer.com/exi-lists.
51 James Rogers, 'Re: THC: Extropian Country – Blueprint undercon-
struction ...', Extropian mailing list, 17 February 1998, 21:32:11,
available at lucifer.com//exi-lists.
52 Mark O'Connell, *Notes from an Apocalypse: A Personal Journey
to the End of the World and Back* (Hamburg: Anchor, 2021).
53 Max More, *Extropy* 1, Introductory Issue (Fall 1988), 11.
54 wce@hogbbs.scol.pa.us, 'Subject: Sea Colonies', in 'A Sample of
Ocean Colonization Discussion on the Extropian E-mail List',
Extropy 12 (1994), 11.
55 Peter Thiel, 'The Education of a Libertarian', *Cato Unbound* 13:4
(2009).
56 Ibid.
57 Maureen Dowd, 'Peter Thiel, Trump's Tech Pal, Explains Himself',
New York Times, 11 January 2017.
58 Joint Special Committee to Conduct, 'A Study Concerning Innovation Zones (SCR11), Legislative Proposal to Authorize Creation of
Innovation Zones in Nevada', September 2021, leg.state.nv.us.
59 EYRC Studio, 'Mission Statement', 2022, eyrc.com.
60 This is a paraphrase of a quote from artist Mierle Ukeles's Maintenance Art Manifesto (1969): 'The sourball of every revolution:
after the revolution, who's going to pick up the garbage on Monday
morning?' PDF available at queensmuseum.org.
61 Prepared by Mary Walker, Representing Storey County, 'Issues
and Concerns Regarding the Innovation Zone Bill Draft 22–1109,
Concern 4', leg.state.nv.us.
62 Ibid., 5.
63 Ibid.
64 Ibid., 2.
65 Jeffrey Berns, Blockchains letter, 30 September 2021, posted in
Daniel Rothberg, 'Blockchains Withdraws Plan for Innovation Zone
Legislation, Citing Lack of Support from State, Governor', *Nevada
Independent*, 7 October 2021, thenevadaindependent.com.
66 Richard Hanania, 'Futarchy: Robin Hanson on How Prediction
Markets Can Take Over the World', transcript of interview, 15
September 2021, richardhanania.substack.com.
67 Mark S. Miller and K. Eric Drexler, 'Markets and Computation:
Agoric Open Systems', *Ecology of Computation* 1 (1988).
68 Robin Hanson, 'Idea Futures: Encouraging an Honest Consensus',
Extropy 8 (Winter 1991–92), 8.

69 Ibid.

70 'Future Forecasts', *Extropy* 15 (7:2; 2nd to 3rd Quarter 1995), 10–13.

71 Davidson and Rees-Mogg, *Sovereign Individual*.

72 Hanson, 'Idea Futures', 8.

73 Geoff Dale, 'Re: Anarcho-Capitalism > Agoric Democracy', Extropian mailing list, 14 April 1998, available at lucifer.com/exi-lists.

74 Friedrich Hayek, 'Competition as a Discovery Procedure', in *New Studies in Philosophy, Politics, Economics and the History of Ideas* (Chicago: University of Chicago Press, 1978), 187.

75 Hal Finney, 'Re: Voting and Idea Futures', Extropian mailing list, 19 January 2000, available at lucifer.com/exi-lists.

76 Mabel Lang, 'Allotment by Tokens', *Historia: Zeitschrift für Alte Geschichte* 8:1 (January 1959), 81.

77 Davidson and Rees-Mogg, *Sovereign Individual*.

78 Aristotle, *Athenaion Politeia* 62: 1.

79 Bill Maurer, 'The Politics of Token Economics, Then and Now', in *Tokens: Culture, Connections, Communities*, ed. Antonino Crisà, Mairi Gkikaki, and Clare Rowan (London: Royal Numismatic Society, 2019).

80 Ibid., 226.

81 A. Guest, 'An Open Letter', 18 June 2016, pastebin.com.

82 Lefteris Karapetsas, 'White Hat Siphoning Has Occurred. What Now?', slock.it blog, 22 June 2016, blog.slock.it.

83 Bryant Joseph Gilot, 'Code Is Cruel', *Medium*, 19 June 2016.

84 Christoph Jentzsch, 'What the "Fork" Really Means', slock.it blog, 18 June 2016, blog.slock.it.

85 Joseph A. Schumpeter, *Capitalism, Socialism and Democracy* (New York: Harper & Brothers, 1942); Anthony Downs, *An Economic Theory of Democracy* (New York: Harper & Row, 1957).

86 Chantal Mouffe, 'Deliberative Democracy or Agonistic Pluralism?', *Social Research* 66:3 (1999).

87 Quinn DuPont, 'Experiments in Algorithmic Governance: A History and Ethnography of "The DAO", a Failed Decentralized Autonomous Organization', in *Bitcoin and Beyond: Cryptocurrencies, Blockchains and Global Governance*, ed. Malcolm Campbell-Verduyn (London: Routledge, 2017).

88 Paul Ennis (@polarpunklabs), Twitter, 6 May 2023, twitter.com.

89 Ethereum, 'Proof of Stake (POS)', 12 January 2023, ethereum.org.

90 Klaus Schwab and Peter Vanham, 'What Is Stakeholder Capitalism?', Davos Agenda 2021, World Economic Forum, 22 January 2021, weforum.org.

7. Outside of Borders

1 Stefan Simchowitz, quoted in Stephen J. Goldberg, 'Sacked and Pillaged; Simchowitz vs. Mahama', *Artillery Magazine*, 23 February 2016, artillerymag.com.
2 Arjun Appadurai, 'Introduction: Commodities and the Politics of Value', in *The Social Life of Things: Commodities in Cultural Perspective*, ed. Arjun Appadurai (London: Cambridge University Press, 1988), 28.
3 Jacob Goldstein and David Kestenbaum, 'The Island of Stone Money', *Planet Money*, 10 December 2010, npr.org.
4 Milton Friedman, 'The Island of Stone Money', Working Papers in Economics, No. E-91-3, Stanford, CA: Hoover Institution, 1991.
5 The British pound sterling had made the move earlier, in 1931.
6 Pierre-Joseph Proudhon, *The Solution of the Social Problem*, [1927], excerpts, transl. Shawn P. Wilbur, revoltlib.com, 2021.
7 'Brothers in Law: When Conceptual Art Certificates of Authenticity Go Up in Smoke', Danziger, Danziger & Muro, LLP, 20 November 2015, danziger.com.
8 Kai Chng, in conversation with the author, 18 January 2018.
9 Maecenas website, 2018, WayBack Machine, web.archive.org.
10 Jérôme Croisier, in conversation with the author, January 2018.
11 Timothy May, 'The Crypto Anarchist Manifesto', in *High Noon on the Electronic Frontier: Conceptual Issues in Cyberspace*, ed. Peter Ludlow (Denver: Bradford, 1992).
12 Kai Ren and Zakie Twainy, 'The Rise of Tokenization', Bank of New York Mellon Corporation, September 2022, bnymellon.com.
13 Appadurai, 'Introduction', 28.
14 Adriano Picinati di Torcello, 'Why Should Art Be Considered as an Asset Class?', Deloitte, 2010, www2.deloitte.com.
15 Marc Spiegler, 'Ten Questions All Gallerists Should Be Asking Themselves Now', Talking Galleries IV Symposium, Barcelona, 2015.
16 Carol Vogel, 'Art for Profit', *New York Times*, 7 July 1995.
17 Ibid.
18 Keller Easterling, *Extrastatecraft: The Power of Infrastructure Space* (London: Verso, 2014).
19 'The freeport contains multiple contradictions: it is a zone of terminal impermanence; it is also a zone of legalized extra-legality maintained by nation-states trying to emulate failed states as closely as possible by selectively losing control.' Hito Steyerl, *Duty Free Art: Art in the Age of Planetary Civil War* (London: Verso, 2017), 142.
20 Ibid.

21 Byung-Chul Han, *Shanzhai: Deconstruction in Chinese*, transl. Philippa Hurd (Cambridge, MA: MIT Press, 2017), 34

22 Kai Chng, in conversation with the author, 18 January 2018.

23 Tina Rivers Ryan, 'Token Gesture', *Artforum*, 2021.

24 Karl Marx, *Grundrisse*, transl. Martin Nicolaus (London: Penguin, 1973), 199–200.

25 McKenzie Wark, *General Intellects: Twenty-One Thinkers for the Twenty-First Century* (London: Verso, 2017).

26 Max Haiven, 'Art after Money', openDemocracy, 10 October 2018, opendemocracy.net.

27 Brian Larkin, 'The Politics and Poetics of Infrastructure', *Annual Review of Anthropology* 42 (2013). Larkin describes the poetics of infrastructure as the 'means by which a state proffers these representations to its citizens and asks them to take these representations as social truths'.

28 Emily Wallington, 'Spread the Wealth', *Art in America*, 5 May 2022, artnews.com.

8. A Celestial Cyberdimension

1 Scott Reyburn, 'Will Cryptocurrencies Be the Art Market's Next Big Thing?', *New York Times*, 13 January 2018.

2 Hal Finney, 'Crypto trading cards', Cypherpunks Mailing List Archive, 17 January 1993, mailing-list-archive.cryptoanarchy.wiki.

3 Yoni Assia, 'Bitcoin 2.X (a.k.a. Colored Bitcoin) Initial Specs', 27 March 2012, yoniassia.com.

4 Ted Nelson, *Literary Machines: Edition 87.1*, self-published, 1987.

5 Ted Nelson, 'Summary of the Xanadu Hypertext System', in ibid.

6 Tim Berners-Lee and Mark Fischetti, *Weaving the Web: The Original Design and Ultimate Destiny of the World Wide Web by Its Inventor* (San Francisco: Harper, 1999).

7 Bob Brown, 'Sony BMG Rootkit Scandal: 10 Years Later', *Network World*, 28 October 2015, csooline.com.

8 ricky8741, 'Joe Rogan Discovers Republic of Kekistan', r/videos, 9 May 2017, reddit.com.

9 McKenzie Wark, 'My Collectible Ass', *e-flux* 85 (October 2017), e-flux.com.

10 Emily Siner, 'When the Internet Is Your Canvas You Paint in Zeros and Ones', *All Tech Considered* (blog), 3 November 2013, npr.org.

11 Walter Benjamin, 'The Work of Art in the Age of Mechanical Reproduction', in *Illuminations*, ed. Hannah Arendt, transl. Harry Zohn from the 1935 essay (New York: Schocken Books, 1968), 217.

12 Byung-Chul Han, *Shanzhai: Deconstruction in Chinese* (Cambridge, MA: MIT Press, 2017), 11.

13 Quoted in ibid., 24.

14 Nick Szabo, who first proposed the idea in the 1990s, described the then hypothetical smart contract as a kind of 'digital vending machine'. Nick Szabo, 'Smart Contracts', Phonetic Sciences, University of Amsterdam, 1994, at fon.hum.uva.nl; Nick Szabo, 'Formalizing and Securing Relationships on Public Networks', *First Monday* 2:9 (1997).

15 Noah Horowitz, *Art of the Deal* (Princeton, NJ: Princeton University Press, 2014).

16 Thorstein Veblen, *The Theory of the Leisure Class* (London: Routledge, 2017).

17 Ruth Catlow, in conversation with the author, June 2018.

18 Jess Houlgrave, in conversation with the author, June 2018.

19 Jean Baudrillard, 'The Art Auction', in *For a Critique of the Political Economy of the Sign* (London: Verso, 2019).

20 Ibid.

21 Pierre Bourdieu, *Distinction: A Social Critique of the Judgement of Taste* (New Haven, CT: Harvard University Press, 1987).

22 Quoted in Erin Woo and Kevin Roose, 'This Social Club Runs on Crypto Tokens and Vibes', *New York Times*, 2 March 2022.

23 Taylor Lorenz, 'Inside "Crypto Woodstock", Where Technologists Plot a Utopian Future', *Washington Post*, 27 August 2022.

24 Kelsie Nabben, 'Inside a Social DAO: How an Online Community Becomes a Digital City', CoinDesk, 17 October 2022, coindesk.com.

25 Woo and Roose, 'This Social Club Runs on Crypto Tokens and Vibes'.

26 Gordon Goner, quoted in Kyle Chayka, 'Why Bored Ape Avatars Are Taking Over Twitter', *New Yorker*, 30 July 2021.

27 Ibid.

28 Jonathan Jones, 'The Bored Ape NFT Craze Is All about Ego and Money, Not Art', *Guardian*, 4 January 2022.

29 Ruth Catlow and Penny Rafferty, eds, *Radical Friends: Decentralised Autonomous Organisations and the Arts* (Lancaster: Torque Editions, 2022), 94.

30 Evgeny Morozov, 'Web3: A Map in Search of a Territory', *Crypto Syllabus*, 2022, the-crypto-syllabus.com.

31 Ruth Catlow, in conversation with the author, January 2023.

32 Kevin Abosch, in conversation with the author, July 2018.

33 Russell W. Belk, 'Possessions and the Extended Self', *Journal of Consumer Research* 15:2 (1988), 139.

34 Ruth Catlow, in conversation with the author, June 2018.

35 Alex Hearn, 'Tim Berners-Lee Defends Auction of NFT Representing Web's Source Code', *Guardian*, 23 June 2021.

36 Kevin Kelly, *New Rules for the New Economy: 10 Radical Strategies for a Connected World* (London: Penguin, 1999).
37 Sergey Brin and Lawrence Page, 'The Anatomy of a Large-Scale Hypertextual Web Search Engine', *Computer Networks and ISDN Systems* 30:1–7 (1998).
38 Stewart Brand, in conversation with Steve Wozniak at the First Hackers Conference, Sausalito, CA, 1984. 'Stewart Brand States Information Wants to Be Free', Videowest Productions footage, 1 November 1984, gettyimages.in.
39 Kevin McCoy, in correspondence with the author, June 2018.
40 Lucy R. Lippard and John Chandler, 'The Dematerialization of Art', *Art International* 12:2 (February 1968).
41 Ibid., 263.
42 Wark, 'My Collectible Ass'.
43 McKenzie Wark (@mckenziewark), 'Hot take on NFTs: it's the art market perfected. The art market is all about provenance: the chain of authentication and verifiable ownership of the art work', Twitter, 4 January 2022, twitter.com.
44 Kimberly Parker, 'Most Artists Are Not Making Money Off NFTs and Here Are Some Graphs to Prove It', *Medium*, 19 April 2021.

9. 'When You Live in a Shithole, There's Always the Metaverse'

1 Logan Flores (loganf1107), 'Favorite Genshin Impact Character and Why?', r/Genshin_Impact, 14 March 2022, reddit.com.
2 Gawain Lucian Lax and Madeleine Mackenzie, 'Against All Odds: Desire and Monetisation in Japanese Mobile Games', *Proceedings of DiGRA 2019: What's Next* (2019), 3, digra.org.
3 'Tamagotchi Graveyard', Tamagotchi Dream World, shesdevilish. tripod.com.
4 Quoted in Shealtielle Blaise De Jesus et al., 'Play-to-Earn: A Qualitative Analysis of the Experiences and Challenges Faced by Axie Infinity Online Gamers amidst the COVID-19 Pandemic', *International Journal of Psychology and Counselling* 1:12 (2022), 394.
5 Richard Heeks, 'Understanding "Gold Farming" and Real-Money Trading as the Intersection of Real and Virtual Economies', *Journal for Virtual Worlds Research* 2:4 (2009).
6 Raph Koster, 'Ownership: How Virtual Worlds Work, Part 5', Raph Koster's Website, 21 October 2021, raphkoster.com.
7 Rebecca Mardon and Russell Belk, 'Materializing Digital Collecting: An Extended View of Digital Materiality', *Marketing Theory* 18:4 (2018); Vili Lehdonvirta and Edward Castronova,

Virtual Economies: Design and Analysis (Cambridge, MA: MIT Press, 2014); Rebecca D. Watkins, Janice Denegri-Knott, and Mike Molesworth, 'The Relationship between Ownership and Possession: Observations from the Context of Digital Virtual Goods', *Journal of Marketing Management* 32:1–2 (2016); Bernadett Koles and Peter Nagy, 'Digital Object Attachment', *Current Opinion in Psychology* 39 (2021); Juho Hamari and Lauri Keronen, 'Why Do People Buy Virtual Goods: A Meta-Analysis', *Computers in Human Behavior* 71 (2017).

 8 Scott Wisniewski, 'Taxation of Virtual Assets', *Duke Law and Technology Review* 7 (2008), 1.

 9 Lehdonvirta and Castronova, *Virtual Economies*; Edward Castronova, 'Virtual Worlds: A First-Hand Account of Market and Society on the Cyberian Frontier', *SSRN* electronic journal (2001); Edward Castronova, 'On Virtual Economies', *SSRN* electronic journal (2002).

10 Julian Dibbell, *Play Money: Or, How I Quit My Day Job and Made Millions Trading Virtual Loot* (New York: Basic Books, 2006).

11 Danny Vincent, 'China Used Prisoners in Lucrative Internet Gaming Work', *Guardian*, 25 May 2011.

12 Jack Cleghorn and Mark D. Griffiths, 'Why Do Gamers Buy "Virtual Assets"? An Insight into the Psychology behind Purchase Behaviour', *Digital Education Review* 27 (June 2015), 97.

13 Viviana A. Zelizer, 'The Social Meaning of Money: "Special Monies"', *American Journal of Sociology* 95:2 (1989).

14 Luc Barthelet, in conversation with the author, January 2023.

15 Lehdonvirta and Castronova, *Virtual Economies*.

16 'The Fortnite Economy', *Stephanomics* podcast, 4 April 2019.

17 Antonino Crisá, Mairi Gkikaki, and Clare Rowan, 'Introduction', in *Tokens, Culture, Connections, Communities*, ed. Antonino Crisà, Mairi Gkikaki, and Clare Rowan (London: Royal Numismatic Society, 2019).

18 Alfred Gell, *Art and Agency: An Anthropological Theory* (London: Clarendon, 1998), 74.

19 'Economy Wipe', Islands Wiki, robloxislands.fandom.com.

20 Evanland Channel, 'Roblox Islands Is Dead! | New Update Wipes Everyone's Data! || Animal XP Update Economy Wipe Islands', 22 January 2021, youtube.com.

21 Sarah Flannery, in conversation with the author, January 2023.

22 Michael D. Murray, 'Ready Lawyer One: Lawyering in the Metaverse', *SSRN* electronic journal, 17 April 2022, ssrn.com.

23 Neal Stephenson, *Snow Crash* (New York: Spectra, 2003).

24 Emma Ruben, 'Indigenous Cultural Embassy Eyes Space in the Metaverse', *National Indigenous Times*, 13 April 2022.

25 Stephenson, *Snow Crash*.

26 Ibid.

27 Cory Ondrejka, in conversation with the author, January 2023.

28 Ondrejka stresses that they are paraphrasing Lessig. Ibid.

29 Ibid.

30 Jorge Luis Borges, 'On Exactitude in Science', in *Collected Fictions*, transl. Andrew Hurley (London: Penguin, 1999).

31 Evgeny Morozov, 'Web3: A Map in Search of a Territory', *Crypto Syllabus*, 2023, the-crypto-syllabus.com.

32 Building the Metaverse, 'Play to Earn Games with Mitch Zamara and Jon: Designs, Opportunities, Misconceptions', 13 December 2021, youtube.com.

33 Matthew Ball, *The Metaverse: And How It Will Revolutionise Everything* (New York: Liveright, 2022).

34 Building the Metaverse, 'Raph Koster and Jon Radoff Talk about the Metaverse, Online Worlds, MMOs and Virtual Societies', 6 October 2021, youtube.com.

35 In the early days of the internet there were standards for rendering 3D images, such as VRMA. None currently exist for virtual worlds.

36 'You'll own nothing and be happy' is a meme levelled at the World Economic Forum (WEF) by critics who argue that the WEF is trying to restrict private property.

37 Alan Butler, *Down and Out in Los Santos (2015–Present)*, alanbutler.info.

38 Alan Butler, 'Bizarro States: Litter and Its Digital Doppelganger', in *States of Entanglement: Data in the Irish Landscape*, ed. Sven Anderson et al. (New York: Actar, 2021).

39 'Interview with Alan Butler by Seanán Kerr, ACW Student', *Art in the Contemporary World*, National College of Art and Design, July 2019, acw.ie.

40 Memo Akten, 'The Unreasonable Ecological Cost of #CryptoArt (Part 1)', *Medium*, December 2020.

41 Alex Heath, 'Meta's Flagship Metaverse App Is Too Buggy and Employees Are Barely Using It, Says Exec in Charge', *Verge*, 7 October 2022.

Index

paper money 53–4, 70–3
Papua New Guinea 50
Pasquale, Frank 66
passion assets 232
Patreon 47
payment, and transactions 36–8
payment in kind 27
payments apps 9
PayPal 40, 43, 47–8, 114
peer groups 125–7
peer-to-peer payments 43
People's Bank of China 109–10
Pepe memes 25, 226
performance art 153
persistent scripts 95
Pettifor, Ann 134
phone credits 2–3, 4
photography 227
phygital economy 267–8
Picasso, Pablo 199, 207–8
Pierce, Brock 251–2
Pierson, Jack 201
Pigou, Arthur C. 136
Pigouvian tax 136
Pistor, Katharina 107, 108
platform capitalism 41–7
platform ecosystem 47
Plato 228
plausible deniability 7–8
Pokimane 17, 18
Polanyi, Karl 85–6
political consequences 11
politics
    code is law 184–9
    escape from 171–4
    human oversight 189
Poovey, Mary 54
Popa, Alina 153–4
Ports Francs et Entrepôts, Geneva 207–8
Posner, Eric 119–20, 200
poverty relief 86–90
power dynamics 33–4, 37–8
precarious workers 8
precariousness 14–15
predictive inventory placement 60
privacy 73, 75, 77, 162–3
private currencies 32, 103, 104
programmable tokens 10–11, 90–9, 99–100, 102
Projekt Melody 23, 24, 25, 40, 44–5, 47
proof of performance 97

proof of stake 188–9
proof-of-work 117, 139, 159, 167, 188
property, tokenisation of 120
prostitution 31–2
Proudhon, Pierre-Joseph 119, 120–1, 195
provenance 201
public key encryption 161
public money 102
purchase profiles 59

QAnon 40
QQ coin 105

Radical Markets (Weyl and Posner) 101, 119, 200
rai stones 193–4
rails 43–7
Rand Visible Filing Systems 55
RARE art platform 218
real money 113
real value 9
realism 271
Red Dead Redemption 2 (game) 255
Reddit 5, 27, 43, 43–4, 220
Redditometro 68–9
redistribution 217
redlining 66–7
Rees-Mogg, William 166, 180, 182
refugees 99–100
refunding 217
regulatory environment 8, 108–11
Ren, Kai 201
rent 45
reparations 217
representation, and things 9, 212–13
representation value 9
reputation capital 101
reputational currencies 101
resale forums 13–14
Rhizome gallery 229–30
Ringley, Jennifer Kaye 16
risk analysis 58, 60
risk-structured financial instruments 63
Ritsema, Jan 154
Robin Hood 150–1
Robin Hood Minor Asset Management Cooperative 151–5
Robinhood app 144, 145–7, 146–7, 151
Roblox 258–9